Designing Effective Digital Badges

Designing Effective Digital Badges is a hands-on guide to the principles, implementation, and assessment of digital badging systems. Informed by the fundamental concepts and research-based characteristics of effective badge design, this book uses real-world examples to convey the advantages and challenges of badging and showcase its application across a variety of contexts. Professionals in education, game development, mobile app development, and beyond will find strategies for practices such as credentialing, goal-setting, and motivation of their students.

Joey R. Fanfarelli is Assistant Professor of Games and Interactive Media in the Nicholson School of Communication and Media at the University of Central Florida, USA.

Rudy McDaniel is Director of the School of Visual Arts and Design and Professor of Games and Interactive Media in the Nicholson School of Communication and Media at the University of Central Florida, USA.

Designing Effective Digital Badges

Applications for Learning

Joey R. Fanfarelli and Rudy McDaniel

Routledge
Taylor & Francis Group

NEW YORK AND LONDON

First published 2019
by Routledge
52 Vanderbilt Avenue, New York, NY 10017

and by Routledge
2 Park Square, Milton Park, Abingdon, Oxon, OX14 4RN

Routledge is an imprint of the Taylor & Francis Group, an informa business

Library of Congress Cataloging-in-Publication Data
A catalog record for this title has been requested

ISBN: 978-1-138-30612-7 (hbk)
ISBN: 978-1-138-30613-4 (pbk)
ISBN: 978-0-203-72855-0 (ebk)

Typeset in Minion
by Swales & Willis Ltd, Exeter, Devon, UK

Dedication

We would like to dedicate this book to our wives, Kristen Fanfarelli and Carole McDaniel. If there were digital badges for spousal excellence, you would both have virtual cabinets full of them.

Contents

Part III. Evaluation and Evolution   145

Illustrations

Acknowledgments

Both authors are appreciative of their many outstanding colleagues in Games and Interactive Media, the Texts and Technology doctoral program, the Nicholson School of Communication and Media, and the School of Visual Arts and Design at the University of Central Florida. In particular, they are thankful for the ongoing support of – and exchange of ideas with – terrific colleagues including: Natalie Underberg-Goode, Cheryl Briggs, Anastasia Salter, Peter Smith, Matthew Mosher, Dan Novatnak, Mel Stanfill, Phil Peters, Terrell Theen, Matt Dombrowski, Eileen Smith, Darlene Hadrika, JoAnne Adams, Max Croft, Maria Harrington, MC Santana, Gideon Shbeeb, Barry Mauer, Stephanie Vie, and Patty Hurter. We are especially grateful to Emily Johnson, mostly for her friendship and support, but also for her delicious baked goods. Anne Sullivan has since left UCF but remains an excellent collaborator. We appreciate her ongoing contributions to our shared Slack channel and her timeless cat photography on Facebook. Finally, we appreciate all of the help and support from editor Dan Schwartz, Jamie Magyar and the editorial staff at Routledge, and our anonymous reviewers – this book is better because of your efforts.

Joey Fanfarelli would like to start by thanking his colleagues. Your constant willingness to discuss your thoughts, ideas, and opinions challenges my own conceptions and helps me to think about problems with fresh perspectives. I must also thank the TKD Club group. At the age of 18, I never knew how important you would be to my growth as a person. Most people will never get to experience the closeness of friendship that we have developed over the past 13 years. I truly value it. Special shout out to my OW team! I am especially grateful to Rudy McDaniel for the friendship and guidance that are integral to the scholar I have become. Your advice has helped me to find my place and my confidence in the academic world. Words are not enough to describe how important this has been for me as a scholar and as a person. I am extremely grateful for my family. From the youngest age, my parents pushed me to be my best and put all the structures in place for me to achieve my goals. My brother Shane has provided support, friendship, and is a fantastic gaming buddy. Last, but certainly not least, I am so incredibly grateful for my wife Kristen who supports me every day, in every way, and brings me more happiness than anyone could ever ask for.

Rudy McDaniel thanks his many colleagues at UCF for ideas and inspiration. In particular, I am thankful to Dean Jeff Moore for his support of this book and to his leadership team in the College of Arts and Humanities. Former research assistants Amanda Hill and Sara Raffel – now Dr. Hill and Dr. Raffel – contributed to this book and deserve the great things coming their way. I owe huge thanks to Janki Maraj and the stellar SVAD staff – our school runs on your talent and dedication. There is no better team to work with than Chuck Abraham, Kevin Haran, Jason Burrell, Larry Cooper, Cheryl Briggs, Steve Spencer, Allen Watters, Hannah Estes, Waheeda Illasarie, and Shannon Lindsey. I thank my hardworking NSCM and SVAD colleagues for exposing me to new ideas in communication and the visual arts, and Drs. Stella Sung, José B. Fernández, and Charlie Hughes for years of mentorship and support. Good friends Joe Muley, Jon Friskics, Peter Telep, Mike Powell, Bryce Jackson, and Eric Main provided important evenings of beer, bowling, videogames, and loud movies. I would like to especially express gratitude to Joey Fanfarelli for his many years of collaboration and friendship. It was truly a pleasure to write this book with him. Finally and most significantly, I am grateful to my family for their encouragement and eternal support, particularly my mom Ann, brother Nathan, sister Cassie, wife Carole, and children Brighton, Benjamin, and Becca. You are the ones that make all the work worthwhile.

CHAPTER 1

Introduction: What Are Digital Badges, and Why Should We Care?

Overview

This chapter introduces *Designing Effective Digital Badges* by explaining why the study of digital badges is timely. We argue that they are important to understand and consider when thinking about how best to educate and train contemporary learners; learning that is happening in an environment filled with unprecedented opportunities, but also significant challenges. We review coverage of digital badging technologies in both research and mass media contexts and then explain why these objects have seen so much attention in the news and media (and, ultimately, why we chose to write a book about them). We discuss common definitions for digital badging and differentiate them from their analog ancestors and from micro-credentials, open badges, and achievements, terms often used interchangeably in the literature. Over the last decade, various researchers, practitioners, and journalists have discussed digital badges at various times in hopeful, hyperbolic, and critical ways, and we briefly discuss each of those perspectives in this Introduction. We close the chapter by providing a personal note from the authors about why we chose to write this book as well as with a concise summary of each of the ten subsequent chapters in the book.

Why Badges?

At the 2017 gathering of the Association for Educational Communications and Technology's (AECT) annual conference, a number of educators and researchers crowded into an auditorium to hear from a panel organized by Dr. Kyle Peck, a researcher at Penn State University. This panel was presenting on digital badging and the format was somewhat unusual in that it also included a collaborative digital activity with the large audience. Dr. Peck and his assembled panelists walked the attendees through a collaborative Force Field Analysis activity, a technique from social science for examining the forces that influence a situation (Lewin, 1946). The idea behind this technique is to articulate the forces that are promoting movement toward a particular goal as well as those forces that are inhibiting movement toward that same goal. These are classified as helpful and hindering forces, respectively, and a collection of each can be useful for understanding the broader context surrounding a particular issue or idea. For example, if one wished to introduce a new technology into an elementary school classroom, this type of exercise reveals those factors that might assist the technology's adoption (e.g., enthusiasm of students, willingness of instructor) as well as those that inhibit it (e.g., complexity of technology, politics of the school district).

In Peck's exercise, attendees typed into a shared online spreadsheet what they considered to be the forces promoting digital badges (in the example spreadsheet, these were referred to as digital micro-credentials) and the forces inhibiting them. In the promoting column, the crowdsourced advantages included entries such as the need for more accurate credentials, the desire of employers for more precise measurements of employee skills and abilities, and the potential to enhance personalized pathways for learners. Attendees also noted that the devices were useful as disruptors to shake up the status quo, that they are useful for training programs, and that they meet the needs of a fundamental human desire for simplicity and clarity.

In the inhibiting forces column, the audience added entries expressing concerns over student privacy, a reluctance of faculty to change, a lack of attention from political support structures, a perceived threat to intrinsic motivation, and federal financial aid restrictions that mean students often cannot begin learning until the semester officially starts. Interesting here was the fact that these forces all came from different places – some from educational practice, some from attitudes and beliefs, and some from specific policies regarding items such as financial aid. Other rows in the inhibiting section of the spreadsheet pointed out a problematic factor with usage and adoption as a chicken-and-egg problem, in that employers are not likely to accept badges until they are widely issued by learning institutions and learning institutions are not likely to widely issue digital badges until employers seem to care about them. As usual, the often-uneasy relationship between industry and academia was noted as a potentially inhibiting force for digital badges.

What became apparent quickly in this exercise was that for every factor listed by an attendee in the promoting column, a factor in the inhibiting column soon followed. By the end of the first phase of this exercise, the group had identified an approximately equal number of promoting and inhibiting forces. Later phases of this Force Field Analysis exercise then walked participants through the process of assigning importance and modifiability scores to each identified item and then collaboratively prioritizing each item in each list. A strategic value for each item could then ultimately be calculated by multiplying importance by modifiability and would allow the master list to be ultimately down-sampled into a trimmed priority list and a final priority list of forces along with an accompanying action plan to address each item. The purpose of this final step is to identify those factors that are most appropriate to tackle if one's goal is to reduce inhibiting forces, augment promoting forces, and ultimately smooth the road for introducing a new type of technological intervention to the educational landscape.

This Force Field Analysis was a great way for this community of educators and researchers to generate a list of the perceived advantages and disadvantages of digital badges, along with the various social and political contexts that they believed could promote or suppress their implementation and adoption. It is clear that this community possessed strong feelings about the potential of this technology, but that they also saw challenges to effectively using and adopting digital badges. Furthermore, many attendees noted during the discussion the potential impact digital badges could have on learning, if deployed thoughtfully and with appropriate supports from necessary infrastructure. Indeed, in one of Peck's co-authored chapters, he acknowledged digital badges' transformative potential as a "disruptive technology that will increase the transparency and quality of educational products, while transforming communication about what has been learned" (Peck, Bowen, Rimland, & Oberdick, 2016, p. 82). The data on the spreadsheet corroborated this vision, but also introduced a number of difficulties that needed addressing. However much in agreement many of the conferences delegates seemed with this long-term utopic vision for digital badges and micro-credentials, the AECT attendees also had numerous short-term concerns about the feasibility and operation of digital badges operating at scale.

We hope that this book can provide some guidance to digital badge enthusiasts and badging novices alike about how to strengthen their chances for successful outcomes with badges. With modern digital media technologies such as learning management systems, online portals, and videogame engines, building a digital badging system has become quite approachable. Many modern systems make implementing digital badges as easy as drag-and-drop. Building an *effective* digital badging system, however, requires careful thinking about desired outcomes, design, implementation, evaluation, usability, and many other factors that we will cover in this book.

Why Now?

Before delving too deeply down into the level of detail that might differentiate an effective system from a non-effective system, let us take a moment to discuss the sociopolitical contexts surrounding digital media technologies for teaching and learning in the early 2010s. This helps us understand why these objects generated so much excitement for many educators and technologists, and some measure of concern or even controversy from others. To set the tone for digital badges' grand unveiling, we need to go back a little further in time from the 2017 AECT conference to some remarks made by Arne Duncan, the

US Secretary of Education, six years earlier (US Department of Education, 2011). These remarks characterize some of the dominant political and educational themes surrounding the launch of digital badging as a major movement in educational technology and the learning sciences.

Speaking at the onset of an event sponsored by the MacArthur Foundation, Secretary Duncan described a need for collaborative partnership and educational reform to address educational challenges and help build and sustain a world-class educational system. Working within the Obama Administration, Duncan spoke of a "cradle-to-career vision for reform," suggesting that the most ambitious educational system reforms should consider education not as a snapshot at a particular moment in one's academic timeline, but rather as the progression of an educational experience. Such an experience runs from the earliest days of early childhood education all the way through college and into career training programs for workforce development. It should capture evidence of formal learning, such as what students do in classrooms and laboratories, but also evidence of informal learning from trips to museums, visits to science centers, scouting expeditions, and projects done at home. Further, a cradle-to-career vision would need to account for a closer relationship between academic experiences and professional internships, better closing the loop between what are often disjointed learning experiences.

There are a number of challenges with such an ambitious initiative. One fundamental challenge deals with understanding and tracking the types of learning that are happening at each of these stages. There are no standardized learning modules, for example, that are flexible enough to map the content of an entire university course's content into a digital form that provides easy interfacing with the informal learning experiences described above. Further, it is difficult to know precisely where a student excels and where she struggles based on a single grade or a summative evaluation at the end of an overall experience. To fine-tune a cradle-to-career educational support system, we need more granularity. Further, our educational support structures must be robust enough to scaffold learning as it occurs longitudinally over time, not just as a snapshot at certain points through the K-12 or higher education experience. As Duncan explained, investing in education does not only mean investing in the physical buildings and instructional personnel that are present during each of these phases of education, but it also means thinking about educational technology and where this technology can assist us with these recognition and evaluation challenges. As it turns out, one of the technologies both Secretary Duncan and the MacArthur Foundation were excited about was digital badges.

Duncan's words kicked off the fourth iteration of the MacArthur Foundation Digital Media and Learning (DML) Competition. Earlier competitions, which distributed funding ranging from $5,000 to $250,000 to help support pilot projects with technology and learning, focused on themes such as innovation and knowledge-networking (DML #1), participatory learning (DML #2), and learning labs for the 21st century (DML #3). This particular challenge focused on the theme of digital badging, which Duncan characterized as systems using digital devices that could "help engage students in learning, and broaden the avenues for learners of all ages to acquire and demonstrate – as well as document and display – their skills." He spoke about the potential for digital badges to "speed the shift from credentials that simply measure seat time, to ones that more accurately measure competency." He further noted the usefulness of digital badges for both informal and formal classroom spaces, in the physical academic classrooms of K-12 and university environments and in sciences, museums, adult education systems, the military, the community, and everywhere in between. Duncan also spoke to the potential usefulness of digital badges for workforce reintegration, and introduced a "Badges for Heroes Challenge" that provided a $25,000 prize "for the best badge concept and prototype that serves veterans seeking good-paying jobs in today's economy." The ambition of the digital badging competition was grand and the scope was broad. MacArthur ended up receiving hundreds of grant proposals from many different types of industry, academic, and nonprofit organizations, all with different ideas for how badges might be used to improve learning.

Ultimately, the MacArthur DML badging competition awarded funding to 30 different projects in two primary categories: (1) badges for lifelong learning, and (2) teaching mastery and feedback (with additional support from the Bill & Melinda Gates Foundation). Grant award amounts ranged from $25,000 to $175,000. Each of these projects proposed different outcomes and purposes for their badging systems: some wished to enable more individualized learning and skills development, some focused on social learning, and others looked to motivate learning in non-academic settings such as after school programs and museums (DML Research Hub, 2012). Winners included many institutions other than traditional universities and colleges, including Disney-Pixar, NASA, the US Department of Veterans Affairs, Peer 2 Peer University, and the National Oceanic and Atmospheric Administration (Carey, 2012a). The hope was that by infusing some of these aspiring projects with both funding and institutional support, researchers could begin to evaluate the conditions in which badging systems could thrive. The projects would also be doing some good for the world at the same time, perhaps by motivating reluctant learners, providing information in a more palatable form to create more user-friendly experiences, or helping out-of-work but skilled practitioners begin new careers.

We will discuss each of these characteristics in detail throughout this book – digital badges as motivational devices, digital badges as informational tools, and digital badges as credentialing devices for performance and skill. We also consider digital badges for other purposes, and we will even speculate about hypothetical uses for the digital badges of the future. For the MacArthur Foundation and a number of government agencies and organizations, however, addressing exigencies within our modern educational landscape was a pressing concern. For such organizations to team up, acknowledge, and fund the potential of a specific educational technology in both formal and informal learning scenarios was significant. This partnership and the launch of this fourth DML competition helped to catalyze a decade of research on digital badging that has since given us much new data to consider with regard to their utility and effectiveness for teaching and learning.

Early Hopes and Concerns

Duncan's remarks were followed by a whirlwind media tour for digital badges, with a number of articles and editorials introducing them more broadly to academics and the general public alike. Kevin Carey, who serves as vice president for education policy and knowledge management at New America, a nonpartisan think tank, wrote a series of editorials and articles about badging for non-technical audiences. In an article for *The Chronicle of Higher Education*, Carey wrote of "a future full of badges," noting the nonprofit organization Mozilla's role in jumpstarting badge-related research and development, notably through the Lifelong Learning Competition Arne Duncan had recently headlined (Carey, 2012a). Major characteristics of this technology, according to Carey, included support from powerful technology partners such as Mozilla, an open-source methodology to design and implementation, and a radical shift in philosophy in thinking about how we credential learning in education.

This shift in philosophy included a migration toward holistic learning techniques such as systems thinking to "organize evidence of both formal and informal learning, from within traditional higher education and without" (Carey, 2012a, para. 6). In this vision, large-scale technology companies would partner with academic institutions and other organizational partners to create open digital repositories to hold and display digital badges. Learners can then export credentials to carry with them to document both informal and formal learning experiences and openly exchange them with academic and occupational partners. This vision carried a powerful narrative of learner empowerment, meeting the occupational skills gap, and injecting stale learning practices with innovative new mechanics. Such a system could easily be used to scaffold new ideas for educating and employing the workers of the future, many of whom it seemed would eventually be working in fields and industries not yet defined.

Carey followed up his *Chronicle* piece with an article in the *New York Times* surveying "some of the most prominent businesses and learning organizations in the world" (Carey, 2012b) that were already using the technology. These included academic organizations such as Purdue University, Carnegie Mellon University, and the University of California, but also business, government, and nonprofit organizations with examples including the Smithsonian Institution, Intel, and Disney-Pixar (Carey, 2012b). In the *New York Times* article, Carey further stressed the utility of digital badges not only for the individuals who earned them, but also for prospective employers. He recounted the story of one Oslo software engineer who earned a relatively rare "legendary" badge for his contributions to the Internet web forum Stack Overflow. The engineer received regular job offers due to the badges he had earned and his reputation within the community (Carey, 2012b). Such anecdotes spoke to the needs of employers, many of whom, when surveyed, expressed a significant preference for hiring people with experience *doing*, not just *knowing*. For example, one survey administered by *The Chronicle of Higher Education* revealed a strong preference for hiring graduates with internship and employment experience over individuals with stronger academic factors such as college reputation and grade point average (GPA) (Thompson, 2014).

Digital badges also gained attention in business circles. In *U.S. News and World Report*, Joanne Jacobs (2012) wrote about digital badges as a disruptive technology, potentially threatening colleges' and universities' market on credentialing for higher education and career preparation. She described how e-portfolios and digital backpacks would allow for the collection and display of learners' digital badges, credentials, and degrees, ultimately allowing employers to have more precise understandings of these potential employees' specific skillsets and knowledge. Better yet, these badges and credentials could be collected from various formal or informal educational experiences, not just university classrooms. This type of thinking emerged in tandem with research in social stratification and career mobility, research that documented the increasing importance of educational credentials in employment and the critical need for credentials to gain access to a growing number of occupations (Baker, 2011). Others wrote books containing information about how to use digital badges to create more engaging business software (Kumar & Herger, 2013) or shared stories about how competitive badges already provide ways to distinguish oneself on the job market (Eisenberg, 2011).

This is not to say that everyone met digital badges with open arms. Many researchers and practitioners also penned carefully considered arguments against the technology. In a blog post titled "How to earn your skeptic 'badge'," prominent academic researcher Henry Jenkins (2012) cautioned against the movement to integrate digital badges too deeply into our educational ecosystems. While he acknowledged their potential usefulness for certain types of learning applications, he worried about using them too widely, noting that the very act of imposing a formal structure on certain types of activities might work against the motivational goals of designers. He also spoke to the social and political complexities of "credit" and the public visibility of credentialing, reminding us that many capable and intelligent students deliberately choose not to earn this credit sometimes because it diminishes their social standing in peer groups. These social and political factors are complex and not always predictable. In fact, many informal learning successes, Jenkins argues, are successful precisely because they *are* emergent, ad hoc, and non-hierarchical, characteristics a digital badging system endorsed by a central authority threatens. Ultimately, Jenkins saw value in making digital badges available as a technology for learning that exists within a broader suite of options, rather than as a "one-size-fits-all solution to a range of ills in the current educational system" (2012, para. 8). He asked the academic communities and the practitioners developing badges to study them more carefully, in addition to and in comparison with other types of learning technologies, before making broader claims about their utility for learning.

Others spoke out about their concerns for the potential commercial misuse of digital badges, likening them to loyalty programs (Bogost, 2010) or comparing them to the beaconing notifications from those other dictatorial, computational taskmasters perpetually directing our attention to new tasks in our online lives (Bogost, 2013). Our mobile phones and devices, for instance, are perpetually signaling for our attention through badges and notification icons. We cover some of these arguments in more detail in Chapter 5, which focuses on badges and videogames, and Chapter 7, which focuses on digital badging in mobile applications.

Gamification: A Brief Aside

It is worth briefly mentioning here that hopes and concerns similar to those discussed above also surround the broader process of gamification. We will take a moment here to define that term. Kapp (2014) defines gamification as "an emergent approach to instruction" that "facilitates learning and encourages motivation using game elements, mechanics, and game-based thinking" (p. 42). So, adding digital badges and a class leaderboard to an online biology course would count as a gamified learning environment, as would a creative writing class that infuses fantasy into the environment to encourage creative writing in new contexts, as one of our creative writing colleagues at our home university has done (Telep, 2017). The hope is that such gamified instructional systems will motivate learners by making the learning experience more fun, perhaps by injecting fantasy into otherwise dry content or by instilling a sense of playful competition among individuals enrolled in a student's academic course or a new employee's onboarding and training program.

The problem that can occur in gamified systems, as Bogost and others have pointed out, is that by making play a requirement rather than an option, the motivational and fun aspects originally present in these game elements are lessened or eliminated entirely. Jenkins also raised this point in his critique, noting the potential danger of gamified structures that "rely so heavily on point schemes that there is far less effort to make the activities meaningful in and of themselves" (2012, para. 12). Gamified structures such as badging systems and leaderboards could also pose problems if they introduce some ideas from videogames, but not others. For instance, As Furdu, Tomozei, and Kose (2017) explain, these mandatory interactions "might create rule-based experiences that feel just like school. The effort, not mastery, should be rewarded, and the students should learn to see failure as an opportunity, instead of becoming unmotivated or fearful" (p. 58). In other words, by taking playful elements out of an environment of one type and putting them into another, we could potentially violate implicit cultural rules about experimentation, risk-taking, and safety that are in fact vital to cultivating and maintaining that fun and playful atmosphere. If we simply take the game components without also taking the game culture, we risk making a serious mistake in how we use digital badges and other gamified constructs in our learning environments.

There are other types of cultural concerns that have also been raised by technology critics and learning theorists. For example, some warn against the potential for digital badges and other gamification techniques for supporting the commodification of education, a phenomenon that might work against the cultivation of deeper types of knowledge or the historical values that undergird learning practices (Olneck, 2015). In a similar vein, Halavais (2012) has pointed out the "moral confusion" of digital badges, which seek to inspire transparency, openness, and networking while borrowing a rich history and culture from organizations like the military, one of the "most regimented and authoritative of organizations" (p. 355). All of these criticisms are valid and point toward the need for a book such as this, one that examines best practices in research and explores tactics and strategies from real-world implementations that we can borrow from and adapt to make our badges the best that they can be.

This is what we aspired to do with this book, and we hope we succeeded in this task. It was never our aim in this book to draw a line in the sand between the positive and negative attributes of digital badges and declare them as "good" or "bad" based on which side has more items. Like any technologies useful for learning, digital badges and other gamified interventions work best when they are carefully considered within a broader context of learners, teachers, technologies, and infrastructure. In supporting this inquiry, our approach is to outline the practices and design techniques we can follow, and review the research that has already provided us with data and evidence about what others have done with these technologies. There are many factors involved in digital badging, ranging from the style and tone of the visual and textual information adorning badges to the specific mechanics used to unlock them and the visibility of the badges once they are earned. This book explores each of these factors in detail in order to study what makes different systems effective in different types of learning contexts.

What Is a Digital Badge?

Having established the modern historical context for digital badges, and having reviewed some of the hopes and concerns regarding these technologies, let us consider the object itself for a moment. What exactly is a digital badge? We will go into much more detail throughout the book, but for now, a few simple definitions will suffice. A digital badge is a visual indicator of skill or accomplishment. The MacArthur Foundation describes it as "a validated indicator of accomplishment, skill, quality, or interest" (Carey, 2012a). An educational book written to teach children about badges presents an even more straightforward definition, which is "an online image that tells people about a new skill that you've learned" (Masura, 2014, p. 9). In essence, all of these definitions point toward the same thing: A digital badge is imagery that provides evidence of activity. The MacArthur Foundation's version adds the word "validated" to the definition, which is important to certain organizations involved in the creation, distribution, and evaluation of digital badges. In essence, though, validation is not a necessary requirement for all digital badges. You could earn one from a website, a formal course, or an online certification program. You could even create your own digital badge for yourself in Microsoft Paint or Adobe Photoshop or make one for your friends. The value of that digital badge, however, will largely depend on the authority of the organization or individual that bestowed it on you.

Operationally speaking, a digital badge is an "image file embedded with information" (Grant, 2014, p. 7), but that simple definition belies a deep complexity and a multitude of purposes for which badges are useful. We discuss many of these functions and purposes throughout this book, but commonly used ones are to provide evidence of authority, expertise, experience, and identity (Halavais, 2012). For example, by viewing a person's collections of earned digital badges in an online portfolio page or digital résumé, a visitor can discern that person's level of expertise, skill, and knowledge about a variety of topics and subjects. One could hypothetically distinguish seasoned participants in a digital community from novice users by comparing their respective collections of digital badges. One might even discern certain behavioral characteristics about different learners based on the specific types of digital badges each has acquired. This assumes the badges are effectively designed and well described.

Effective design is the topic of this book, but effective design requires effective description, both on a surface level and in terms of their underlying digital codes. Both levels of description are important for the human badge-seekers and for the computational systems that must process, store, and issue them. For example, most digital badges also contain metadata, or data describing the badges, that indicate how the badges were earned and include other information that ties particular digital badges to particular users (this comes in handy later, when we discuss integration with other systems). Common uses of metadata are to indicate the badge issuer, the description of the badge, and the evaluation criteria for learning (Gamrat, Zimmerman, Dudek, & Peck, 2014). Theorists interested in learning more about metadata and its powerful relationship to how we construct knowledge using digital media technologies might wish to read *The Rhetorical Nature of XML* (Applen & McDaniel, 2009). For technical enthusiasts interested in more of the nitty gritty details of metadata implementation for digital badging, a specific metadata system used for digital badges is the Open Badges 2.0 specification authored in JavaScript Object Notation (JSON). The full specification is available for review online (IMS Global Learning Consortium, 2017), and will be discussed in more detail in Chapter 2.

In discussions of digital badges, comparisons are often made between analog badges, digital badges, and different types or variations of digital badges. In the following sections, we will briefly differentiate digital badges from these other categories and provide some background context about each group.

Digital Badges vs. Analog Badges

Digital badges borrow heavily from their physical ancestors: military medals recognizing performance, Boy Scout and Girl Scout merit badges recognizing skills or accomplishments, and religious jewelry denoting prestige or authority. As Halavais (2012) notes, "the metaphor of the online badge draws on centuries of use in the offline world" (p. 354) and examples of physical badges can be traced back to roots in Roman armies where insignia were used to identify cohorts, mark units as friend or foe, and show the functional roles of different army segments (Halavais, 2012). They later evolved as objects worn on clothing or embossed on metals to be used in armor or weaponry. These objects served as durable physical credentials, providing a fast visual mechanism for showing one's allegiance, one's status, or one's relative position within a larger group. In Chapter 10, we will go back even further in history to discuss a form of very similar physical credentialing used in Ancient Mesopotamia.

The difference between digital badges and physical badges is that in relation to their analog ancestors, modern variants inherit both the advantages and disadvantages of digital technology. They are malleable, but physically impermanent. They are exceedingly flexible, but less durable. They can be copied in exact form, bit-by-bit, but they open up concerns about the privacy and security of our online information. They are networkable and immediately sharable with broad or targeted audiences, but their ease of use and distribution can diminish their perceived value. Many of our most optimistic dreams for digital media technologies, such as the democratizing potential of the medium and the instantaneous networked availability of information, can also be applied to digital badges. However, many of our deeper fears about emerging digital technologies, such as concerns about privacy, negative social effects, and a reduced control of our own personal and professional information, are also applicable.

Digital Badges vs. Micro-Credentials

In the literature, one will often find the terms "digital badges" and "micro-credentials" used somewhat interchangeably. Indeed, both terms refer to digital badges, but we agree with Elliott, Clayton, and Iwata (2014) who maintain that there are subtle differences. The term micro-credential, to these researchers and to us, implies an additional level of validation by a central authority such as an academic institution, professional organization, governing body, or a similar entity with a reputation and a body of expertise that qualify them to do this validation. Digital badges, however, can be used even to recognize work in progress that has not yet been centrally validated. Elliott, Clayton, and Iwata (2014) suggest that micro-credentials are summative and digital badges are formative, but we see the potential for digital badges to be both formative and summative. For example, digital badges might be useful for motivating certain types of behaviors in an interactive system or they might recognize performance but not require an outside central authority's blessing to do so. Nonetheless, understanding these nuances is useful as both terms will appear frequently in both academic references and applied examples of badging projects. We use "digital badges" as our preferred terminology throughout this book.

Digital Badges vs. Open Badges

Another commonly used term to describe a specific type of digital badges is "open badges." Open badges are digital badges built using open-source technologies, allowing them to be used interchangeably between different systems. This openness is important for meeting the long-term goals espoused by Arne Duncan and the Mozilla Foundation as discussed earlier in the Introduction. If each company, employer, and university were to develop their own proprietary system for managing digital badges, it would be impossibly difficult to manage the exchange and distribution of digital badges as a learner progresses through his or her lifelong learning experiences. Open badges are associated with particular open technical specifications, such as the Open Badge Infrastructure (Mozilla Open Badges, 2012) and the Open Badges 2.0 Specification (IMS Global Learning Consortium, 2017) described previously. Developers who build open badging systems must adhere to such standards in order to ensure the badges learners acquire in their courses, games, or simulations will be exchangeable and interoperable with future open badging-compatible systems that learner might use. Although we do not always use the word "open" in front of the badging systems we discuss throughout this book, we strongly support the philosophy behind open badges and believe this openness of design is a critical element to effective badge design.

Digital Badges vs. Achievements

We commonly see digital badges in videogames, often referred to as achievements, when players accomplish something inside games that developers wish to recognize. In fact, badges are often described as technologies that are "being used to improve education itself, by borrowing techniques from video games that keep users playing, until they advance to the next level" (Carey, 2012b). However, we often increasingly see them in other types of non-entertainment domains: websites, mobile fitness applications, online course management systems, simulations, adult education programs, community volunteer initiatives, and many other types of formal and informal digital learning spaces. In modern society, digital badges have gone viral.

Modern Contexts

Since Duncan's remarks and the launch of the MacArthur Foundation's badging challenge in 2011 and the subsequent national media coverage in 2012, both the media and academic research continued to focus attention on digital badges and many projects were developed and profiled in the literature. A high school in New York implemented a digital badging system to document learners' technical competencies so that they could "train students in economically challenged communities to be the technology and web literacy experts for their schools" (O'Byrne, Schenke, Willis III, & Hickey, 2015, p. 451). Badges are also heavily used to support the user experience of browsing news, informational, travel, and technical repositories, with sites such as Google News, the Huffington Post, Stack Overflow, TripAdvisor, Foursquare, and dozens of other commercial websites using their own implementations of digital badges (Halavais, 2012).

An International Phenomenon

The sustained attention has not just focused on North America, either. For example, the Waikato Institute of Technology in New Zealand is now using digital badges in a system that empowers learners with a more holistic approach to learning. The system awards digital badges that can then be shared with peers, employers, and professional organizations (Elliott, Clayton, & Iwata, 2014). An article in 2016 profiled a pilot program in Germany designed to support refugees with reintegrating into the German workforce (Ruff, 2016). The program, called Beuth Bonus, allowed migrants to earn digital credentials to provide evidence of their expertise in skills such as information technology, teamwork, and communication. Participants entered the program from countries including Afghanistan, Ghana, Nigeria, and Syria (Ruff, 2016). In addition to these smaller pilot projects, many of the large academic, nonprofit, and commercial projects that now support digital badging, such as the Mozilla Open Badge Framework, the Massachusetts Institute of Technology's MITx Program, Khan Academy, and the Joint Educational Project at the University of Southern California also support both national and international audiences (Ellis, Nunn, & Avella, 2016).

A Hybrid Approach

At this point, we have more data than ever before about digital badges, including case study reports and research findings from all 30 of the funded MacArthur Badges for Lifelong Learning projects (Grant, 2014). Mozilla keeps an accounting of hundreds of other organizations using their Open Badges platform (Mozilla, 2015) and Educause offers both a microcredentialing program with 108 digital badges in five different categories and a badging and credentialing library with resources, videos, and presentations offering tips on effective digital badge usage (Educause, 2018a, 2018b).

We mention this to explain that this book is not intended to be a purely practical guide to effective badge design, although we certainly hope readers will come away from reading the book with many ideas for how to do this. There are already a number of resources that exist with tips and practical advice for how to design with digital badges in different learning contexts. One major resource is the Design Principles Documentation Project (DPDP), which outlines recommendations for using digital badges for recognizing learning, assessing learning, motivating learning, and studying learning (Otto & Hickey, 2014). The DPDP website even provides a downloadable card deck with ideas for systems design using digital badges (Design Principles Documentation Project, 2018). Another is Sheryl Grant's book *What Counts as Learning*, which includes a very good chapter on different approaches to badging system design (Grant, 2014, chapter 10).

Rather, we hope this book is a more broad analysis of effectiveness, learning, and technology, with digital badging as the focal point of this investigation. We adopt a hybrid approach for this task, integrating a multidisciplinary approach that draws from research in both academia and industry and pulls together empirical, practical, philosophical, and theoretical ideas at various times to consider multiple perspectives on each chapter's topic. By doing so, we hope to extend the already excellent collection of emerging research on digital badges in exciting and interesting new directions.

Why We Care

We hope the information above has presented a cogent argument for why we, in the collective as educators and technologists, should care about digital badges and should better understand how they work. However, we would also like to take a brief moment to explain why we; as in the authors, personally; have chosen to invest our time over the past several years researching and writing this book. What is it about the medium and its potential that we find exciting?

For McDaniel, the ability to compress such a powerful behavioral tool into such a simple package is a fascinating conundrum. At their essence, badges are just pictures with a little text on them. Underneath the hood, though, is a sophisticated system of cause-and-effect decisions, psychological strategy, and precision engineering. The best badging systems, which we argue are often found in videogames, do all of these things synergistically to motivate users, encourage exploration, and credential expertise, all without negatively impacting the user experience. As with many of our most popular and frequently used digital media technologies, simplicity atop a sophisticated infrastructure makes for a powerful combination. For McDaniel, this makes the topic well worth studying in careful detail.

For Fanfarelli, the digital badge represents a versatile tool that can serve a variety of purposes in nearly any field. With careful design, badges can be playful goal-setting mechanisms in videogames, transferrable credentials in large institutions, feedback mechanisms in learning scenarios, and more. By understanding the way design impacts purpose, the badging designer can custom tailor their badging system to improve performance and affect across a number of different scenarios. For Fanfarelli, the expansive realm of possibilities and broad applicability make badging an exciting topic.

For both of us, we ultimately hope to both build upon existing badging research and encourage ideas for new studies and badging implementations. For example, in terms of existing research, in 2014, a report was published by the Digital Media and Learning Research Hub outlining several years' worth of progress in theorizing and implementing digital badging systems, with feedback from the MacArthur Foundation, Mozilla, HASTAC (Humanities, Arts, Science, Technology Alliance and Collaboratory) and badging researchers and practitioners from various communities (Grant, 2014). Open digital badges, which implement open-source technologies that are interoperable between various systems and implementations, were highlighted prominently in this report. As Grant (2014) writes, such badges are receiving so much attention "because they meet needs not currently being met, not only for learners ranging from Kindergarten through college, but for lifelong learners transitioning from one career to another, or for employees staying current with their careers" (p. 5). Indeed, this ability of digital badges in general, and open badges in particular, to work inside the nebulous networks that exist in contemporary academic and occupational practices is one of their key strengths. To be successful, argues Grant (2014), these systems must also be socially, academically, and technologically relevant. They must carefully consider the nature of the learning, the technologies available to certain populations of learners, and the academic learning outcomes most conducive to success. Without relevance, even the flashiest and most technologically robust badging system will fail.

Book Structure

This book is structured into three main sections. For easy reference and to aid those readers who wish to jump directly to specific topics, each of these sections and chapters is briefly summarized below.

Part I: What Is a Badge and How Should I Use It?

Part I deals with the fundamentals: how badges are built, what they can do, and how they are useful for shaping behavior. Our aim for this first section is to review the basics of badging. In Chapters 2 through 4 we cover the core components of digital badges and discuss their functionality and some common purposes and areas in which they are used. We then talk specifically about the relationship between badges and humans and how badges are useful for shaping behavior in digital environments.

Chapter 2: How Are Badging Systems Constructed?

Chapter 2 examines the composition, qualities, and types of badges, and identifies the difference between badges, badging systems, and badging backpacks. We discuss some of the different forms badges can take, from Open Badges to ranking badges. We also identify the component parts of individual badge construction. By referencing past literature and defining components such as completion logic, signifier, and reward, we present the common badging language that can be used to better understand and describe badges.

Chapter 3: What Can Badges Do?

Chapter 3 describes the variety of functions of badges, including credentialing, providing feedback, reward and so on. We also explore three psychological dimensions of badging, presenting the cognitive, affective, and social considerations for badging design to help designers acquire a more holistic picture of how badging design affects users. Design considerations are described for each function and dimension to promote an applied understanding.

Chapter 4: How Do Badges Shape Behavior?

Chapter 4 focuses on badges and human behavior. We discuss behavior from the perspective of effective design; what does an effective badge design look like in terms of eliciting particular types of behaviors from a badging system's users? We review early research on behaviorism as well as more contemporary ideas about behavior and then consider particular types of behavioral categories we might be looking to see in our digital systems. We also discuss motivation, feedback, and reward in relation to behavior.

Part II: Contexts and Practice

In Part II, we move into the nitty gritty details of digital badging. What do researchers think about when developing badges for specific implementations in videogames, online learning systems, mobile applications, and military training simulations? We chose these different contexts to highlight the different applications and audiences that exist for digital badges. Studying specific examples from each of these areas provides us with useful insights about effective design in different domains.

Chapter 5: Using Badges in Videogames

Chapter 5 discusses the digital ancestors of digital badging: game-based achievements. Videogames have developed some of the most effective strategies for gainfully using digital badges to encourage replayability and to motivate players to explore virtual worlds and invest time in complex problem-solving. While doing these things, the players are also usually having fun. In this chapter we review published research on effective strategies for videogame-based badging and review how these strategies can be carried over into other application areas.

Chapter 6: Using Badges in Online Learning Systems

Chapter 6 examines the role and possibility space for badges within the educational realm. Online learning has been steadily rising in prevalence and poses some unique challenges. We consider the different purposes that educators might want to fulfill with badges, and provide specific design recommendations and example badges to help design badges for these purposes.

Chapter 7: Using Badges in Mobile Applications

Chapter 7 reviews digital badges in mobile applications. Mobile technologies have reshaped our interactions with computers in fundamental ways. We discuss these changes and also consider some of the unique challenges introduced by this type of technology. Some of these challenges include limited screen real estate, unique power requirements to prolong battery life, and security and privacy implications.

Chapter 8: Using Badges in Military Applications

Chapter 8 identifies the role of badging in military applications. Military organizations have a long history with physical badging, and have shown interest in digital badging initiatives. In this chapter, we identify how digital badges might fill different roles from the physical badges, primarily in more niche learning situations. We identify different types of training and present examples of how badges might be designed to enhance them.

Part III: Evaluation and Evolution

Part III ventures into what might be the biggest challenge for using digital badges: measuring whether or not they actually work and predicting how they will evolve. In these two chapters, we first discuss how digital badges can be measured in various ways and we talk about different procedures for testing, data collection, and assessment using these technologies. We then consider how novelty occurs in digital badging and how we can approach themes of novelty and invention within badging systems.

Chapter 9: Badging System Testing and Evaluation

Chapter 9 is all about evaluating the success of badging systems. We describe specific badging subsystems that should be tested, and progress to discuss specific steps that are important in the testing process. We also discuss a number of different metrics and methodologies that might be useful, describing each one, and noting any special considerations.

Chapter 10: Novelty and Badging

Chapter 10 looks toward the future in considering the types of badging systems that we might wish to build to solve tomorrow's challenges with digital interactions. We discuss two different techniques for thinking about novelty – recurrence and recombination – then describe how evaluation fits into those different frameworks for thinking about novel badging systems.

Conclusion: The Future of Badging

The book closes with a number of thought exercises that consider how badges might evolve in coming years. As a young technology immersed in an environment of rapidly changing technologies and human practices, it is very likely that the digital badges we see a decade from now might look and operate somewhat differently from our badges of today. In this chapter we speculate about new designs, genres, contexts, and functions for the digital badges of tomorrow.

Next Up

In our first chapter, we will dive right in to a discussion of digital badges and their construction. We will discuss basic terminology and review the differences between different types of badges and common purposes for these technologies. In this chapter and throughout the book, we will include examples from both academic research and industry practice to frame our discussion.

References

Applen, J. D., & McDaniel, R. (2009). *The rhetorical nature of XML: Constructing knowledge in networked environments.* New York: Routledge.

Baker, D. P. (2011). Forward and backward, horizontal and vertical: Transformation of occupational credentialing in the schooled society. *Research in Social Stratification and Mobility, 29*(1), 5–29.

Bogost, I. (2010, February 10). Persuasive games: Check-ins check out. *Gamasutra.* Retrieved from www.gamasutra.com/view/feature/4269/persuasive_games_checkins_check_.php.

Bogost, I. (2013, November 8). Hyperemployment, or the exhausting work of the technology user. *The Atlantic.* Retrieved from www.theatlantic.com/technology/archive/2013/11/hyperemployment-or-the-exhausting-work-of-the-technology-user/281149/.

Carey, K. (2012a, April 8). A future full of digital badges. *The Chronicle of Higher Education.* Retrieved from www.chronicle.com/article/A-Future-Full-of-Badges/131455.

Carey, K. (2012b, Nov. 2). Show me your badge. *The New York Times*. Retrieved from www.nytimes.com/2012/11/04/education/edlife/show-me-your-badge.html.

Design Principles Documentation Project (2018). Retrieved from http://dpdproject.info/.

DML Research Hub (2012, March 1). Badges for lifelong learning competition winners announced. Retrieved from https://dmlhub.net/newsroom/media-releases/badges-for-lifelong-learning-competition-winners-announced/.

Educause (2018a). EDUCAUSE microcredentialing program. Retrieved from www.educause.edu/microcredentialing.

Educause (2018b). Badges and credentialing. Retrieved from https://library.educause.edu/topics/teaching-and-learning/badges-and-credentialing.

Eisenberg, A. (2011). For job hunters, digital merit badges. *The New York Times*. Retrieved from www.nytimes.com/2011/11/20/business/digital-badges-may-highlight-job-seekers-skills.html.

Elliott, R., Clayton, J., & Iwata, J. (2014). Exploring the use of micro-credentialing and digital badges in learning environments to encourage motivation to learn and achieve. In B. Hegarty, J. McDonald, & S.-K. Loke (Eds.), *Rhetoric and Reality: Critical perspectives on educational technology*. Proceedings ascilite Dunedin 2014 (pp. 703–707).

Ellis, L. E., Nunn, S. G., & Avella, J. T. (2016). Digital badges and micro-credentials: Historical overview, motivational aspects, issues, and challenges. In D. Ifenthaler, D. Mah, & N. Bellin-Mularski (Eds.), *Foundations of digital badges and micro-credentials: Demonstrating and recognizing knowledge and competencies* (pp. 3–21). Switzerland: Springer International Publishing.

Furdu, I., Tomozei, C., & Kose, U. (2017). Pros and cons: Gamification and gaming in classroom. *BRAIN: Broad Research in Artificial Intelligence and Neuroscience, 8*(2), 56–62.

Gamrat, C., Zimmerman, H. T., Dudek, J., & Peck, K. (2014). Personalized workplace learning: An exploratory study on digital badging within a teacher professional development program. *British Journal of Educational Technology, 45*(6), 1136–1148.

Grant, S. (2014, Aug. 31). *What counts as learning: Open digital badges for new opportunities*. Irvine, CA: Digital Media and Learning Research Hub. Retrieved from https://dmlhub.net/publications/what-counts-learning/.

Halavais, A. M. (2012). A genealogy of badges: Inherited meaning and monstrous moral hybrids. *Information, Communication & Society, 15*(3), 354–373.

IMS Global Learning Consortium (2017, March 8). Open badges 2.0 IMS candidate final/public draft. Retrieved from www.imsglobal.org/sites/default/files/Badges/OBv2p0/index.html.

Jacobs, J. (2012, Jan. 20). Digital badges threaten colleges' monopoly on credentials. *US News & World Report*. Retrieved from www.usnews.com/education/best-colleges/articles/2012/01/20/digital-badges-threaten-colleges-monopoly-on-credentials.

Jenkins, H. (2012, March 4). How to earn your skeptic 'badge.' *Confessions of an aca-fan*. Retrieved from http://henryjenkins.org/2012/03/how_to_earn_your_skeptic_badge.html.

Kapp, K. (2014). Gamification: Separating fact from fiction. *Chief Learning Officer*, March, 42–52.

Kumar, J., & Herger, M. (2013). *Gamification at work: Designing engaging business software*. Berlin, Heidelberg: The Interaction Design Foundation.

Lewin, K. (1946). Force field analysis. *The 1973 Annual Handbook for Group Facilitators*, 111–113.

Masura, S. (2014). *Digital badges*. Ann Arbor: Cherry Lake Publishing.

Mozilla (2015). Who's issuing Open Badges? Retrieved from https://openbadges.org/about/participating-issuers/.

Mozilla Open Badges (2012). *Badges/onboarding-issuer*. Retrieved from https://wiki.mozilla.org/Badges/Onboarding-Issuer#A._Mozilla_Open_Badge_Infrastructure_.28OBI.29.

O'Byrne, I., Schenke, K., Willis III, J., & Hickey, D.T. (2015). Digital badges: Recognizing, assessing, and motivating learners in and out of school contexts. *Journal of Adolescent & Adult Literacy*, *58*(6), 451–454.

Olneck, M. (2015). Whom will digital badges empower? Sociological perspectives on digital badges. In D. Hickey, J. Jovanovic, S. Lonn, & J. E. Willis III (Eds.), *Proceedings of the Open Badges in Education OBIE 2015 Workshop @ LAK* (pp. 5–11). Poughkeepsie, New York. March 16, 2015.

Otto, N., & Hickey, D. T. (2014, August). Design principles for digital badge systems: A comparative method for uncovering lessons in ecosystem design. In *International Conference on Web-Based Learning* (pp. 179–184). Cham: Springer.

Peck, K., Bowen, K., Rimland, E., & Oberdick, J. (2016). Badging as micro-credentialing in formal education and informal education. In L. Y. Muilenburg & Z. L. Berge (Eds.), *Digital badges in education: Trends, issues, and cases* (pp. 82–92). New York: Routledge.

Ruff, C. (2016, April 16). Online badges help refugees prove their academic achievements. *The Chronicle of Higher Education*. Retrieved from www.chronicle.com/article/Online-Badges-Help-Refugees/236278.

Telep, P. (2017). Role-playing, simulations, and game design techniques to increase student engagement and motivation. *UCF Faculty Focus*, *16*(3), 1–2.

Thompson, K. (2014, Aug. 19). The thing employers look for when hiring recent graduates. *The Atlantic*. Retrieved from www.theatlantic.com/business/archive/2014/08/the-thing-employers-look-for-when-hiring-recent-graduates/378693/.

US Department of Education (2011). Digital badges for learning: Remarks by Secretary Duncan at 4th Annual Launch of the MacArthur Foundation Digital Media and Lifelong Learning Competition. Retrieved from www.ed.gov/news/speeches/digital-badges-learning.

PART I

What Is a Badge, and How Should I Use It?

CHAPTER 2

How Are Badging Systems Constructed?

Overview

Before we can begin discussing how to create badges for specific applications, we need to understand the parts of a badge that can be manipulated by designers. We also need to recognize the different badging terms and systems, and how they relate to one another. This knowledge primes the designer to consider the variety of factors that accompany the design of both simple and complex badging systems and enables her to have greater mastery over each individual component. This chapter describes these various structures and hierarchies not only to achieve these goals, but also to denote a common language that will be used throughout the rest of this book. We begin with a description of how individual badges are constructed and then proceed to describe badging hierarchies. Through this sequence, we will show how individual badges can be grouped into various badging systems and subsystems and illustrate their relationships with one another. Finally, we present several different types of badging sub-structures that can be used, depending on the designer's goals. Ultimately, this chapter will help you to understand what a badge is, which badging components exist and can be manipulated, and how to start thinking about the bigger picture of badging design.

Individual Badges

Before we get into the larger systems and components, it is useful to start with the basics. The individual badge is the smallest complete unit within a badging system. This section takes an in-depth look at the components of badges and their permutations in order to facilitate future discussion of how to design, alter, or otherwise customize badges to achieve the designer's goals.

Breaking Down the Badge: Components

Just as combinations of different molecules make the different objects in our world, different components combine to form badges with varying qualities.

Understanding these components is important for visualizing how a badge is constructed. This understanding also helps us become better badge designers; each component is a point of manipulation, design, or improvement, and is something that can and should be designed with care and purpose.

Hamari and Eranti (2011) presented a digital badging framework that deconstructed badges into three distinct components: the signifier, completion logic, and reward. These are defined as follows:

1. Signifier – The visual portion of the badge that might include images and/or text. The signifier typically includes:

   - *Name* – A unique identifier for each badge.
   - *Description* – A string of text that describes the badge and may include hints or direction on how to earn the badge.
   - *Visual* – An image that is representative of the badge.

2. Completion Logic – The actions that must be completed in order to earn the badge. The completion logic is composed of:

   - *Trigger* – Denotes what a player has to do or what change must occur in a system before a user can be evaluated for potential badge awarding (e.g., end of a patient treatment training scenario).
   - *Pre-requirements* – Requirements that must be met before the trigger can occur (e.g., hard difficulty setting).
   - *Conditions* – Conditions that extend the earning requirements (e.g., trainee performed no unnecessary procedures on patients).
   - *Multiplier* – Specifies how many times the user must meet the requirements before a badge can be earned (e.g., trainee successfully treated five patients).

3. Reward – What the earner will be given once the badge has been earned.

In addition to Hamari and Eranti's physical components, we also include the *metadata* component, which includes information beyond what is shown on the badge's signifier. The metadata accompanies the badge and can usually be accessed by clicking the badge or a related hyperlink. This metadata might include information such as the date the badge was earned, who was awarded the badge, evidence of badge earning (e.g., material submitted for completion), or other relevant information. Let us examine each component in greater detail, beginning with the most frequently considered part of the badge – the signifier.

Signifier

Badges include a visual element (deMaine, Lemmer, Keele, & Alcasid, 2015) that most users would consider to be the actual badge. This visual portion of the badge is called the *signifier*, and typically includes the badge's name, description, and an image. It does not include the earning mechanisms or rewards associated with the badge, but it might include descriptions of these things.

Name

The *name* of each badge should be unique and descriptive. For instance, while a badge named "Team Leader" does not inform exactly how that particular badge can be earned, it does provide some sense of the types of qualities the earner might exhibit to earn the badge, especially when earned in a specific context (e.g., team-based competitive videogame, group work in a classroom, military command). Naming conventions are often context-specific – while playful or humorous names are often appropriate in a videogame, they are probably less appropriate for most military combat simulators, although exceptions exist. Similarly, badge names are commonly themed along with the system they are badging within. Classroom-based badges might have names like "Head of the class" or "Easy A." However, the themes do not necessarily need to be quite so stringently related to the context; some instructors have used fantasy-based names for their badging system (e.g., "Knight of the Multiplication Table"). Creativity in the name and description of a badge can help a badging system align with pre-existing themes (e.g., role-playing exercises in class), or might simply infuse a bit of fun to a scenario where more engagement is desirable.

Description

The *description* of the badge is the text-based descriptor that is visible on a badge. This most often includes text that hints or tells the user how the badge can be earned, but it might also include other information such as rewards, narrative-based text, or congratulatory messages. The text description's level of specificity should be tailored to the badge's goals. For example, when badges are being used to help users set appropriately difficult goals, care should be given to ensure that the description is clear and explicit.

On the other hand, sometimes descriptions might be better left vague, or only hinting at the requirements of earning. Badges can be useful for encouraging students to explore, whether in learning, gameplay, or for leisure. Sometimes we want users to experiment in an environment in order to identify the conditions for unlocking the badge. Oftentimes, if we tell the user exactly what we want them to do – especially in educational settings – they will do precisely what was asked of them and no more. However, leaving goals a bit nebulous can encourage users to try to figure out what is being requested of them in order to acquire the badge and any associated rewards.

Consider a medical simulation where trainees are learning to treat burn victims. You might have badges with the following names and descriptions:

- Ouch – "Treat 5 burn victims."
- Just Warming Up – "The criteria for earning this badge are locked."
- Hot, Hot, Hot – "The criteria for earning this badge are locked."
- On Fire! – "The criteria for earning this badge are locked."

If you know the simulation requires trainees to treat at least ten burn victims in order to be successful, you could help the user progressively build toward that goal by making the Ouch badge's description explicit, as we have done in this example: "Treat 5 burn victims." After treating five more burn victims, the trainee would then stumble upon the "Just Warming Up" badge. Now, the trainee has learned that there was a second badge for treating burn victims. She might now begin to wonder if there are more badges for treating even more burn victims, and continue to treat victims to see if she can figure out how to unlock the other badges.

The description can also be used to provide information to the user beyond the earning conditions, such as feedback. When a human grades an assignment, provides feedback on a trainee's skill, or critiques someone's gameplay, she takes into account a variety of factors and provides the most appropriate information to help that person improve. Likewise, badges are unlocked only under certain conditions and may deliver feedback via the badge's description. Consider a scenario where students commonly make a mistake in programming. For example, perhaps they retype the same code over and over again instead of using a loop, which would more efficiently do the same task. If a badge is awarded for successful completion of the task, but repetitive content is detected, the badge can include a description that says, "You've completed the assignment, but you seem to repeat your code quite a bit. Have you considered using a loop?" A follow-up badge might be named "Looped" and be given for students who not only complete the task, but do it efficiently, providing incentive to listen to the feedback and achieve a greater level of proficiency.

Visual

The *visual* is the image associated with a badge. In tandem with the other subcomponents of the signifier, the visual forms each badge's unique identity. It is the face of the badge that, when well-designed, can make it instantly recognizable to users. Just as visuals can form unique identities for each badge, so too can they create cohesive group identities for badges within the same system.

Individuality vs cohesiveness is an important balance, and constitutes two critical considerations in visual design. When badges within a system share a color scheme, theme, shape, font, or other qualities, they are more recognizable as being from the same group. For instance, a school-wide badging system could utilize school colors in the background of each badge. Likewise, another organization might use their logo in the background of each badge to show ownership of badges in a system.

Designing the visual to support badging individuality can help individual badges to be recognizable by experienced users. While a first-time user reads the badge's description to understand what the badge represents, returning users can be more efficient by associating the description with the visual and instantly recognizing the badge on sight. To achieve this, it is useful to ensure that badges are not *too* similar. While cohesiveness can be established through badge shape, colors, logos, and so on, individuality may be promoted by using a unique image or icon for each badge. When developing the visuals for badges in a badging system, the designer should consider which common features will be shared by all badges and which features will be manipulated to show individuality.

Consider a badging system from a particular school whose colors are black and gold. While all badges might have a black and gold background, the chemistry badge might contain an image of an Erlenmeyer flask. With cohesiveness established by the background design, the flask and other elements within the image are free to use color schemes that accent their uniqueness or otherwise help to create the badge's identity. For instance, using subdued professional colors might be prudent for a badge that is likely to be used in a portfolio, while vibrant playful designs might be more appropriate for badges that are meant to reward children.

It is important to note that not all badges must have all three elements. Some badges, especially ranking badges (McDaniel & Fanfarelli, 2016) are often much simpler. These types of specialized badges might exclude the description, name, or both, potentially leaving only the image which acquires meaning through external or non-text means. A ranking badge is a unique type of badge that will be discussed later in this chapter.

Completion Logic

While the signifier is the visible face of the badge, the completion logic makes up the inner workings. If a badge is a vehicle for encouraging or rewarding actions or behaviors, then the completion logic is what lies "underneath the hood" of the vehicle, so to speak. The completion logic and its subcomponents were first detailed by Hamari and Eranti (2011) in reference to videogames. It is defined as the set of requirements that users must complete in order to earn the badge. Note that the logic denotes the actual requirements and is thus separated from the badge's description. While a description might give hints or outright tell a user how to earn the badge, it might also omit this information completely or even be intentionally misleading, according to the designer's goals. The completion logic and badge description are two separate points of manipulation for the badging designer and should be considered as such in order to open the designer's full toolkit. Let us look at the subcomponents of completion logic in greater depth. These include the trigger, pre-requirements, conditions, and multiplier (Hamari & Eranti, 2011).

Trigger

The trigger is the primary action that must be completed before a badge can be earned. Consider a videogame that awards a badge for defeating ten enemies.

Defeat ten enemies would be the trigger. Likewise, a meditation app might have a trigger of *meditate for 15 minutes.* These two examples show two different types of triggers: (1) *player-invoked actions* and (2) *system-invoked events* (Hamari & Eranti, 2011). While the first trigger is assessed for completion when a player kills an enemy (player-invoked action), the second is assessed after the app clocks 15 minutes (system-invoked event). The trigger may stand alone, as in the examples described above, or might be accompanied by other requirements that must be satisfied.

Pre-Requirements

While a trigger specifies what must be completed during a use session, the *pre-requirements* dictate what must happen before a use session even begins (Hamari & Eranti, 2011). A marksmanship simulator might have three levels of difficulty: (1) easy – static targets, (2) medium – lateral moving targets, and (3) hard – moving enemies. If a trigger mechanism is created that specifies that the trainee must *neutralize ten targets* for a badge award, a pre-requirement might specify that it has to happen *in medium difficulty mode.* Likewise, a math game with a trigger that requires the player to *complete 100 math problems* might require them to complete the problems *in time attack mode,* where there is a countdown timer that ends the session when it reaches zero. The pre-requirements can include any number of requirements before the use session begins, including specific system settings (e.g., in-game tips disabled), modes (e.g., time attack), difficulties (e.g., easy or hard), avatar or ability customizations (e.g., wizard or knight), time of play (e.g., day or night), or anything else that can be chosen before the use session begins.

Conditions

The conditions fall somewhere between the trigger and pre-requirements. While the pre-requirements specify what must happen before the use session begins and the trigger denotes what must happen during the use session, the conditions describe what must occur during the use session, but before the trigger is satisfied (Hamari & Eranti, 2011). To extend our marksmanship simulator example, the trainee might need to neutralize ten targets in medium difficulty mode *while in prone position.* During the session, the trainee must move into the prone position and then complete the trigger mechanic, assuming the difficulty was set before the session started (pre-requirements).

Multiplier

The multiplier is simply how many times the user must complete all other portions of the completion logic. We have actually already been talking about this one in our examples. Neutralizing *ten* targets or completing *100* math problems specifies the multiplier for those particular completion logics. Respectively, the logics must be satisfied ten or 100 times.

Reward

After the completion logic is fulfilled and a badge is earned, some type of *reward* might be given to the earner. Rewards can include digital or real-world perks. Typical rewards include advantages such as power-ups or special cosmetic items in a game, extra credit in a course, or a discount at the local coffee shop. Additionally, the badges might be considered rewards in and of themselves (Blair, 2011). The word reward is used in a complex way here, as badges might or might not be viewed as rewards, and they might or might not be accompanied by other rewards, depending on the system's design. Just as sports enthusiasts value medals for significant physical achievements (e.g., completing a marathon), digital badges that are given for significant achievements will likely feel more rewarding.

However, if the tasks being badged do not feel challenging, the badge is unlikely to be valued by the user and might simply be seen as a digital image. If a user is given a badge for creating an account in a web forum, she is unlikely to feel accomplished and will probably not feel that the badge is rewarding. That said, sometimes we, as designers, want to encourage mundane tasks – such as account creation – and can encourage other rewards that go along with the badge (e.g., currency or reputation points). The link between badges as rewards and proper design to support this use is a complex topic that will be discussed in greater depth in Chapter 3.

Metadata

While some digital badges might be formed by only an image and associated text, some badges might contain a clickable hyperlink that allows a viewer to see more information about the badge. This is a mechanism for viewing the badge's underlying *metadata*. When clicked, the metadata might provide the user with information that describes how the badge was earned, why it was earned, or even with evidence of the work that earned the badge (deMaine, Lemmer, Keele, & Alcasid, 2015). Metadata can be embedded in a few different ways; one example of a JSON-LD (JavaScript Object Notation for Linked Data) metadata file is shown below (Figure 2.1).

Whether or not you are familiar with JSON-LD or key-value pair notation, a quick scan of the text communicates information about the specific badge, who issued it, and why it was issued. It is important to note that this is a partial example of metadata for a particular type of badge, called the Open Badge; we will discuss Open Badges a bit later in this chapter. A full metadata file will include even more information regarding the badge, issuer, and earner. A complete list of specifications for Open Badges metadata can be obtained from IMS Global (2017).

```
...
"badge": {
  "type": "BadgeClass",
  "id": "https://ucf.edu/badges/php/5",
  "name": "PHP – Strong Start",
  "description": "This badge is awarded for acquiring an A on the PHP coding module at the University of Central Florida.",
  "image": "https://ucf.edu/badges/php/php1/image",
  "criteria": {
    "narrative": "Students demonstrate mastery of simple variable use through a PHP project."
  },
  "issuer": {
    "id": "https://ucf.edu/jfanfarelli",
    "type": "Profile",
    "name": "University of Central Florida",
    "url": "https://ucf.edu",
    "email": "joey@ucf.edu",
      "verification": {
        "allowedOrigins": "ucf.edu"
      }
  }
}
...
```

Figure 2.1 Abridged metadata file

Metadata extends the usefulness and credibility of badges because it "provides context, meaning, process and result of an activity" (Gibson, Ostashewski, Flintoff, Grant, & Knight, 2013, p. 404). While metadata is most often associated with credentialing badges (i.e., badges that serve as indicators of learned knowledge, acquired skill, or accomplished feat in the educational domain to provide evidence of learner accomplishments), it can be used in other ways and in other domains. For example, some videogame badge logics require players to be playing a particular game mode or difficulty level when they accomplish the tasks required to earn the badge (i.e., pre-requirements, as discussed above). While most contemporary badges tend to explicitly state the requirement in the badge's description, these badges could be modified to incorporate mode and difficulty metadata to allow players to see the various conditions under which they have fulfilled the badge's completion logic. A player who has only earned the badge in easy mode would have "easy" reflected in the badge's difficulty metadata.

- "difficulty":"Easy"

Likewise, a player that has completed the logic against both AI and human players would have both of these reflected in the badge's game mode metadata.

- "versus":"AI,Human"

This sort of metadata allows the earner and other users to understand the earner's accomplishments in order to be appropriately competitive or support the player in her successes.

Badging Hierarchy

With an understanding of the badging components, we are ready to consider how badges fit into the larger badging ecosystem. Badges are integrated into different organizational structures that designate which badges are related, how they are related, and where they can or cannot be shared or accessed. Here, we describe the relationships between individual badges, metabadges, badging systems and subsystems, and, ultimately, badging backpacks.

Metabadges

A *metabadge* is a badge that is awarded after earning a series of other badges (deMaine, Lemmer, Keele, & Alcasid, 2015). These badges are useful for signifying the achievement of larger milestones, complex competencies, or simply a combination of related accomplishments. For example, consider a badging system for a biology course. Individual badges might be given out for demonstrating competency using different pieces of lab equipment (e.g., microscope, centrifuge). Once a student receives all of the different equipment badges, she will be issued the "Equipment Master" badge, which signifies her mastery over a range of different laboratory tools (Figure 2.2).

Badging Systems

A *badging system* is a collection of explicitly related badges. Each of the badges in a particular videogame, website, app, class, or training course may constitute its own badging system. However, badging systems vary widely in scale and are often defined in slightly different ways. For instance, while one videogame might have its own badging system, the badging systems of all videogames on a particular console might constitute a badging system, too. Likewise, all badges in one course might compose a badging system, but so might all badges in all courses at a particular university. Thus, a badging system could be composed of five badges, or five thousand; in the case of classifying a group of badges as a system, the number of badges is less important than the relationships between badges. Badging systems can stand alone, or be part of another larger system, such as a videogame or website.

Figure 2.2 Illustration of badges required to earn the Equipment Master metabadge

Badging Backpacks

Badges in a badging system might be stored in a badging *backpack* (deMaine, Lemmer, Keele, & Alcasid, 2015). A backpack is a place for earners to store badges from different issuers (Devedzic & Jovanovic, 2015) and thus is a place where badges from different badging systems can be combined into one centralized location.

When considering adopting or developing a badging backpack, you should consider the importance of *portability*. Here, portability refers to the extent of your ability to transfer and display badges across different platforms. For instance, earning a badge for exceptional programming ability in a learning management system would be far more useful if the earner could also display this badge on an ePortfolio site for viewing by potential employers. Likewise, a user using a running app would benefit from being able to share badges on social media and other places that might provide social support for achieving her fitness goals. Thus, portability is especially important when the effects of badging can be enhanced by the addition of social factors.

Badge Qualities and Types

Badges come in a variety of shapes and sizes, but differ in other ways that are arguably more important than their visual differences. Badges can be viewed, awarded, or modified in many different ways. The research is already beginning to show that the ways in which badges differ are not superfluous; not only can a badge's properties affect how well it fits its purpose, it can also affect the badge's actual effectiveness (e.g., how it interacts with earner motivation). Here, we discuss these differences.

Expected and Unexpected Badges

Badges can be designed to be either *expected* or *unexpected* (Blair, 2011). An expected badge is one that can be viewed before earning. In other words, when it was received, it was expected to be received. The user knew exactly when it would be awarded. An unexpected badge is hidden until earned. The user has no way of knowing what it takes to unlock the badge; receiving it is an unexpected event.

While these two qualifiers are useful for describing badge design, badging systems do not need to be wholly expected or unexpected. Blair (2011) suggested mixing both expected and unexpected badges within a badging system to acquire the benefits of both types of badges. This makes sense when you consider the effects each type of badge can have. For example, expected badges facilitate goal-setting – by knowing which badges exist and what it takes to acquire them, users can intentionally set out to earn the badges they want. This can be quite useful whenever you want the user to perform specific actions (e.g., rote learning through completing an action ten times) as you can use these actions to let her know about important and worthwhile goals.

However, any teacher will tell you that some students will often do only what is required of them, sometimes limiting creativity, effort, and ability to reach their full potential. Thus, if all badges are prescribed, the user might take a linear and rigid path to earn them, stifling exploratory inclinations. This is where unexpected badges shine. While a user cannot set a specific and targeted goal to earn a badge they do not know exists, they can set a goal to find whatever mysterious badges do exist within a system. In other words, unexpected badges can lead to experimentation or exploration.

Consider a simple example where a badge is awarded for completing five chemistry exercises (e.g., creating stable compounds). The user does not know this badge exists, but perhaps the system is designed in such a way that she will end up completing five exercises without much effort – maybe ten exercises are required by the instructor. Now, in this same badging system is a badge that is awarded for completing ten exercises. The user might begin to think, "I wonder if there is a badge for 15 exercises?" If you have a task that benefits from repetition, this could be a useful strategy, especially in learning or training applications.

In games, designers can use these unexpected badges to encourage users to spend more time exploring and discovering game content to increase playtime and showcase more nuanced aspects of design, such as hidden parts of the game world, or to discover special features within the software. Blending expected badges and unexpected badges can make for a multipurpose badging system that facilitates goal-setting while encouraging exploration and creativity. We will return to badging in videogames in Chapter 5, where expected and unexpected badges will reemerge alongside measurement and completion badges.

Measurement and Completion Badges

Completion badges (Blair, 2011) are awarded when a user completes a particular task. As long as the user completes the required task, the badge will be awarded – no matter how efficiently or skillfully the task was completed. The previously described chemistry badge is an example of a completion badge. As long as the exercises are completed, the badge will be awarded.

Measurement badges (Blair, 2011) are awarded when a user completes a particular task *to a certain degree*. While completion badges are unconcerned with performance, measurement badges demand demonstration of a particular level of skill or efficiency. If a completion badge is given out for completing a set of 50 math problems, a measurement badge might be awarded for completing 50 math problems within five minutes. Similarly, a measurement badge might be awarded for 90% accuracy in the answers given to those 50 math problems. Both of these examples move beyond mere completion to include skill or efficiency along the way to completion.

Functionally, these two types of badges are likely to be quite similar, except for the types of activities they badge; you will never use a completion badge for a measurement task, or vice versa. However, you may carefully design your tasks so that they are measurement or completion tasks, and then use the correct badges. Asking a player to complete the first level (and badging for it), will likely encourage them to do just that, but they might not put much effort into doing much else in the first level. Conversely, asking the player to complete the first level without defeating any enemies will cause the player to play that level in a very different way than they otherwise would have. This change in gameplay might extend the total play time, make the game more interesting, or alter player behavior in other ways. If we connect this with the previous section and make this an unexpected badge, the player might begin to wonder what other ways they can complete the level to potentially earn other badges. This encourages players to try new play styles.

Of course, measurement badges are not always better; sometimes you just need the user to complete a task without any regard for degree of success. It probably does not matter how a web forum user sets a profile picture. There is probably no benefit to making the process more difficult. You just want the user to set their picture so that the forum feels more like a community. Each task should be intentionally designed, and then badged appropriately; while badges can sometimes be used to alter the way a user approaches a task, task design and badge design are often strongly linked.

Ranking Badges

Ranking badges are badges that denote an individual's rank within a ranking system. These types of badges are closely related to the types of credentials given out by military or scouting organizations. These badges are often quite different from other badges in both their looks and underlying logics. Just as with military ranks, ranking badge signifiers almost always have an image that denotes the particular rank of the earner, but they often lack a name or description. These missing components do typically exist somewhere and are typically well known by the community of potential earners, but they are not part of the badge's signifier. Instead, they are often located externally. For example, Blizzard Entertainment's team-based competitive first-person shooter game, *Overwatch* (2016), uses ranking badges to denote the relative skill of players (Figure 2.3).

In *Overwatch*, each ranking badge has an associated name (i.e., Bronze, Silver, Gold, Platinum, Diamond, Master, Grandmaster, Top 500), yet each player's ranking badge is shown without its name or any description before, during, and after every match. Players can visit other places within the game, *Overwatch*'s official website, or other places on the web (e.g. YouTube), in order to learn the name that goes with each image. They can also learn more about the underlying hierarchy of the badging system, ultimately understanding that there is an order to the badges (e.g., bronze is less prestigious than silver).

Ranking badge completion logics often position the earner's performance relative to other potential earners. At the end of *Overwatch*'s 8th competitive season, only the top 1% of players held the Grandmaster or Top 500 badge. Ranking in

Figure 2.3 Ranking badges in Blizzard's *Overwatch* (Blizzard Entertainment, 2016)

comparison to other players is determined by a number called Skill Rating, which increases or decreases after every game win or loss, making it a number that is influenced by performance against other players. The completion logic for each badge requires an in-game Skill Rating number to be within a particular range (e.g., the Master badge is given for players with Skill Ratings between 3500 and 3999). Not all games have a number like this available to players. Instead, they might use relative completion logics based on social factors, such as success relative to other players (McDaniel & Fanfarelli, 2016).

One new dimension introduced by ranking badges is the permanency of the digital objects. In other words, badges can be removed if the requisite conditions are no longer met, or added when new conditions allow for it. For example, in most types of badging systems, when a badge is earned, it is permanently given to the user. In contrast, ranking badges can be upgraded or downgraded, and typically only one badge can be held at a time. In *Overwatch*, a player might attain the Top 500 badge for being one of the best players. However, if the player falls to 501st place, the player's badge could be downgraded to the Grandmaster badge. Similarly, climbing back into the 500th spot will upgrade the player back to the Top 500 badge.

Ranking badges are typically valuable because they are earned along with social capital and prestige. A player's ranking badge is publicly showcased so that the community can approximate the earner's skill level and competitive success. Thus, the badge becomes not only an indication of the earner's hard work, but can also serve as a symbol of social status (Antin & Churchill, 2011) among peers within a competitive community. In addition, other, more tangible rewards might also be provided. In *Overwatch*, at the end of each season, a player is given in-game currency in an amount dependent upon her earned rank. While most badges provide rewards at the time of earning, ranking badges that provide additional rewards typically provide these rewards on a delayed timeframe, requiring the earner to maintain their ranking until a particular triggering event takes place (e.g., end of a competitive season). Overall, these badges are unique and might not be a good fit for all systems. However, they have been quite successful in their implementation for certain applications, both in their historical tangible form (e.g., military medals), and in their current digital form (e.g., competitive gaming).

Credentialing Badges and the Open Badges Standard

Similar to how ranking badges tell the story of the earner's current skill level at a particular task, *credentialing badges* serve as evidence of particular skills or competencies. Earlier, we discussed the importance of portability in badging backpacks. These portable systems enable users to transfer their badges from their badging systems to backpacks and from backpacks to other digital locations (e.g., ePortfolios, or social media). While portability is a necessary requirement for credentialing badges, it is not the only requirement.

Trust is another concern that accompanies portability. The issuer's credibility is important to the badge's worth (Gibson, Ostashewski, Flintoff, Grant, & Knight, 2015). For instance, a friend can provide you with a gold star for your efforts, but an employer is unlikely to be impressed by such a gesture. Conversely, future employers might be more impressed by a Microsoft-issued badge for computer science prowess. But, can that employer trust the badge actually came from Microsoft? If a badging display platform is too lax, it is possible that a user could create a badge for herself and claim that it came from a prestigious authority. Thus, both issuers and badging backpacks need to have a transparent and understandable validation system in place. The Open Badges standard is one such system.

Open Badges (Mozilla, 2016) is a badging standard for creating free, distributable, and understandable badges that contain descriptive metadata. Badges that conform to the Open Badges standard are called open badges. This standard packages a badge into a single image file that contains the badge's image; metadata about the badge, earner, and issuer; and evidence that the earner satisfied the badge's completion logic. The Open Badges standard allows earners to store and display badges from multiple different issuers in one centralized location; the standardization of these badges makes them portable, enabling users to move their badges between any systems that support the Open Badges standard.

This is important because credentialing is not typically a unidimensional endeavor. The Open Badges standard combines with backpacks and display sites to enable users to display the badges they have earned from multiple issuers, thus providing a more complete representation of a particular user. Consider a biology student applying to graduate school. It might be worthwhile to know that she did very well in several aspects of her Biology I course, but it is perhaps more useful to know how she did in the multitude of courses that are relevant to the graduate program in which she is applying. Beyond courses, it might also be worthwhile knowing that she served as president of her student organization, that she received special recognition during a summer internship at a prestigious lab, and that she was awarded an undergraduate research award.

With Open Badges, each of these courses and organizations could create their own badging systems and issue badges to the earner. This earner could then decide which of these badges are most relevant to her application and selectively display them on a badging site or in a backpack, helping reviewers better understand the person they are reviewing. While this sounds very much like the current process of crafting the perfect résumé, it offers the additional benefit of traceability. The Open Badges metadata not only includes information about the issuer, but also provides proof of the student's prowess, providing evaluators with more information and confidence about the credentials in front of them.

Incremental Badges

Incremental badges are awarded in sequence as a user completes more of a task, or at increasing levels of difficulty, complexity, or proficiency (Blair, 2011). These badges are useful for scaffolding processes in order to break complex tasks down into simpler, more manageable tasks. Users can feel more confident achieving these smaller milestones, ultimately building up to the most difficult or complex form of the task. For example, badges in a marksmanship simulator might be given out for achieving 25%, 50%, 75%, and 100% accuracy, or for hitting all targets within increasingly smaller time limits. A new badge can be given out for each individual accomplishment, or the badge can simply be upgraded each time a new level of success is achieved. In the latter case, the 25% accuracy badge might be bronze in appearance or designation (e.g., in the badge's name or description). Subsequent badges might upgrade the badge to the silver, gold, and platinum variants, respectively, with corresponding updates in the badge graphic and associated text.

Incremental badges may work in tandem with, or as a substitute for, metabadges. In the latter situation, users might receive progressively better badges for completing more tasks on a list of tasks (e.g., 1 task = bronze, all = platinum). Refer back to the laboratory equipment example. Learning to use the first piece of equipment might award a bronze badge, while learning to use all of the equipment might upgrade the badge to platinum. Incremental badges are sometimes also called *leveling badges* due to their similarity to a level-up system within a videogame (Hamari & Eranti, 2011).

Conclusion

We have described how badging systems are constructed, paying particular attention to the varying points of manipulation within badging design. The thoughtful designer will consider each component as an opportunity for intentional design and take care to make purposeful design decisions. In addition to allowing designers to be more specific and intentional in their design, this chapter also serves as a beginning roadmap for badging researchers. Badging research has shown variable effectiveness of badges. Frankly, sometimes they work and sometimes they do not. By understanding how badges are constructed, researchers can study a range of different configurations of these components in order to identify the most effective permutations of badge designs for each situation. These badging components and types will be revisited in later chapters as we discuss how they can be designed for more specific applications, within several domains and for several purposes.

Next Up

Now that we know about the components and construction of badges and badging systems, we move on to discuss some of the functions of badges. While many consider badges for their reward or credentialing purposes, and these are two very important purposes, their potential extends far beyond these two functionalities. In the next chapter, we identify what badges are capable of and discuss the many ways in which they can be used.

References

Antin, J., & Churchill, E. F. (2011). Badges in social media: A social psychological perspective. *In CHI 2011 Gamification Workshop Proceedings (Vancouver, BC, Canada, 2011)*. Retrieved from http://gamification-research.org/wp-content/uploads/2011/04/03-Antin-Churchill.pdf

Blair, L. (2011). *The use of video game achievements to enhance player performance, self-efficacy, and motivation* (Doctoral Dissertation). University of Central Florida, 1–30.

Blizzard Entertainment (2016). *Overwatch* [PC]. Irvine, California: Blizzard Entertainment.

deMaine, S. D., Lemmer, C. A., Keele, B. J., & Alcasid, H. (2015). *Using digital badges to enhance research instruction in academic libraries*. In B. L. Eden (Ed.), *Enhancing teaching and learning in the 21st century academic library* (pp. 59–78). Lanham, MD: Rowman & Littlefield.

Devedzic, V., & Jovanovic, J. (2015). Developing open badges: A comprehensive approach. *Educational Technology Research & Development, 63*(4), 603–620.

Gibson, D., Ostashewski, N., Flintoff, K., Grant, S., & Knight, E. (2015). Digital badges in education. *Education and Information Technologies, 20*, 403–410.

Hamari, J., & Eranti, V. (2011). Framework for designing and evaluating game achievements. *Proceedings of DiGRA 2011*, Hilversum, Netherlands.

IMS Global (2017). Open badges v2.0: IMS candidate final/public draft. *IMS Global Learning Consortium*. Retrieved from www.imsglobal.org/sites/default/files/Badges/OBv2p0/index.html

McDaniel, R., & Fanfarelli, J. (2016). Building better digital badges: Pairing completion logic with psychological factors. *Simulation & Gaming, 47*(1), 73–102.

Mozilla (2016). What's an open badge? Retrieved from https://openbadges.org/get-started/

CHAPTER 3

What Can Badges Do?

Overview

In the previous chapter, we discussed the component parts that make up badges and badging systems as well as some of the different forms badges can take. Now, we shift our focus to what we can actually *do* with badges. While the credentialing and reward functions of badges are those most often covered in the academic literature and popular press, there are many other purposes badges can fulfill. In this chapter, we discuss those credentialing and reward functions for badges, but we also review some other less-often considered badging functions and some associated considerations regarding their design for these other uses. We begin by examining some of the common psychological dimensions that can be affected by badges and progress to explore specific targeted functions of badges.

Psychological Dimensions of Badging

At this point, we have discussed the physical components of badges, how they work together to construct individual badges, and how individual badges combine to form badging systems and subsystems. Certainly, the rest of this book would not be possible to write without this foundation. However, this tells only a part of the badging story, which extends beyond the physical and into the psychological (McDaniel & Fanfarelli, 2016). McDaniel & Fanfarelli proposed three psychological dimensions of badges – cognitive, affective, and social – focusing specifically on how these dimensions pair with Hamari and Eranti's (2011) completion logic. As badges are designed, it is important to consider the psychological ramifications of design considerations; how do badges affect users? Construction is more than just physical, after all. The way a badge affects a user's mental state is important to promoting a positive user experience. Moreover, badges can be designed in many ways and for many purposes, and the particular design concoction can have psychological impacts – whether they facilitate thought processes, impact emotions, or help users feel more connected to one another. This section describes how badging design impacts users along these three dimensions and provides some examples of how digital badges can be used within each psychological domain.

Cognitive

Those with learning or training goals in mind will likely see the immediate importance of designing badges to support cognition, which includes constructs such as memory, information processing, choice, decision-making, and creativity, among others (Runco & Chand, 1995). Cognition is a key component in learning, which is often associated with educational applications. However, the importance of learning, education, and cognition should not be estranged from other applications, even those made purely for entertainment. After all, even recreational videogames require players to undergo advanced learning processes to acquire information or learn complex procedures. This holds true even in games that are fairly simplistic compared to most modern-day games.

Consider the case of *Super Mario Bros.* (Nintendo, 1985). On the surface, this game has no clear learning objectives. The player must traverse obstacles and avoid pits, flying turtles, and fireballs to make it from the beginning to the end of each stage, ultimately saving the princess from the evil Bowser. However, all of these tasks must be learned. The user must understand the controls, how they impact the avatar in the game, which obstacles are helpful, hurtful, or have no effect, and how to dispatch or avoid each enemy type. Thus, even entertainment applications incorporate cognitive processes. Designers who understand where application design and cognition intersect will be more successful in creating badges that promote user experience and meet their design goals.

Now, let us consider an application that blends both entertainment and learning. *Medulla* (Fanfarelli & Vie, 2015) is an educational game that teaches brain structure and function through a single-player platformer game. In order to succeed in the game, players must undergo the three stages of memory: encoding, storage, and retrieval (Poon, Fozard, Cermak, Arenberg, & Thompson, 1980). The game places the player in a world in turmoil, where mental maladies have taken over the citizens' brains. The player is tasked with curing these citizens and ultimately saving the world. At the beginning of each level, the player is taught, via text-based dialogue, about a new part of the brain and one of its primary functions (e.g., the occipital lobe is important for vision). The player must first undergo the relevant cognitive processes to examine the text and identify which pieces of the text are relevant learning content. The player then attempts to relate the content to prior knowledge in order to understand its meaning (encoding). Following this, she places the information into semantic memory so that it can be accessed when needed (storage). Finally, she must recall the information when it comes time to use it to cure a citizen (retrieval).

While the game incentivizes students to do these things by tying them to gameplay advancement, digital badges are used to encourage students to do more than is required. The badging system uses exclusively unexpected badges, so that players do not know of all of the badges available to them. The first relevant badge is unlocked when a player cures a single citizen. More badges unlock using multiplier-based logic when she cures three citizens, five citizens, and so on. The awarding of the initial three- and five-citizen badges hints to the player that badges might exist for curing more and more citizens. While the player must cure a certain number of citizens to advance in the game, there are many more citizens that are optional, and require the player to move off the main path in order to find and cure. If users hope to attain the highest levels of badges, they must cure many more citizens than the minimum required to complete the game (thus, performing the three stages of memory more times). Thus, the badges used in *Medulla* are designed to motivate the user to undergo additional cognition in order to solidify the learning process.

Affective

Affect is the psychological dimension of emotion. Affect can take many different forms, both positive and negative. This dimension is particularly important for the consideration of users' feelings of motivation, arousal, and curiosity, which are often targeted by badge designers (McDaniel & Fanfarelli, 2016). Affect is important to consider because it tends to impact a range of domains such as motivation to engage in training, enjoyment of gameplay, or satisfaction with an interface. For example, students who feel positively about a particular teacher are more likely to be receptive of that teacher's instruction and then engage in the cognitive processes required to learn what is being taught. Likewise, users who are embarrassed or ashamed of their lack of technology skills will probably be less likely to actively participate in a social community on a technical web forum.

Often, we tend to think of happiness or sadness when considering affect, but equally important are other affective states such as being stressed or fearful, which can heighten the user's engagement in the present experience. When it comes to badges, it is important to consider how they might affect users, and how we want our users to feel. Learners and game players alike might benefit from feelings of accomplishment, curiosity, pride, enjoyment, or other affective states that make them feel positively during the experience. Consider another affective state: bravery. One of the greatest benefits of a learning environment is that it allows for failure in a low-risk environment. This is true on different levels across different domains, whether it be a military combat trainer or a K-12 learning game. Thus, we might want to encourage our badge earners to experience bravery so that they feel comfortable taking those risks, rather than playing it safe to ensure they succeed on the first try. While marginal success can be useful, it is also useful to make mistakes and learn from them in order to avoid making those same mistakes in the future.

We can also design badges to elicit humor. Consider the Adidas *miCoach* personal fitness tracker and game for the PlayStation 3 videogame console. One of its badges is called "Everybody Do the Dinosaur" and has a description of "Lifted a triceratops (10,000 kg) total." In the game, players can grab a weight, tell the game how much they are lifting, and then lift the weights while the *miCoach* registers the lifts. When the player reaches 10,000 kg of weight lifted, the badge is earned. The badge description could have simply read "Lifted 10,000 kg total," but the designers decided to infuse a bit of humor and playfulness into the description by incorporating the notion of lifting a dinosaur. Moreover, the thought of lifting an amount of weight that exceeds the weight of a hefty dinosaur likely also inspires feelings of pride and accomplishment in the user. Here, only a very slight modification was made to the badge description, impacting the affective dimension, while retaining the original goal of the completion logic. Sometimes the slightest modification can add a new dimension to a badge. Designers should think creatively about how to be efficient, but impactful. Thoughtful affective design can aid in this endeavor.

Social

Humans are social creatures. We engage in daily discussions across a number of mediums we have developed in order to facilitate communication (e.g., phone, texting, video calling, social media) and often find ways to engage socially even in pursuits that do not require other people (e.g., running or meditation). Sociality occurs in both competitive and cooperative manners and takes on a variety of forms. The way we incorporate social factors into our applications can improve or lessen their effectiveness. For instance, designing for sociality in applications can create support systems or knowledge-sharing communities, improve motivation, or aid in the formation teams of people that can more efficiently achieve a goal. However, some designed sociality can be harmful; for example, incorporating competition into an application can either improve or harm motivation and affect depending on how it is designed. Among other factors, individual differences play a substantial role in how social information is perceived (Lyubomirsky, 2001). Thus, social aspects of design should be done intentionally and in an informed manner.

Researchers and developers incorporate social designs for badging in a number of ways. While many different systems allow their users to see which badges their friends have, Microsoft's Xbox achievement system takes the process a step further and generates a sort of social currency called Gamerscore. Each badge (called an "achievement" by Microsoft) rewards the user with a certain number of points that contribute to the player's Gamerscore. The Gamerscore can only be incremented by earning badges in games. Over time, an active player can accumulate a high Gamerscore relative to other players, showing that she has completed many achievements and is an active player. However, a higher Gamerscore does not automatically mean that the player is a *more skilled* player, as players can acquire games that have easy to earn badges and boost their Gamerscore without much effort. Thus, while Gamerscore can convey some measure of social status (Antin & Churchill, 2011), the status is limited to conveying active or extensive play and not necessarily high skill. We will revisit this topic in Chapter 5, as we discuss badging in videogames.

On the other hand, Valve's Steam PC gaming platform allows users to see what percentage of players have unlocked each badge. Some of the badges are quite rare. For example, *Devil Daggers* (Sorath, 2016) has a badge that is earned after surviving for 500 seconds, which is quite difficult in this fast-paced action shooter game. It is so difficult that only 0.1% of the estimated 300,000 players (Steamspy, 2018) earned this achievement. To earn it, players must combine advanced movement, aim, game knowledge, and rapid decision-making ability, making its awardees appear to be highly skilled players. Of course, a low percentage of players who have earned the badge is not always indicative of the badge's required skill. At the very least, this outcome does indicate rarity that might have social ramifications. When designing difficult-to-earn or rare badges, designers should consider how the presence or absence of them might influence how these badges are perceived by other users.

What Can I Do with Badges?

Now that we have examined some ways in which badges can psychologically impact users, let us consider some more specific functions of badging. Perhaps most often, designers and others interested in badges consider them for either their credentialing or reward functions – both of which are quite important and will be discussed here. However, badges can be used for a variety of other purposes that will also be described. At their core, badges are tools for transmitting information (Fanfarelli, Vie, & McDaniel, 2015); information is created by the badge's designer, transferred using the badge as a vessel, received by the earner, and may be further passed on to those looking at a user's badge (e.g., other players, educators, or employers). When examining badges in this way, we can begin to consider the different types of information that can be transmitted using badges and thus tease apart the functions of digital badges. Here, we investigate several of these functions.

Credentialing

One way we commonly use badges is for credentialing purposes (White, 2018; Deterding, Dixon, Khaled, & Nacke, 2011). Here, badges are supplemental to grades or degrees and might even serve as alternatives to these more traditional credentials (Rughiniş & Matei, 2013; Terrell, 2014). When a potential employer looks at an applicant's résumé and notices a bachelor's degree in web development, it is probably safe for that employer to assume that the applicant can make some sort of a website. The employer might even go a step further and examine the transcripts, perhaps noticing that the applicant received a B letter grade in a server-side scripting course. She might now assume that the applicant probably learned one of the server-side languages and performed acceptably in the course, but was not stellar.

At this point, we approach some ambiguities. What language(s) did the student attempt to learn in the course? Why did the student not earn an A? Did the student attempt to step out of her comfort zone and learn new skills that challenged her in ways that made the course quite difficult, or was she simply lazy and decided to not complete assignments to the fullest extent? Maybe, instead, she suffers from text anxiety (Zeidner, 1998) and demonstrated great coding skill on the websites she made, but was unable to perform well on the examinations. Clarifying these ambiguities would allow an employer to know if it would be better to hire this applicant, or a different one who earned an A in the same course. After all, the A student might have completed all assignments to satisfaction, but never attempted to move beyond the requirements of the course and thus had an easier time meeting all requirements.

Here, credentialing badges are quite useful. Consider, now, a case in which the professor of the applicant's course provided several different badges to students. Badges are designed for more specific areas of competency and skill, including specific badges for:

1. MySQL Database Coding – the student has demonstrated effectiveness in performing CRUD (Create, Read, Update, Delete) operations on a MySQL database integrated with a website.
2. PHP – the student has demonstrated effectiveness in using variables, conditional statements, loops, and functions within the PHP language.
3. Exceptional Creativity – the student demonstrated creative problem solving on two or more web projects, above and beyond that of her peers.
4. Top Project – the student submitted a project that was deemed to be of the highest quality in the course, as judged by the professor.

Whether or not you know what CRUD operations or conditional statements are, you can probably see the value of understanding an applicant's skills to this level of specificity. With these particular badges, an employer can learn what the student actually knows and can likely do in the work place. Further, they are able to see whether or not the student demonstrated advanced skill in the classroom, despite the generalized letter grade on her transcript. All of this facilitates a finer granularity of assessment (Fanfarelli & McDaniel, 2017). Additionally, by using the Open Badges standard, the badges issued by the professor can be transferred to the student's badging backpack and then transferred again to an ePortfolio, which could be linked on the student's résumé.

As discussed in the previous chapter, the Open Badges standard allows for the linking of metadata, which can include valuable information. For example, metadata could embed a link to the assignment that earned the badge, the name and contact information of the professor who issued the badge, and a link showing the badges that were available in the course. This would allow the employer to gain a better understanding of the origin and meaning of these badges and thus trust them with greater confidence. This is especially true if she has come to know about this professor's badges through other students that have applied to job openings, or through a partnership with the university. Even if the employer does not yet trust the professor, she can view the student's work through a link in the metadata and decide for herself how the student's work stacks up to other applicants or current employees. In other words, credentialing badges empower both the student and the employer; the student can better showcase her skills and the employer can make more informed decisions about applicants. Credentialing badges backed by metadata-based evidence are more meaningful in this sort of scenario (Casilli & Hickey, 2016). Recall that badging backpacks can pull in badges from multiple sources, beyond just a single professor, and the employer can now gain a more well-rounded understanding of the applicant. While it would be useful to see badges from other courses, other interesting badges might come from local web development meet-up organizers, coding competitions, or other organizations that would be able to verify that the student has gone above and beyond the minimum coursework.

While credentialing discussions have primarily taken place in the educational realm, there is room to explore this badging function in other spaces, such as training or even videogames. For example, the U.S. Army offers physical badges for marksmanship. Credentialing badges might be given for a number of different weapons-based competencies with a variety of weapons (e.g., hitting 26 of 30 targets to earn the expert badge) or in non-combat applications (e.g., cybersecurity). We will expand upon badging for both marksmanship and cybersecurity in Chapter 8, when we discuss badging for military applications. In videogames, players are often respected for reaching particular skill levels of competitive play or for having completed especially difficult single-player games. These things are badged fairly often already, but cross-platform badging backpacks that maintain and extend the uses of credentialing badges are currently uncommon and have room for growth. Credentialing badges have a number of potential purposes beyond the formal learning realm that have yet to be explored.

Reward and Motivation

Another common use for badges is to motivate users through reward. In the past, there has been some contention in the literature when pairing reward with motivation, because badges are often considered to be extrinsic forms of reward (Blair, 2011). Researchers theorize that users might perceive these rewards to be controllers of behavior, thereby reducing the autonomy (i.e., feelings of free choice) necessary to foster intrinsic motivation. While *extrinsic motivation* describes the motivation to complete a task to obtain a reward unrelated to the task (e.g., currency, candy, physical prizes), *intrinsic motivation* is the motivation to complete a task for the value inherent in its completion and not to obtain some external reward (Ryan, 1982; Deci, Koestner, & Ryan, 1999).

While some studies have failed to improve motivation through badges (Munson & Consolvo, 2012), others have succeeded (Facey-Shaw, Specht, van Rosmalen, Börner, & Bartley-Bryan, 2017), indicating that there is still much to learn about how badging-based rewards interact with motivation. Interestingly, the negative effects associated with rewards only appear to emerge under very specific circumstances. A meta-analysis of 96 studies found that rewards only produced negative effects when rewards were expected, tangible, and provided for mere completion of a task (Cameron & Pierce, 1994) as opposed to rewarding degree of completion or exceptional effort. Consequently, we argue that specific badging *design* is the deciding factor on whether or not reward badges will be motivational or demotivational. When it comes to reward badges that are designed to improve intrinsic motivation, designers should probably avoid these particular criteria unless there is (a) a compelling reason to use them; and, (b) an accompanying strategy for dealing with potential demotivational effects.

Of course, not all badges are meant to be rewarding, even within the same badging system. In the last chapter, we discussed how some users expect to see and earn some badges in order to facilitate goal-setting. We call these *expected* badges. Other badges users encounter and earn are *unexpected* badges. In this case, the badge-earning criteria are not communicated to the user until the badge is earned. Unexpected badges can be useful to foster motivation. These unexpected badges are motivating because they infuse the element of surprise, which releases dopamine into the brain. Dopamine is a neurotransmitter associated with reward and happiness (Anderson, 2011). It plays a significant influence on freeform, pleasure-seeking behaviors, but also on goal-directed behaviors, since many users are motivated toward trying to do things that will ultimately make them feel good. Sometimes, however, this goal-directed behavior can backfire. For example, when badge criteria are known, users might actively engage in badge-hunting behavior, setting a goal of obtaining a badge and potentially losing the original purpose of the activity as desired by the system designers (Fanfarelli, Vie, & McDaniel, 2015).

Aside from being unexpected, reward badges should use completion logic that specifies effort above mere task completion. For example, in an academic course, students are expected to do their homework and complete exams. There is inherent value in these activities, such as self-improvement or enhanced reasoning capabilities in that subject. If students become used to receiving badges for completion of these activities, the reward could undermine the original intrinsic reasons for completing them. The students might find lower inherent value in doing them in a later course, wondering why they are pursuing them if they are not getting a reward for their completion. In this scenario, the original justification for using badges in the first place is lost. The *overjustification effect* (Lepper, Greene, & Nisbett, 1973) occurs when users receive more justification than necessary for completing a task. Consequently, they undervalue the original intrinsic reasons for their effort. Here, the value of the original justification is re-assigned to the newer extrinsic reward and the badge becomes the primary motivator for doing the homework. The intrinsic value of important underlying psychological motivators, such as feelings of self-improvement, are perceived as less valuable by the user.

To avoid this, reward badges should be given for tasks that are completed *to an exceptional degree* (Fanfarelli, Vie, & McDaniel, 2015). While completing a homework assignment might not be badge-worthy, completing an additional set of optional practice problems might be exceptional. A player in a videogame might be expected to complete the levels, but completing the levels without losing any health would be an example of exceptional effort. Notably, most students or players would not perform these actions on their own; thus, intrinsic motivation here is insufficient to motivate action and this is a potentially useful scenario for a badging application. On the other hand, most students are naturally motivated to earn a passing grade, so a badge for a passing grade in a course is unnecessary and could undermine students' original intrinsic motivation. In Chapter 4, we will expand upon the importance of fostering motivation to meaningfully redirect user behaviors.

Goal-Setting

Proper goal-setting has been shown to motivate individuals to exert greater effort, increase persistence toward goal achievement, and adopt behaviors and strategies that are more likely to help them achieve the goal (Wegge & Haslam, 2003). Badges are uniquely poised to facilitate the goal-setting process. Goal-setting is useful not only because it helps users to see a clear path forward, but also because it helps users to forecast and plan for obstacles that could obstruct progress toward the goal. Having this knowledge available ahead of time can improve user self-efficacy. This construct refers to a user's beliefs regarding his or her ability to succeed in a particular action (Zimmerman & Kitsantas, 2005).

When we discuss goal-setting as a constructive activity, we are not talking about setting just any sort of goal. Goals should be productive, specific, and of moderate difficulty in order to foster intrinsic motivation (Locke & Latham, 2002). A learner in a math course can set a goal to memorize all of the solutions to the practice problems, and she might do so, hoping that these problems might come up on the future exam. However, a better use of the time would be to try to learn the methodologies used to come up with the solutions to the problems so that her skills would be transferrable and useful, extending beyond a single-use case. Thus, setting specific productive goals is more important than setting just any sort of goal.

Likewise, setting goals that are too difficult can reduce motivation. If you were asked to read 100 novels in one day, you probably would not think you were capable of accomplishing such a feat. Likely, you would decide that your time would be better spent elsewhere, not even attempting the goal or even a milestone toward the larger goal. Similarly, if you were asked to read five novels in one day, you might put forth a valiant effort initially, only to feel frustrated and quit once you feel as though the goal is not possible. On the opposite side of the scale, a user that sets a goal that is too easy will achieve it effortlessly, but will feel boredom due to lack of challenge. Those pursuing too difficult or too easy goals will both be disadvantaged; neither will achieve their full potential in an efficient manner.

Intentionally designed badges can help users set specific, useful, and moderately difficult goals to motivate them to exert effort in digital spaces. In the last chapter, we discussed completion logic, or the underlying requirements that must be fulfilled by the user in order to earn the badge. We also discussed the badge's written description that is shown to the user. By intentionally linking these two aspects of badges with appropriate goals, badges can serve as a roadmap through a system. Further, by using the badge's description to point to the next badge that should be earned, each goal-setting badge can act as a pointer to the next goal, creating a learning pathway that is constructed one step at a time through the attainment of badges (Gibson, Ostashewski, Flintoff, Grant, & Knight, 2015).

Consider an app that teaches users to speak French. While a traveler visiting France in the summer might only need to learn a few common phrases, a French major in college will need to learn much more. While the student might think it is best to start learning these phrases, it might be more useful for her to learn the alphabet and the pronunciations of each letter, followed by individual words, and then move on to how these elements combine to form complete sentences. Taking this route, the user will be able to form, recite, and understand far more sentences by understanding the sentence components (words, phrases, and pronunciations) than if she had simply learned a series of phrases. A complementary set of badges could point to each of these activities in succession, requiring module/activity completion or assignment/exam mastery in sequence along the desired learning pathway.

This might seem obvious, but badge descriptions should be explicit and accurate when being used for goal-setting purposes. In the previous chapter, we discussed the potential for designers to create descriptions that are vague, misleading, or otherwise poorly aligned with the underlying completion logic of the badges. Badges used for goal-setting should clearly point users toward the goal in order to ensure they exert their efforts in the proper direction.

Feedback

Well-designed badges are also useful tools for providing feedback. Feedback is defined as information provided to a learner that is meant to enhance their understanding of their performance or comprehension (Hattie & Timperley, 2007). Learners are not necessarily from traditional educational contexts. Learners might be students in a formal academic setting, but they could also be players learning the skills necessary to succeed in a game, or users learning to use an app. Feedback is important because it allows learners of all varieties to understand their performance, good or bad, after completing an action.

Feedback has strong positive benefits when properly implemented (Hattie & Timperley, 2007).

In an educational context, a user who incorrectly answers a question might be given feedback to understand why she was incorrect and what she can do to improve in the future. Likewise, feedback received for a correct answer might tell her that she is performing adequately and should continue using the same learning strategies. In videogames, feedback performs a similar function, helping players understand how their actions positively or negatively affect in-game progress.

Many times, badges are used in systems that have very large numbers of users. This is important, because it can be difficult for human agents to provide adequate and consistent feedback when there are too many people that require feedback. In these instances, badges might be strong candidates for automated feedback delivery when they are designed using effective feedback structures.

Let us consider a non-badged typical classroom scenario. The teacher requires assignment completion in order to test students' developed skills. The students submit assignments which are graded by the teacher. The grade serves as a rudimentary form of feedback. It might be accompanied by more in-depth feedback, like a short written or verbal blurb that goes into the details of the grade and explains why deductions occurred and what could be done to avoid similar pitfalls in the future.

Now, let us consider how this might translate to a feedback-based badging system. A badge's completion logic and description can be used to set a goal for the user (assignment). The user completes that goal (submitting an assignment) and is provided with the badge (feedback). Now, consider the fact that a badge's description can be designed to change after a badge is awarded. While the original description can point the user toward earning the badge, the revised description after earning can contain specific feedback. Thus, the user receives feedback immediately upon earning a badge. Even better, if the badge's awarding can be automated, as most current systems allow, the badge will provide *instantaneous* feedback.

Note that these sorts of badges are completely separate from the credentialing badges discussed earlier in the chapter. These badges are not meant to serve as evidence or showcase skills. They might never even be shared with anyone beyond the learner. Instead, they are meant to help users see that they are reaching milestones in their learning and to provide information on how to reach the next milestone. Imagine a single-player car racing videogame where playtesting reveals that most players experience significant difficulty on the third race. One of two issues commonly prevents players from progressing. Either they fail to brake and accelerate at the correct parts of turns, reducing their overall speed through the course, or they enter turns at the inside instead of the outside of the turn. This improper pre-turn positioning causes them to brake hard and lose speed. Automated player data could be collected during gameplay and fed into the badging system. As the player completes the prior race and earns a badge, the badge's description can be tailored to the player's current shortcoming:

- Feedback Badge Variation A – Congratulations on finishing race 2! Race 3 is a tough one. You're doing great, but to beat this race you should *brake a little bit earlier and start accelerating after the turn's apex.*
- Feedback Badge Variation B – Congratulations on finishing race 2! Race 3 is a tough one. You're doing great, but to beat this race you should *be sure to take your turns at the widest possible angle so you can maintain speed.*

Just as a teacher would tailor feedback to the student's proper scenario, a game can do the same thing by having multiple badging variations at the ready. These then provide specific and relevant feedback as they recognize the player's accomplishment. While we have primarily discussed automated feedback badges in this section, manually awarded badges can be pre-prepared in the same manner and awarded by the issuer in the same way.

Social Status

Social groups tend to organize themselves into hierarchies, over time, where members with higher status tend to have advanced access to power, influence, skill, or dominance (Koski, Xie, & Olson, 2015). As such, social status can be a motivating factor in a variety of scenarios. Some people buy expensive cars and houses simply to create tangible examples of their hard work. Likewise, in some sports, players win and wear rings, jackets, or other items that can be worn to show their status as champions among their peers. In *World of Warcraft* (Blizzard Entertainment, 2004), users can acquire different items that are shown on the player's avatar. While some of these items are quite powerful, others are simply rare and are worn to display the player's tenacity or skill in acquiring them. These virtual adornments provide evidence that their player owners are exceptionally powerful or dedicated, at least within their social system of other game players.

Likewise, badges can convey reputation (McDaniel & Fanfarelli, 2016) and status (Antin & Churchill, 2011; Gibson, Ostashewski, Flintoff, Grant, & Knight, 2015), primarily in situations where earners can see each other's earned badges. People who achieve particular feats, as dictated by their social group, are often looked upon with greater reverence than those who do not. For example, when discussing credentialing, we mentioned students who have submitted the top project in the course and received a badge for it. Such a badge, if viewable by peers, could also convey a level of status for that student: she is a high achiever and has advanced skills in a level that is relevant to her interests and professional development. Likewise, peers might see her as someone from whom they can learn.

Social status badges are also present in videogames. *Counter-Strike:Global Offensive* (*CS:GO*) is a first-person shooter game where players compete in team vs team objective-based gameplay. Ranking badges are incorporated into the game to denote a player's skill relative to other players. Players who hold The Global Elite ranking badge have attained the most prestigious badge in *CS:GO*'s 18-badge sequence. These players are known to be among the best at their craft, which is noteworthy as videogame mastery is a means of advancing social status in particular gameplay communities (Olson, 2010). As such, these and other highly ranked players are asked gameplay questions via online communities, engage in player–player coaching, and create advice videos which are more likely to be seen as trustworthy than those made by someone who is of a lower rank. Thus, higher ranked badges in *CS:GO* convey a similar status to performance-based badges in a classroom. These badge holders are seen as highly skilled individuals within their social group and might take on the status of leader or trusted teacher.

These examples suggest several important factors to consider when designing social status badges. Perhaps most obviously, the badge must actually be viewable by others within a social group. Some badges are only viewable by the earner, which might be useful for certain other badging purposes, but a badge's attainment cannot influence an individual's social status if the social group is not able to see and verify the badge's award. Of course, not just any viewable badge is going to elevate status; the badge must represent an achievement that is held in high esteem by the social group. Such esteem might come from a badge's rarity or from signifying achievement that is difficult to attain. In a mobile running app, a user is unlikely to improve her social standing among peer runners by earning a badge that is given out for running for the first time. However, earning a badge for running the full 26.2 miles of a marathon could be seen as a milestone achievement that places the runner into a different level of social achievement. Even more impressive might be a scenario where a running app collaborates with a major race (e.g., the Boston Marathon) and provides badges for achieving 1st, 2nd, or 3rd place in a setting where the world's best marathon runners are competing. This digital badge mirrors the physical awards typically given out at such events, but can be shareable on a much wider scale. Aside from holding up a trophy on a stage, it is difficult to show a physical trophy to 100 other people at the same time. However, sharing a digital badge on social media can quickly reach numbers well beyond 100.

A degree of caution should be used when using badges for social status. While it can be useful to recognize your highest achieving users, social status can also be used for less than noble causes. Creating a social divide that incites elitism or discrimination within your users is unlikely to be desirable. Thus, social status badges should be used carefully and their effects should be examined regularly to ensure undesirable effects do not result from the badging system.

Next Up

While this chapter provided an overview of some of the different capabilities of badges, the next chapter dedicates more time to a larger function of digital badges, behavioral redirection, which necessarily incorporates many of the capabilities presented in this chapter. Badges can be used to help users behave in ways that improve their interactions and experiences within the badged system. In the next chapter, we examine how to intentionally design for these purposes.

References

Anderson, S. P. (2011). *Seductive interaction design: Creating playful experiences.* Berkeley, CA: New Riders.

Antin, J., & Churchill, E. F. (2011). Badges in social media: A social psychological perspective. In CHI 2011 Gamification Workshop Proceedings (Vancouver, BC, Canada, 2011). Accessed 10 April 2018. Retrieved from http://gamification-research.org/wp-content/uploads/2011/04/03-Antin-Churchill.pdf.

Blair, L. (2011). The use of video game achievements to enhance player performance, self-efficacy, and motivation. Doctoral Dissertation. University of Central Florida, 1–30.

Blizzard Entertainment. (2004). *World of Warcraft.* [PC]. Irvine, CA: Blizzard Entertainment.

Cameron, J., & Pierce, D. W. (1994). Reinforcement, reward, and intrinsic motivation: A meta-analysis. *Review of Educational Research, 64*(3), 363–423.

Casilli, C., & Hickey, D. (2016). Transcending conventional credentialing and assessment paradigms with information-rich digital badges. *Information Society, 32*(2), 117–129.

Deci, E. L., Koestner, R., & Ryan, R. M. (1999). A meta-analytic review of experiments examining the effects of extrinsic rewards on intrinsic motivation. *Psychological Bulletin, 125*(6), 627–668.

Deterding, S., Dixon, D., Khaled, R., & Nacke, L. (2011). From game design elements to gamefulness: Defining gamification. In *Proceedings of the 15th International Academic MindTrek Conference: Envisioning Future Media Environments* (pp. 9–15). doi:10.1145/2181037.2181040

Facey-Shaw, L., Specht, M., van Rosmalen, P., Börner, D., & Bartley-Bryan, J. (2017). Educational functions and design of badge systems: A conceptual literature review. *IEEE Transactions on Learning Technologies.* doi: 10.1109/TLT.2017.2773508

Fanfarelli, J. R., & McDaniel, R. (2017). Exploring digital badges in university courses: Relationships between quantity, engagement, and performance. *Online Learning, 21*(2). doi:10.24059/olj.v21i2.1007

Fanfarelli, J. R., & Vie, S. (2015). Medulla: A 2D sidescrolling platformer game that teaches basic brain structure and function. *Well Played, 4*(2), 7–29.

Fanfarelli, J., Vie, S., & McDaniel, R. (2015). Understanding digital badges through feedback, reward, and narrative: A multidisciplinary approach to building better badges in social environments. *Communication Design Quarterly Review, 3*(3), 56–60.

Gibson, D., Ostashewski, N., Flintoff, K., Grant, S., & Knight, E. (2015). Digital badges in education. *Education and Information Technologies, 20*(2), 403–410.

Hamari, J., & Eranti, V. (2011). Framework for designing and evaluating game achievements. *Proceedings of DiGRA 2011*, Hilversum, Netherlands.

Hattie, J., & Timperley, H. (2007). The power of feedback. *Review of Educational Research, 77*(1), 81–112.

Koskie, J., Xie, H., & Olson, I. R. (2015). Understanding social hierarchies: The neural and psychological foundations of status perception. *Social Neuroscience, 10*(5), 527–550.

Lepper, M. P., Green, D., & Nisbett, R. E. (1973). Undermining children's intrinsic interest with extrinsic reward: A test of the overjustification hypothesis. *Journal of Personality and Social Psychology, 28*(1), 129–137.

Locke, E. A., & Latham, G. P. (2002). Building a practically useful theory of goal setting and task motivation: A 35-year odyssey. *American Psychologist, 57*(9), 705–717.

Lyubomirsky, S. (2001). Why are some people happier than others? The role of cognitive and motivational processes in well-being. *American Psychologist, 56*(3), 239–249.

McDaniel, R., & Fanfarelli, J. (2016). Building better digital badges: Pairing completion logic with psychological factors. *Simulation & Gaming, 47*(1), 73–102.

Munson, S.A., & Consolvo, S. (2012). Exploring goal-setting, rewards, self-monitoring, and sharing to motivate physical activity. *Proceedings from 6th International Conference on Pervasive Computing Technologies for Healthcare*. San Diego, CA: IEEE.

Nintendo. (1985). *Super Mario Bros.* [Nintendo Entertainment System]. Kyoto, Japan: Nintendo R&D4.

Olson, C. K. (2010). Children's motivations for video game play in the context of normal development. *Review of General Psychology, 14*(2), 180–187.

Poon, L. W., Fozard, J., Cermak, L. S., Arenberg, D., & Thompson, L. W. (1980). *New directions in memory and aging*. Hillsdale, NJ: Lawrence Erlbaum.

Rughiniş, R., & Matei, S. (2013). Digital badges: Signposts and claims of achievement. In C. Stephanidis (Ed.), *HCI international 2013-posters' extended abstracts* (pp. 84–88). Berlin, Germany: Springer.

Runco, M. A., & Chand, I. (1995). Cognition and creativity. *Educational Psychology Review, 7*, 243–267.

Ryan, R. M. (1982). Control and information in the intrapersonal sphere: An extension of cognitive evaluation theory. *Journal of Personality and Social Psychology, 43*, 450–461.

Sorath. (2016). *Devil Daggers* [PC]. Melbourne, Australia: Sorath.

Steamspy. (2018). Devil Daggers. Accessed 10 April 2018. Retrieved from http://steamspy.com/app/422970

Terrell, S. S. (2014). *The 30 goals challenge for teachers: Small steps to transform your teaching*. London: Routledge.

Wegge, J., & Haslam, S. A. (2003). Group goal setting, social identity, and self-categorization. In S. A. Haslam, D. van Knippenberg, M. J. Platow, & N. Ellemers (Eds.), *Social identity at work: Developing theory for organizational practice* (pp. 43–59). Philadelphia, PA: Taylor & Francis.

White, M. (2018). Gamification of nursing education with digital badges. *Nurse Educator, 43*(2), 78–82.

Zeidner, M. (1998). *Text anxiety: The state of the art*. New York: Plenum Press.

Zimmerman, B. J., & Kitsantas, A. (2005). Homework practices and academic achievement: The mediating role of self-efficacy and perceived responsibility beliefs. *Contemporary Educational Psychology, 30*(4), 397–417.

CHAPTER 4

How Do Badges Shape Behavior?

Overview

In our previous two chapters, we discussed how badges are constructed and considered some of their applications and capabilities. In this chapter, we consider the behavioral relationships between digital badges and their human collectors. We first discuss behavior broadly and consider what effective behavior looks like in different circumstances. We then consider how digital badges might be used to catalyze certain types of behaviors that are effective for particular purposes, such as learning or cooperation. We explain how thoughtful designers can use digital badges to shape behavior by motivating, providing feedback, and rewarding. The chapter concludes with some recommendations for designing digital badging systems with behavior in mind.

Badges and Behavior

There are a number of ways that we might interpret the meaning of the word *effective* in our book's title. In this chapter, we use the word effective to refer to digital badges that shape behaviors in ways that are useful for the system's stakeholders. They, too, will have different ideas about what is effective depending on their objectives. For example, a media company intent on soliciting as much participation and engagement with their users as possible might see effective digital badges as those that capture the interest of their user base and persuade those users to return repeatedly to interact with the company's media platform. On the other hand, a teacher might interpret effective digital badges as those that encourage students to spend more time reviewing difficult content rather than breezing by without fully understanding the material. Likewise, a military simulation specialist might see effective badges as those that require the simulation participants to engage in meaningful after-action review – to learn from their mistakes and understand their successes.

Regardless of each stakeholder's interpretation of *effective*, each of these outcomes is in part measured by the actions of the users who are interacting with a badging system. Taken collectively, these actions are behaviors – systems with underlying activities that interact with other activities and are linked to specific times and places within environments (Sherry, Lucas, Greenberg, & Lachlan, 2006). People *do* things both individually and with other people. The things they end up doing result, among other things, from their cognition, their memories, histories, and external stimuli emerging from their locations. In a nutshell, we behave based on the way we think and the way we react to things that happen in our environments. It is easy to observe human behavior, but much more difficult (even for the person doing the behaving) to understand precisely why someone is behaving a certain way at a certain moment.

We often consider badges from a behavioral perspective when we study how humans use badges in designed systems. In these situations, we investigate the possibilities for using badges in a way that changes or discourages destructive behaviors and promotes the constructive behaviors we would like to encourage or sustain. In this chapter, we refer to such possibilities as behavioral shaping, or adjusting behavior according to design objectives. External credentials have long been used for behavioral shaping in this way throughout history and in fictional media. Examples range from the real-world military medals and awards and certificates given by employers for exceptional performance to the fictional scarlet letter "A" made infamous in Hawthorne's well-known novel (1850). Earning a credential of this nature shapes the behavior of both the earner and the people around them. In the previous chapter, we talked about how badges affect social status. An individual with a sufficient number of military medals might be looked upon favorably, especially by other soldiers, while Hawthorne's scarlet letter invokes quite the opposite range of reactive behaviors.

Understanding the behavioral significance of badges is important for a number of reasons, but one major reason is the effort and investment that is required of both the designers and the earners. It probably does not make sense to carefully design a system for badging and credentialing if the ultimate acquisition of the badges and credentials has a net neutral effect on behavior. The same is true of the most successful types of external credentials we have seen throughout history, which require significant time and effort to obtain. One striking example is the Eagle Scout merit badge awarded by the Boy Scouts. The Eagle Scout award has been given to only two percent of scouts since 1912 and requires advancement through seven required ranks (Scout, Tenderfoot, Second Class, First Class, Star, Life, and Eagle). This involves a great deal of work and requires extensive service commitments and years of adhering to Scout Law and its principles (DBailye, 2017).

As a motivator for behavioral change, the Eagle Scout badge might or might not be significant, depending on the scout. On the one hand, certain scouts will find its exclusivity compelling and see this elite badge as something worth pursuing. On the other, considering that only two percent of scouts have earned the badge, one can argue that the badge is insufficiently motivating to the general population of scouts. It is likely an effective credential in the eyes of its designers, however, since those who ultimately earn it will be in the company of a very limited group, thus experiencing the ethos of exclusivity intended for this badge. The deep service commitments required of this badge also provide many opportunities for repeatedly shaping behaviors in a way the Boy Scouts sees as congruent with their organizational mission. This ensures that only individuals with the proper appearance of scout-specific character, as demonstrated by their long record of mission-specific activities, are elevated to their highest honor.

Not all behavioral shaping strategies for digital badges will require such commitments of time, nor are such longitudinal approaches likely to be successful in the rapidly evolving virtual spaces we inhabit. That does not mean that prolonged interaction is not valued, however. For instance, in the case of the hypothetical media company mentioned above, stakeholders might be most interested in producing repeated visits and active engagement from consumers. The point is that the behaviors we are most interested in will vary depending on audience, context, and purpose. What is effective in one context might not be effective in another. What does not vary, however, is the underlying idea that these behaviors are important to us as designers, developers, and researchers of digital badges. Because of this, it is useful for us to better understand behavior, both broadly as a human activity and specifically as we see behaviors occurring in digital environments.

Studying Behavior

B. F. Skinner observed in his work on behaviorism that studying behavior is not complex because behavior as an idea is difficult to understand. Since we all behave and are behaving in various ways throughout our lives, observing discrete behaviors is rather easy and it is simple to understand this concept operationally. Simple behaviors can be boiled down to what people do and how they act. It would not be difficult to discern someone who is behaving in an extroverted fashion from someone who is behaving in an introverted fashion; ten minutes observing both individuals at a dinner party would do the trick. However, what makes a more comprehensive scientific observation of behavior difficult is the fact that behavior "is a process, rather than a thing" and that "it cannot easily be held still for observation" (Skinner, 1953). In other words, we cannot easily separate behavior and study it in isolation from other human phenomena. We can only observe it as it is happening and attempt to understand what types of conditions might encourage certain behaviors to occur. We can also investigate what other types of conditions might emerge as the result of behaviors.

Behavioral study is also complicated because we cannot determine whether a behavior is natural or contrived based solely on what we observe. Context is critical here. It could be that an individual behaves in an introverted fashion at a social gathering but is quite extroverted at home with his family, for example. In any case, we are limited to commenting on behaviors based upon what we can observe at any given moment as it is occurring. This strategy is the basis for Skinner's ideas about operant conditioning, in which Skinner and colleagues looked at observable actions and studied how different types of reinforcement could cause different actions to reoccur over time. This idea of operant conditioning has, not surprisingly, been linked to a number of studies about digital badges (Buffardi & Edwards, 2014; Landers, Bauer, Callan, & Armstrong, 2015; Zellner, 2015).

This book does not intend to provide a detailed treatment of operant conditioning or of the psychological or sociological theories of behavior or behaviorism. In fact, many of the core ideas of behaviorism have since been found to be flawed in one way or another and they fail to explain the more complex abilities of humans, such as memory and language (Naik, 1998). However, core ideas about behaviorism, and even Skinner's theories of oper-ant conditioning, are useful when we consider designing the types of badges that are effective in different types of scenarios. In order to build such badges, it is necessary to think about the types of behavior you wish to encourage or discourage through badging. With this in mind, we can conceptualize a typol-ogy for behavior in digital environments that allows us to group behavior into different types of categories.

Behavioral Categories for Badges

We discuss some detailed methods for listing out desirable behaviors, with design in mind, toward the end of this chapter. Before going into this level of detail, however, a good starting point when considering behaviors is to classify them into broad categories. There are specific types of behavior that we com-monly see in digital environments that badges might be useful for shaping, sustaining, or preventing.

Here are six types of behaviors that are useful to consider in relation to digital badges:

- *Connective behaviors* bridge activities between virtual and real environments. For example, a task in a nutrition game that requires its players to take pho-tographs of healthy groceries at a real-world grocery store in order to earn a digital badge links the physical and digital worlds.
- *Cooperative social behaviors* require users to work together for the sake of completing a more challenging objective, learning how to work as a team, or dividing a larger problem into more manageable chunks. An online course management system can encourage cooperative behaviors by awarding badges for collaborative tasks such as peer-review or group project work.
- *Exploratory behaviors* encourage users to seek out the hidden nooks and crannies of the digital environment. Exploratory behaviors are useful when a designer is seeking to immerse a player more fully in the virtual experi-ence. For example, exploratory behaviors can use hidden journals scattered throughout a level to provide narrative backstories to a videogame, thereby outsourcing some of the game's exposition to these optional game objects.

They can support learning objectives by requiring the learner to explore in order to find necessary information to progress in the game.

- *Productive, task-specific behaviors* are those that are most useful for solving a particular class of problem within the interactive environment. For example, a productive behavior within an oil maintenance simulator might be spending time learning how various valves and safety features work rather than aimlessly chatting with non-playable characters.
- *Prolonged behaviors* are exhibited when users spend more time interacting with a digital system. Prolonged behaviors are useful for many different applications such as increasing time on task for mastery of materials and knowledge building. A common prolonged behavior in role-playing games is "grinding," or battling virtual characters or completing minor quests to build up experience points and "level up" the character to strengthen him for future battles (Kaiser, 2012). A similar grinding mechanic for virtual badges could prove useful when the desired objective requires a significant amount of time doing repetitive activities.
- *Risky* or *atypical behaviors* are evident when users do something differently or in contrast to their normal style of interaction in order to earn a badge. For example, a badge that directs a normally methodical videogame player to seek a "speed run" badge encourages her to play more recklessly than usual since time is a critical factor in earning that badge. Conversely, a player who is generally more casual with her gameplay style will suddenly become investigative and careful if seeking to unlock a hidden badge nestled deep within a puzzle.

These are just a few examples of behavioral categories. The six behavioral types listed here are not mutually exclusive, nor is this list exhaustive. A digital designer could easily come up with many more categories and it is not difficult to imagine behaviors that are both prolonged and atypical, or cooperative and productive. What is important is to recognize that badges are tremendously useful for shaping behavior because they can provide users with different types of experiences. These experiences can shape different types of behaviors that are useful for the end goals of the system. In other words, effectively designed badges, like the operant conditions studied by Skinner, can reinforce and encourage different behaviors. Because of the critical importance of both motivation and feedback in relation to behavior, we will talk about each of these areas in more detail. We discussed some of these concepts previously in Chapter 2, but here we discuss them more specifically in relation to behavioral shaping.

Motivation

One of the primary ways that designers hope their digital badges will shape user behavior is by increasing motivation. When we are enticed to earn digital badges, we are motivated to do what is necessary to obtain them. In fact, Ryan and Deci

(2000) define motivation as being "moved to do something" (p. 54). When a person is motivated to learn, for example, there exists an underlying impetus, urge, or inspiration that is causing her to behave in a way that initiates or prolongs a learning experience. Similarly, when that person is not motivated to learn, then she is not moved to behave in a way conducive to learning. She might find excuses to avoid the content, she might procrastinate, or she might find something else entirely to occupy her time. Thus, motivation and behavior are naturally linked, particularly when we talk about learning in digital environments.

We can separate motivation into different typologies depending on its features. For example, as we discussed in the last chapter, one well-known classification is to separate motivation into *intrinsic* and *extrinsic* forms. Intrinsic motivation is found when one does an activity just for the sake of doing it; the activity is engaging and pleasurable all on its own, without external reward. On the other hand, extrinsic motivation has what Ryan and Deci (2000) describe as "instrumental value" (p. 60). Extrinsic motivation means being motivated by an external reward or a lack of an external punishment (Ryan and Deci, 2000). External rewards might be financial, social, or virtual, but they are perceived as having value by the individual who is behaving in a certain way to earn them. When badges are used as rewards similar to praise, stickers, grades, or points, they are serving as positive reinforcers that increase extrinsic motivation (Zellner, 2015). However, specific badge designs that help users feel more competent, autonomous, or socially successful can also impact users' intrinsic motivation. An example is a badge that helps users improve their abilities through progressive goal-setting.

While Ryan and Deci's research on intrinsic versus extrinsic motivation is important to our consideration of badges and behaviors, there are other classical theories about behavior that are also useful for our analysis. For example, perhaps the most well-known theory of motivation is described in Abraham Maslow's 1943 paper "A Theory of Human Motivation" where he presented his hierarchy of needs. According to Maslow's model, basic physiological needs must be addressed by behaviors before other more complex needs can be addressed. A person unable to meet basic physiological needs will be hard pressed to find motivation for doing more complex tasks. As Maslow (1943, p. 373) explained:

> [I]n the human being who is missing everything in life in an extreme fashion, it is most likely that the major motivation would be the physiological needs rather than any others. A person who is lacking food, safety, love, and esteem would most probably hunger for food more strongly than for anything else.

While Maslow's hierarchy of needs is broadly important and useful for understanding motivation theory at large, what is most useful to our understanding of motivation as it pertains to behavior is his conceptualization of motivation as a goal-centered principle. In other words, Maslow considered motivation through the lens of goal-setting – as a means of urging behaviors toward goals that would meet the current needs of the individual.

This goal-setting paradigm is useful for behavioral brainstorming in badge design. It helps us think about the goal states we wish our interactive products to promote. After all, activities in digital environments such as games are generally goal-oriented and steer players toward "win states" that allow them to gain new abilities or proceed to more difficult levels (Glover, 2013). As designers, we want these same outcomes in digital learning environments; we want our students to reach particular learning goals so that they can proceed to master concepts that are more difficult. This enables them to acquire skills that are more sophisticated, too. Properly designed badges can provide milestone markers toward incremental goals that gradually lead toward the larger goals.

In videogames, for instance, players are awarded digital badges for completing objectives within individual levels as well as additional badges, often with greater rewards, for completing the entire level. It is also true that digital users or game players are likely to ignore badges for the most part until they have an understanding of the basic mechanics and interactions of the system; a player that cannot properly control her avatar is unlikely to care about badges that recognize advanced strategic victories. The goal-setting paradigm and the design strategy of meeting basic needs before higher-order needs are both helpful for effectively shaping behaviors with digital badges.

As another example, consider an online learning application designed to teach introductory physics to college freshmen. If we were to divide this course content based on what a learner needs in order to be successful in this subject, we might broadly structure the content into two categories: (1) basic needs and (2) advanced needs. Basic needs might include pre-requisite formulas and principles of physics and advanced needs might include facility with word problems where students must apply the principles of physics to arrive at a correct answer. In such an arrangement, it makes logical sense that learners would need to understand basic formulas and principles of physics – gravity, acceleration, mass, friction, and so forth – before they could adequately work toward solving the more advanced word problems.

Motivating learners to spend sufficient time meeting mastery goals for these word problems would be difficult without them first possessing the pre-requisite knowledge. They would lack the competence that is a key factor in fostering intrinsic motivation (Ryan, 1982; Deci, Koestner, & Ryan, 1999). So, it seems reasonable in a case like this to extrapolate Maslow's hierarchy of needs from the biological realm to instructional design. Many classical learning theories, such as Bloom's Taxonomy, have done exactly that (Bloom, 1956). One of the core ideas behind Bloom's Taxonomy, for example, is that one needs to master basic competencies such as factual recall and understanding before progressing to higher forms of learning such as analysis, evaluation, and creation.

Increasing the motivation of users is a good goal for digital badges because motivation is potentially helpful for increasing effort and prolonging time on task. In particular, research indicates that intrinsically motivated students perform better on classroom scenarios, adjust better to school, employ more effective learning strategies, expend more effort on more complex tasks, persist for longer amounts of time on assigned tasks, and feel more confident than non-motivated peers (Brewster & Fager, 2000). In badging scenarios, the trick is to use what on the surface appears to be an extrinsic motivator to support intrinsic motivation. One view is that the rewards of these digital objects are the credentials themselves, potentially valuable for future coursework or to future employers. However, as we stress throughout the book, viewing digital badges merely as extrinsic rewards is shortsighted. These objects can also build skill competencies and behaviors that are necessary for intrinsic motivation. Even if a user is first motivated by earning the badge itself, the behavioral satisfaction of performing better and more capably is, in and of itself, intrinsically satisfying. Badges might also open up the possibility of new pedagogical opportunities, such as having a better chance of getting into college or empowering students to be more active in selecting their own learning strategies (Davis & Singh, 2015).

We discuss reward in more detail later in this chapter, but it seems logical to acknowledge that motivated individuals are individuals who are open to behavioral change. However, while motivation can increase certain types of behaviors over time, like focusing more carefully or spending more time on task, there are some situations in which we need behaviors to change more immediately. This might be necessary for the sake of our learning objectives or immediate goals in a game, learning system, or simulation. For these cases, properly delivered feedback is a useful tool.

Feedback

In order to shape behaviors in productive ways, it is critical that badges make use of one of their most powerful features: providing feedback in a concise, engaging, and palatable way. Feedback is information that is provided to a learner to enhance her understanding of her performance or comprehension (Hattie & Timperley, 2007). As individuals who have progressed through different types of formal and informal learning experiences, we are all accustomed to varying sorts of feedback. The feedback we receive throughout our lives ranges from formal feedback delivered through examination grades and comments to more casual feedback delivered through conversations with staff members or docents when visiting museums or science centers on field trips.

What is critical for behavioral shaping is that the feedback we receive causes us to adjust our current or future behaviors. This feedback can support or diminish our motivation to act. For instance, when a student tanks an examination and receives feedback about this poor performance, the student might study harder, review materials more thoroughly, or seek out additional help from the teacher. However, if feedback is provided too frequently, is inaccurate, or otherwise discourages or frustrates the learner, it can lead to reduced effort and even less studying for the next exam. As Abramovich, Schunn, and Higashi (2013) explain, both over-assessment and inaccurate assessment have "clear negative consequences on motivation" (p. 218). Inaccurate feedback is particularly bad because "it can cause a drop in motivation to learn for a student who thought they were learning but is provided feedback that contradicts their self-assessment" (p. 218). As these examples show, improperly structured or inaccurate feedback can lead to negative outcomes for motivation and learning.

A good strategy is to determine which types of feedback enhance positive outcomes and diminish negative ones. Fortunately, this is a fairly well-researched subject in the literature, at least in certain types of instruction. For example, in one study, researchers examined the effect of different feedback strategies on ESL student writing (Bitchener, Young, & Cameron, 2005). They examined a variety of feedback types including direct, written feedback; individual conferences with the instructor; and no corrective feedback (although they did provide feedback about organization to this third group). For certain learning objectives, such as accuracy in using the past tense and the definite article, the study found a significant effect for accuracy when using the combination of written and conference feedback.

Feedback is also frequently given in informal learning environments. For example, consider a science museum that has a device to demonstrate how potential energy is converted into kinetic energy. The demonstration is composed of a ramp, a track, several balls of different masses, and some large domino tiles. Visitors drop their selected ball from various heights on the raised ramp and then it rolls down the track. The goal is to drop the ball from a sufficient height that it will knock down a series of large dominoes at the bottom of the ramp. When a visitor interacting with this device recognizes that their domino-toppling strategies are not working, they use any feedback they receive to adjust their interactions to ensure a better possibility of success. Perhaps they need to select a ball with more mass, or drop a ball from a higher point on the track so that it accumulates enough kinetic energy to break down the dominoes at the bottom of the ramp. Failure to knock down the dominoes, in this case, is one type of feedback, but young visitors might also receive feedback from their teachers or from museum staff. Ideally, motivation is high enough to continue trying even when the solution is not immediately clear. In these situations, the information the participants receive during each subsequent trial becomes part of an ongoing feedback loop since they are adjusting behavior and receiving feedback in a continuous cycle.

Although receiving feedback during formal or informal educational moments is critical to how we think and understand, feedback is not limited to learning contexts. We receive other types of feedback from books, relationships, conversations with friends and colleagues, disciplinary situations, and even from our interactions with common machines in the world (e.g., vending machines, traffic lights, ATM kiosks, and so on). For example, if we push a button to purchase a snack item from a vending machine and have not yet inserted the correct amount of change, the machine provides feedback that we did not satisfy the conditions necessary to dispense our food. We then adjust our behavior at that moment to add the correct number of coins. We will also behave differently in the future because our background knowledge has changed about the situation. Feedback is critical to understanding what we are doing right and what we are doing wrong – it is what Hattie and Timperley call a "'consequence' of performance" (2007, p. 81). Because almost all of us experience these types of interactions throughout our lives, we are very accustomed to receiving and acting upon feedback.

There are many different ways that users receive feedback in digital systems. The feedback can be verbal, visual, or haptic, for instance, and each of these modes may contain multiple levels of feedback. For example, a real-time strategy videogame might use verbal feedback in written form during gameplay to inform the player about items and resources. This written verbal feedback could also be augmented with voiceover actors who relay auditory feedback as action unfolds. The controller might also shake during battle and the music might vary in intensity depending on a player's actions. With digital systems, the type of feedback can vary widely due to the wealth of multimedia possibilities at a designer's disposal.

How, then, does feedback relate to digital badges? Although we have been discussing badges as behavior shapers in this chapter, they are also informational vessels. As transporters of information, badges carry information created by a designer to an audience. This information is transmitted by the badge system and received by its users. In this model, we can envision how badges transfer information containing feedback that the receiver can use to better understand her performance.

One way badges function in this fashion is as just-in-time feedback tools. *Just-in-time* refers to a badge's ability to be triggered at specific times within an automated system to respond to user actions. This enables the delivery of feedback information just as a mistake is made or a correct action is performed. To properly modify behaviors for the purposes of learning, feedback should be tied to goals and just-in-time feedback can immediately reorient behaviors toward these goals. We can design a system in other ways to encourage goal orientation, such as by including badges that chunk larger and more formidable tasks into smaller, more manageable, and more achievable goals.

There are also examples of more novel ways that digital badges use feedback to enhance learning or communication. For example, Resnick and colleagues (1998) developed a prototype for toys they called "digital manipulatives," which could play a role in learning through the manipulation of different types of toy-like objects. One version of their digital manipulatives was their "thinking tag" toy which used digital badges that contained information about the backgrounds, interests, and opinions of the wearers. In describing how the thinking tags worked, Resnick et al. (1998) wrote, "When two people met, their badges exchanged information and turned on lights to show how much the two people had in common. In this way, the badges acted as a conversational prop to get people talking with one another" (p. 285). In this case, badge-based visual feedback was used creatively to act as a social lubricant to help ease the anxiety of first time introductions between strangers.

Reward

Another powerful feature of digital badges is their ability to provide rewards to the people that earn them. Rewards and behaviors are deeply and intricately linked in our everyday activities and interactions. Effective professional behavior, for example, is probably most significantly rewarded through the paycheck that accompanies one's workplace effort on a regular cycle. Other professional rewards could be recognitions in the forms of bonuses, employee awards, or preferential treatments. Not all rewards are material, of course. Expressions of affection are rewards for behaviors that reinforce relationships and deepen bonds between family members and friends. Professional or personal rewards can also emerge internally through cognition and emotion, in feelings of self-sufficiency and accomplishment.

Some rewards, like a paycheck, are expected. Other rewards, such as a surprise bouquet or a friendly phone call, are not. This dimension can be an important factor in the way badging systems are designed. For example, research has shown that in digital badging contexts, expected rewards can negatively influence intrinsic motivation, while unexpected rewards do not (Zellner, 2015). This presents an opportunity to think about badging reward in two complementary ways: (1) as an expected reward to scaffold particular types of learning content; and (2) as a set of unexpected rewards to encourage other behaviors you might wish to elicit from your users.

We can operationalize digital badge rewards in different ways to influence behaviors. For example, a videogame badge might reward a player by demonstrating achievement and elevating social status, as discussed in the previous chapter. Consider a badge that a player can publicly display in their badging showcase or backpack that displays a cumulative score of total points earned across all games. The Xbox Live's "Gamerscore" is one such example of this (Qualls, 2016). In Xbox's system, earned badges have virtual currency that establishes a reputation for the player. A person with a relatively low Gamerscore, for example, might be considered as a less serious gamer. A person with a higher Gamerscore might be considered a more experienced gamer and might be more likely to be selected for multiplayer invitations. In cases such as these, the rewards of earning a badge are essentially a heightened credential that provides the earner with greater social status or other digital stature within a particular community.

Badge rewards are not always so direct as to simply generate points or credentials, however. Sometimes, there are deeper principles at work in learning that can be engaged with carefully crafted badges. For example, Zellner's (2015) case study of badges used in Khan Academy, a popular online learning community, revealed that relatedness, autonomy, and competence needs – the criteria for fostering intrinsic motivation – were all rewarded in one way or another through digital badge acquisition. In terms of relatedness, the badges revealed clear directives showing online learners how to contribute to the community, thus empowering them to build relationships with other users of the system. Autonomy was also seen as being rewarded, since the badges were implemented in a way that was not mandatory for continued course progression, but enabled learners to choose their own routes through the learning content without having to depend on acquiring badges to continue. Finally, badges can reward learners in Khan Academy by increasing their feelings of competence and self-efficacy. Clear goals combined with strategic feedback of badges and points motivate learners by enhancing their feeling of success and encouraging them to continue down the paths they have already started.

One challenge with reward as a behavioral motivator is the way in which that reward is transferrable, as a credential, outside the system that does the rewarding. In order for certain types of credentials to be properly recognized outside the digital system, they must be recognized as credible outside that environment. Research has shown that perceived legitimacy is one of the major challenges associated with digital badges. For example, in their research studying digital badges in afterschool learning, Davis and Singh (2015) interviewed students, teachers, and a college admission director to study how they used badges and to investigate the perceived opportunities and challenges around digital badges. In their research, credibility was the most frequently cited challenge of digital badges. In fact, almost a third of the total challenges coded by the researchers in their interviews related to credibility. A number of participants described credibility as a "chicken or egg" situation in that they did not know if the correct approach was to create a robust badge system and then have external stakeholders buy into the approach, or secure the necessary stakeholder buy-in first and then develop the badging system. However, it is clear that one of the main benefits of digital badges – their ability to assess knowledge and skill at a more granular level than transcripts have traditionally allowed – is greatly impacted in a negative fashion if the badges are not widely recognized by other systems in the future educational or career pathways of the students.

Last, curiosity fulfillment is another human emotion that can serve as a reward for users or players. When we seek out a new puzzle or challenge simply to see what happens in a game, we are motivated by our curiosity. Satisfying that curiosity is our reward. Badges that are unknown, or hidden from the user until they earn them, can inspire curiosity within users (Fanfarelli, 2018). They might wonder what they need to do to earn that particular greyed-out, mysterious badge, or they might peruse online communities or wikis or talk to their friends to determine if anyone else has figured out how to earn the badge.

Behavioral Variations

While it would be nice to talk about all human behaviors as though they were uniform from one person to the next, we know from our real-world observations and experiences that this is certainly not the case. Real people behave differently, sometimes quite differently, even when faced with the same situation. Human beings are also motivated by different factors. Words such as "personality" and "temperament" are often used to refer to different behavioral patterns in humans; for example, someone might be described as having an introverted personality and a calm temperament. Another person might show signs of an extroverted personality and an excitable temperament. These two individuals would probably respond quite differently to certain stimuli, such as being asked to give an impromptu speech to guests at a social gathering. Even though the prompt is the same, the resulting behaviors would be quite different.

The same is true for digital behaviors. On social media, for example, some users are content to lie behind the scenes and "lurk" for content, while others are much more active in communicating and exchanging ideas in online spaces. Similarly, some videogame players will be aggressive and almost belligerent on the chat channel, while other players will be more strategic and less verbose. Other research has explored what interests and motivates videogame players and inspires them to play games. For example, Sherry, Lucas, Greenberg, and Lachlan (2006) identified six reasons why people play games: competition, fantasy, social interaction, challenge, diversion, and arousal. We could devise potentially motivating digital badges to accompany each of these. To motivate competitive players, we might develop a badge to award the highest score on the leaderboard for a particular game level in a platformer like *Super Mario Brothers* or *Crash Bandicoot*. To reward players who enjoy fantasy, we might offer a badge earned by delving deeply into the history of a forbidden order of priests. Earning it would require acquiring and reading all of the hidden journals placed strategically throughout the kingdom in a role-playing game. For social gamers, a badge might be unlocked after completing at least ten quests with one's online guild members.

More specifically in the domain of digital badging, research shows that badges work differently for different types of learners. For example, those who have high expectations for learning and who value learning tasks respond more positively to badges than those who have lower expectations (Reid, Paster, & Abramovich, 2015). This research suggests that while attempting to use digital badges to encourage reluctant or remedial learnings is a noble and worthy cause, we do not yet have evidence that such endeavors will be fruitful. Or, perhaps we have just not yet determined the right scope, type, and format of the badges that will work for learners with low expectations about learning.

As these examples show, behavioral variations in digital environments are common and in some ways similar to behavioral variations in real-world environments. As a result, it is important to design and develop a sufficiently diverse set of badges so that your application will support different motivating factors for a wide variety of players and play styles. Otherwise, a designer risks isolating a particular fragment of her audience or creating an interactive digital environment that uses badges that are only motivating to certain types of people.

Designing with Behavior in Mind

A good starting activity for thinking about behavior in an interactive digital system is to write down the types of behaviors you hope to encourage. The simplest way to do this is to write them down in paragraph form or using a bulleted list as we did at the beginning of this chapter. However, you could also use a more formal method, such as a use-case diagram, which shows the various actors who will use your system and the types of activities they will perform in your environment. The benefit of the former approach is simplicity, but in certain development environments for larger projects, the latter approach might be more useful. This is because other members of your team, such as software developers, might prefer more formalized models for user activity mapping. You could also map out behaviors using personas, or hypothetical scenarios describing how different audiences might interact with your system. Regardless of method, the important thing to do as a first step is to think carefully about behaviors and get a list down on paper in one form or another.

Then, using the same technique as for your productive behaviors, list out the undesirable or unproductive behaviors that are potentially emergent within your system. For example, is there the potential for digital badges to be distractions that break immersion and cause your users to become frustrated or upset? Do not worry about trying to fix those issues yet, just spend some time articulating the potential negative behaviors so that you can then determine how best to address them in the next step.

After the constructive and destructive behavior list has been generated, you next need to think about how your badges will reinforce desired behaviors and suppress undesired behaviors. It is likely not possible to build the perfect system right off the bat. It might be that there are unexpected behaviors that you did not anticipate that you will need to deal with further down the line. The appeal of creative and original solutions to problems in digital complex systems should not be underestimated. Consider this description of emergence from game designer Richard Rouse:

> It is the development of numerous robust and logical systems that leads to player-unique solutions to situations in a game. One could describe these solutions as "emergent" from the systems design of the game, a popular buzzword in game design circles. Establishing a game universe that functions in accordance with logical rules players can easily understand and use to their advantage allows those same players to come up with their own solutions to the problems the game presents. Nothing is more rewarding for players than devising some obtuse, unobvious method for solving a puzzle or a combat situation and then having it actually work. The more complex systems work correctly and concurrently with each other, the more interesting and varied the solutions to situations become.
>
> (Rouse III, 2005, pp. 117–118)

Once you have listed out the behaviors and acknowledged the potential for new emergent behaviors, it is time to think about the tools at your disposal. Three such tools were discussed at length in this chapter: motivation, feedback, and reward. Each of these can be tricky to get right because they can vary widely depending on play styles and demographics. However, as with much learning assessment, the trick is to find a compromise that seems "good enough" to account for as much of your target audience as possible. As you consider each of these three factors, you might ask questions such as the following to determine your overall strategy for behavioral shaping:

1. How can I use badges to motivate my users to seek out productive behaviors in my system?
2. How can I use badges to discourage nonproductive behaviors in my system?
3. What types of rewards will users find most motivating?
4. Can rewards be used to discourage unproductive behaviors?
5. What types of feedback should I use to encourage players to continue engaging in productive behaviors?
6. Should just-in-time feedback be used, or feedback after the level is done, or some combination?

While these questions are certainly useful for designing with behavior in mind before a level or application is built, we often do not have the luxury of joining a project at its onset. Perhaps we want to add badges to a course in a learning management system with content that has already been added and assignments that have already been drafted. Or, maybe we are tasked with adding achievements to a game level that has already been scripted and populated with art and characters. Fortunately, in these situations we can still rely on digital badges to help shape behaviors. This is because another important feature of digital badges is their ability to redirect behaviors after a system has already been designed.

We have written about this feature in earlier work (McDaniel & Fanfarelli, 2016), but the gist of the matter is this: badges can change the way humans interact with already designed systems. In other words, strategically deployed badges can persuade a player to play a level that has already been designed, in an atypical way – perhaps faster, slower, more strategically, more cooperatively, or just differently, in any other number of variations. We should not underestimate this powerful capability. Designing digital environments is costly. Art takes a long time to develop and so does dialog, learning content, sound, and all of the other digital and procedural assets and scripts that we use in our learning games, simulations, and online course management systems. To be able to redirect behaviors in already designed spaces using a comparatively simpler designed object, such as a digital badge, is a useful tool in our digital toolbox. Of course badges used in this fashion must be designed thoughtfully and they should integrate as seamlessly as possible into the digital environment in order to have a stronger and more meaningful impact on user behaviors.

Next Up

In Part II of this book, we move into designing effective digital badges for specific applications. We will discuss badges' use in videogames, online learning systems, mobile applications, and military training simulations. Each of these contexts challenges us as designers to think about audience, function, and behavior in slightly different ways in order to build successful systems for different purposes.

References

Abramovich, S., Schunn, C., & Higashi, R. M. (2013). Are badges useful in education? It depends upon the type of badge and expertise of learner. *Educational Technology Research and Development, 61*(2), 217–232.

Bitchener, J., Young, S., & Cameron, D. (2005). The effect of different types of corrective feedback on ESL student writing. *Journal of Second Language Writing, 14*(3), 191–205.

Bloom, B. S. (1956). *Taxonomy of educational objectives. Vol. 1: Cognitive domain.* New York: McKay.

Brewster, C., & Fager, J. (2000, October). Increasing student engagement and motivation: From time-on-task to homework. Northwest Regional Education Laboratory. Retrieved from https://educationnorthwest.org/sites/default/files/byrequest.pdf.

Buffardi, K., & Edwards, S. H. (2014, June). Responses to adaptive feedback for software testing. In *Proceedings of the 2014 Conference on Innovation & Technology in Computer Science Education* (pp. 165–170). ACM.

Davis, K., & Singh, S. (2015). Digital badges in afterschool learning: Documenting the perspectives and experiences of students and educators. *Computers & Education, 88*, 72–83.

Deci, E. L., Koestner, R., & Ryan, R. M. (1999). A meta-analytic review of experiments examining the effects of extrinsic rewards on intrinsic motivation. *Psychological Bulletin, 125*(6), 627–668.

DBailye (2017, June 1). From the community: Eagle Scout Award: What is the big deal? *Chicago Tribune.* Retrieved from www.chicagotribune.com/suburbs/orland-park-homer-glen/community/chi-ugc-article-eagle-scout-award-whats-the-big-deal-2014-02-16-story.html.

Fanfarelli, J. R. (2018). Using digital badges to foster curiosity: Adjusting the knowledge gap through strategic design. *Foundations of Digital Games '18*, Malmö, Sweden.

Glover, I. (2013). Play as you learn: Gamification as a technique for motivating learners. In J. Herrington, J. Couros, & V. Irvine (Eds.), *Proceedings of World Conference on Educational Multimedia, Hypermedia and Telecommunications 2013.* Chesapeake, VA: AACE, 1999–2008.

Hattie, J., & Timperley, H. (2007). The power of feedback. *Review of Educational Research, 77*(1), 81–112.

Hawthorne, N. (1850). *The scarlet letter.* Retrieved from www.gutenberg.org/cache/epub/33/pg33.txt.

Kaiser, R. (2012, August). 'Grinding' and its relationship with the RPG genre. *Engadget.* Retrieved from www.engadget.com/2012/08/05/grinding-and-its-relationship-with-the-rpg-genre/.

Landers, R. N., Bauer, K. N., Callan, R. C., & Armstrong, M. B. (2015). Psychological theory and the gamification of learning. In T. Reiners & L. C. Wood (Eds.), *Gamification in education and business* (pp. 165–186). Cham: Springer International Publishing.

Maslow, A. H. (1943). A theory of human motivation. *Psychological Review, 50*(4), 370.

McDaniel, R., & Fanfarelli, J. (2016). Building better digital badges: Pairing completion logic with psychological factors. *Simulation & Gaming, 47*(1), 73–102.

Naik, P. (1998, August). Behaviorism as a theory of personality: A critical look. Retrieved from www.personalityresearch.org/papers/naik.html.

Qualls, E. (2016, December 4). What is a Gamerscore? Lifewire. Retrieved from www.lifewire.com/what-is-a-gamerscore-3563172.

Reid, A. J., Paster, D., & Abramovich, S. (2015). Digital badges in undergraduate composition courses: Effects on intrinsic motivation. *Journal of Computers in Education, 2*(4), 377–398.

Resnick, M., Martin, F., Berg, R., Borovoy, R., Colella, V., Kramer, K., & Silverman, B. (1998, January). Digital manipulatives: New toys to think with. In *Proceedings of the SIGCHI Conference on Human Factors in Computing Systems* (pp. 281–287). ACM Press/Addison-Wesley Publishing Co.

Rouse III, R. (2005). *Game design theory and practice* (2nd ed.). Plano, TX: Wordware Publishing.

Ryan, R. M. (1982). Control and information in the intrapersonal sphere: An extension of cognitive evaluation theory. *Journal of Personality and Social Psychology, 43*, 450–461.

Ryan, R. M., & Deci, E. L. (2000). Intrinsic and extrinsic motivations: Classic definitions and new directions. *Contemporary Educational Psychology, 25*(1), 54–67.

Sherry, J. L., Lucas, K., Greenberg, B. S., & Lachlan, K. (2006). Video game uses and gratifications as predictors of use and game preference. *Playing Video Games: Motives, Responses, and Consequences, 24*(1), 213–224.

Skinner, B. F. (1953). *Science and human behavior.* New York: The Free Press.

Zellner, A. (2015, March). 21st century rewards: A case study of Khan Academy and digital badges from an educational psychology perspective. In *Society for Information Technology & Teacher Education International Conference* (pp. 1899–1906). Association for the Advancement of Computing in Education (AACE).

PART II
Contexts and Practice

CHAPTER 5

Using Badges in Videogames

Overview

In Part I of this book, we discussed digital badges at a high level and introduced fundamental information about their construction, capabilities, and behavioral shaping potential. As we begin Part II, we will examine these objects more closely in specific domains and contexts. We discuss areas in which digital badges have the potential to be particularly effective. These include areas such as videogames, online learning systems, mobile applications, and military training simulations. We begin this mission in this chapter by discussing how badges are used in game-based environments and exploring the history of badges in videogames. We explain that digital badges work in videogames fundamentally the same way they operate in other media, such as simulations and learning management systems, but with some special affordances made possible by their design. We discuss the specific *completion logics* required to earn badges in games, how the *visual representations* of badges can change in fantasy-based environments, and how associated *rewards* translate into game-based points or other virtual currencies. We note that in some cases, even without external currencies attached, earning the badge is sufficient reward for game players. For these players, each badge becomes a trophy that is meaningful in and of itself for bragging rights or a sense of self-fulfillment. We conclude the chapter with a discussion of effective design principles for digital badges used in videogames. We can learn from many of these design principles, even when designing badges outside of game-based environments. Designing badges that are fun, motivating, and effective is important for a wide variety of learning, credentialing, and training applications. Studying the badges found in videogames can help us do this better.

Why Do We Care about Badges in Games?

There are three important reasons we start our discussion of the applications and contexts of digital badges with videogames. First, digital games were precursors to many of the modern techniques we now see that attempt to improve virtual experiences by adding more fun or engagement. It is no accident that the term "gamification," which refers to the use of game-like features such as badges, leaderboards, and levels (Deterding, Dixon, Khaled, & Nacke, 2011), has the word "game" in its root. Games are integral and fundamental to our understanding of achievements and videogames are central to our understanding of digital badges. Furthermore, many of the earliest usages of digital badges, if not *the* earliest usages, appeared in early videogame environments.

Second, because of the long history of videogames with badges and their successful use of these objects for shaping player behavior, it makes sense to spend some time better understanding their history and usage trends. For example, why are badges so prevalent in entertainment media? A study conducted by the Electronic Entertainment Design and Research (EEDAR) organization found that games that included many achievements were better reviewed and generated more sales than games with fewer achievements (Arent, 2007; Jakobsson, 2011). Thus, there is also an economic incentive for using achievements in videogames and we can learn from techniques honed over time to encourage replayability and help distributors sell more games.

Third, and most importantly for our purposes, there are some very specific behavioral characteristics that videogames elicit. These are useful for our understanding of badges. For example, a primary characteristic that we find compelling in games is their ability to maintain player attention and encourage players to return repeatedly to the game they are playing. This characteristic has obvious benefit to us as designers who want our users and players to spend a lot of time immersed in what we design, but it also has a major economic impact on the businesses and organizations that bankroll these projects. Not surprisingly, these stakeholders, who are invested in continuous revenue generation in digital environments, have long been interested in better understanding these phenomena. Economists coined the term *stickiness* of content to reference online digital content with the ability to focus users' attention over sustained periods and encourage repeat visits (Kominers, 2009). Sticky content is highly valuable for advertisers and bloggers because it ensures repeat traffic and creates a pipeline for new readers and return visitors over time. Like these successful commercial websites that have developed methods for creating and sustaining this type of content, popular and well-designed videogames are sticky and use this property to capture and sustain players' attention. Often, as we are considering how digital badges could be useful for our own goals and purposes for shaping behavior in a productive way, a pre-requisite is keeping a person's attention focused on our digital environment for prolonged periods.

Another behavioral reason that games are useful testbed environments in which to study badges relates to their ability to encourage productive types of deliberate or repetitive behaviors. In *What Video Games Have to Teach Us about Learning and Literacy*, James Paul Gee (2003) argues that one of the reasons videogames are so successful for allowing players to learn is because of their utility in facilitating practice. As Gee explains, learning is largely a phenomenon that depends on practice, since human beings must regularly work on relevant exercises in order to develop mastery in particular learning domains. With videogames, these exercises are facilitated in an environment that is fun, that rewards experimentation and risk, and that provides immersion and engagement. Game players will spend many hours practicing their skills in order to learn the content necessary to succeed in the virtual environments. Videogames have track records showing many decades' worth of sustained performance in the area of facilitating learning and practice in digital environments. When motivated properly, players will spend many hours deliberately practicing tasks within the environment, and digital badges can be used to steer that practice in particular directions (Fanfarelli & McDaniel, 2015). Game designers have become very good at using achievements and trophies for precisely this purpose.

This ability to shape behavior within games has proven broadly useful for many other types of objectives found within games, too. In some contexts, designers construct digital badges to serve as markers of progress, to show players that they have successfully completed portions of a mission or made progress toward the broader objectives of a game level. In others, developers use them to change the method of gameplay itself, such as by awarding a badge for stealthy, speedy, or strategic types of gameplay behaviors. In still others badges are used to promote social behaviors, perhaps by encouraging players to socialize with one another or to work together collaboratively to complete missions or quests. Using modern game engines, developers can easily access each of these metrics through gameplay analysis or even entirely behind the scenes using performance data gathered by the software.

One final point that should be made early in regards to badges used in video games is that these objects are sometimes referred to by different names within this medium. We have already been doing this to some extent throughout the book, but the terminology difference is especially noticeable in game-based media. Most commonly within videogames, digital badges are described as *achievements* or *trophies*, for example, and learning pathways are called *skill trees* (Blair, 2016). However, the basic functionality is the same. Badges, trophies, or achievements are awarded to videogame players based on their ability to complete particular objectives within games. Once awarded, these badges sometimes reward the player with additional forms of currency, such as point values or credentials of rank that provide the player with additional evidence of reputation or success within video game communities. In this chapter, we may use the term achievement, badge, or trophy to refer to the same object: an in-game virtual token used to provide players with feedback and reward after they accomplish objectives.

A Brief History of Badges in Videogames

While the history of analog badges can be traced back to military awards, wreaths, and medals appearing in Greek society (Schwarz, 2016), credentialing has also always been an important part of gaming culture in contemporary society. At the height of arcade gaming in the 1980s, the high scores keyed in by players (generally limited to three characters and comprised of one's initials or gaming nickname) were digital calling cards that issued challenges to up-and-coming gamers seeking to unseat the champion and claim their own small slices of glory. The competition surrounding such gaming environments is deeply embedded in popular culture. A number of films and books speak about the fierce rivalries in early console gaming, but this is perhaps most notably portrayed in the 2007 documentary film *King of Kong* (Cunningham & Gordon, 2007) in which newcomer Steve Wiebe sought to unseat longtime *Donkey Kong* (Nintendo, 1981) champion Billy Mitchell in order to claim a new world record and have his high score listed in the official *Twin Galaxies* online forum.

Even outside of arcade environments in which these digital credentials were tied to specific physical machines, there were other, more traditional venues for displaying records of one's accomplishments in gaming. For example, Steve Wozniak, cofounder of Apple Computers, noted the importance of the "NES Achievers" section of the gaming periodical *Nintendo Power*. NES Achievers was a "two page spread that listed the names of people who either completed or got exceptionally high scores on popular NES or Game Boy games. The competition to get on the list was fierce and not always restricted to kids" (Kent, 2001, loc. 5964). Wozniak mentions that he held a number of achievements in the periodical, including some top scores for *Game Boy Tetris* (Nintendo, 1989). In fact, he eventually had to submit his scores using a fake name because his name began to be printed too frequently and the editors stopped including the scores. Eventually, he simply reversed the letters of his name, turning Steve Wozniak into Evets Kainzow, in order to claim additional real estate on the page (Kent, 2001). Even before we had the precursors to our modern digital achievements, then, there were activities unfolding that spoke to the need for gamers to be recognized for their virtual accomplishments.

Although high scores and printed evidence of game achievements appeared early in gaming history in the mid- to late-1980s, there was physical credentialing of gaming accomplishment that appeared even earlier. For example, Jakobsson (2011) notes that the early videogame *Chopper Command* (Activision, 1982) on the Atari 2600, a console now more than 40 years old, offered an option for players to mail in high scores. Upon verification, they received a special patch that they could sew onto their jackets or backpacks to demonstrate their gaming prowess. This was a physical badge, but it was also an achievement offered for success in a digital environment and it serves as one of the earliest mechanisms of this type of reward in game-based media. Although Boy Scouts had been doing this for decades at this point, there was now a special legitimacy ascribed to virtual achievements that we had not seen before. Just like wilderness survival or automotive maintenance, gaming success was something that could be recognized and endorsed by a central authority.

Since the mail-in days of *Chopper Command* and the stories printed in *Nintendo Power*, achievements have grown more complex, polished, and pervasive, ultimately evolving into what we now see in modern gaming consoles such as the latest Xbox or PlayStation. (Notably, as of the time of this writing, Nintendo does not yet have a modern achievements or trophy ecosystem, although they are said to be working on it (Davidson, 2017)). Early consumer technologies in the mid-1990s gradually matured to include more sophisticated media, such as hypertext, and more sophisticated digital storage mechanisms, such as databases. These allowed digital achievements to be both more persistent and more accessible. While the patch earned in *Chopper Command* needed to be seen in person and the achievements listed in "NES Achievers" needed to be read inside the magazine, it was suddenly possible for any gamers with a dial-up Internet connection to see the achievements displayed by their competition. In the early days of the World Wide Web, these systems were relatively unsophisticated, but they still provided the base functionality that would be adapted into our modern achievement ecosystems. For example, Jakobsson (2011) notes that the MSN Games website, which was acquired by Microsoft in 1996, was perhaps the earliest environment hinting at what would later become the Xbox achievement system we know today. The Games website served as a repository for both free and paid videogames and also included badges that could be earned for certain games within the repository.

Microsoft's earlier initiatives with digital badging eventually grew into the Xbox Live system with the introduction of the Xbox 360 console in 2005 and its initial use of the term "achievement" (Blair, 2016). Shortly after, Steam achievements for PC gamers appeared in 2007 and the PSN Trophy system was introduced in 2008 (McDaniel, 2016). With modern game consoles, there are many different competing badging systems. Some of the most popular game-based environments with support for digital badges include Apple's iOS Game Center, Xbox Live, PSN, and Steam (McDaniel, 2016). In addition to the native badge environments, there are also numerous websites and Internet forums dedicated to researching, listing, and discussing digital badges in videogames. For example, there is a website that exhaustively lists every trophy available for the PlayStation 3, PlayStation 4, PlayStation VR, and PlayStation Vita consoles (PlayStation Trophies, 2018). Similar communities exist for Xbox achievements (Xbox Achievements, 2018) and a number of websites and community forums also provide guides for earning achievements on PC and Mac computing platforms.

Although digital achievement systems are now robust and rich with features, there are also examples of more recent initiatives that return credentialing in games back to its analog roots. Game-related badges continue to emerge in different cultural and economic contexts, even outside of digital game environments. For example, the Girl Scouts organization recently created a videogame developer badge to encourage young women to pursue science and technology careers (Yandoli, 2013). In order to earn the "Game Visionary" badge, Girl Scouts seeking this credential must demonstrate imagination and community mindedness to "bring people together for creative and thoughtful fun" (Girl Scouts, 2018).

As this brief history demonstrates, the use of badging in videogame environments is not a modern phenomenon. In fact, there is a rich history of credentialing in gaming. Over the years, designers and resellers alike have used variants of badging to motivate players to hone their skills and improve their performance. These early efforts using analog and print media have evolved into robust digital platforms where game achievements are not only useful for shaping behavior, but also serve as valuable economic forces for selling more games and persuading players to spend more time playing them. Because of these useful and important properties, it seems obvious that we should spend a little time understanding how they work.

How Badges Work in Videogames

An achievement earned by playing a game in a modern game system looks similar to a digital badge we can earn in a mobile application, simulation, or learning management system (LMS). The achievement generally includes a visual signifier in the form of an icon or badge, an achievement name, a description of the objective required to earn the badge, and an associated reward. Recall from Chapter 2 that these can be grouped into three primary components: a signifier (form factor for the achievement), a completion logic (set of conditions to earn the achievement), and a reward (Hamari & Eranti, 2011). Figure 5.1 provides an example of an achievement we might see in a videogame designed for education. Here the badge's signifier is a mad scientist icon, the completion logic is achieved by applying the scientific method within the context of the game, and the reward is 100 game points (as well as the earning of the digital badge itself).

An example of a game-based badge created for a commercial entertainment game is found in Jakobsson's (2011) two-year study of Xbox 360 badges and the stakeholders who create, use, and write about them in the press. He describes in detail how digital badges work within the Xbox Live Achievement System. Here, as we noted earlier in the chapter with regard to terminology, the digital objects are referred to as achievements rather than badges. The principle, however, is the same. Jakobsson uses the *Body Juggler* achievement from the game *Crackdown* (Realtime

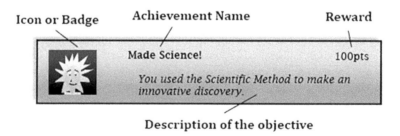

Figure 5.1 Game-based achievement (Fanfarelli, 2014)

Worlds, 2007) as his first example. This achievement requires the player to "use explosives to keep a body up in the air for 10 seconds" (Jakobsson, 2011). While this is visually gruesome, it is typical of the types of achievements we see in videogames. Beneath the grisly description is an opportunity for a player to use creativity to try to solve the particular problem laid out in the achievement's description.

Should the player find a way to accomplish this objective and fulfill the terms of the achievement's completion logic, she will be rewarded with an icon and a Gamerscore reward. In Chapter 3 we introduced the Gamerscore as a form of social currency. As a reminder, each Xbox achievement provides a certain number of points to the earner, which add up to form the player's Gamerscore. The Gamerscore exists within the player's account profile and does not go away when the game ends. In other words, the Gamerscore is persistent beyond the game itself. It exists not just as a cumulative total of all achievement points earned within the Xbox ecosystem, but also as an indicator of the overall time and effort a particular player has invested toward playing games and accomplishing these targeted objectives (Qualls, 2018).

Someone who has a very high Gamerscore, for example, will be generally recognized as someone who is quite experienced in seeking achievements from a broad variety of games. Someone with a very low Gamerscore might either be a rookie player or someone who is completely uninterested in seeking achievements within games. Even by default, though, a player will earn a good number of Gamerpoints simply by following the main game objectives laid out by designers. So, it is possible to assess the longitudinal experience of an Xbox gamer merely by gauging their Gamerscore. The Gamerscore mechanism is unique to the Xbox console, but similar principles apply to the PlayStation console. An equivalent relationship exists between a player's experience and the number of trophies she has displayed in her profile.

Special Characteristics of Videogames

Achievements and trophies in videogames are able to take full advantage of the idiosyncrasies of the medium. Simply put, when compared to other media forms, games offer deeper interactive experiences. Players of games can *do* more virtual things than they can in other media. Compare a videogame to an electronic book, where a player's range of motion is limited to flipping a virtual page or highlighting a selection of text. Or contrast a videogame to a digital video where a player can only play, pause, or advance frames forward or backward as the video plays. Not only do games have an increased range of physical interactions, but players are also cognitively and emotionally protected from the consequences of failure tied to their virtual decisions. The worst that will happen when a player fails at an objective in a game is that she will need to respawn and try again. Finally, game environments are steeped in fantasy. This offers additional design opportunities for storytelling and imaginative interaction design that might not be present in other forms of media.

When designing badges for games, game designers can and should take advantage of the flexibility of game affordances, the fantasy of characters and environments, and the lowered consequences of failure. They can manipulate each of these elements to inspire different types of behaviors from players. Even when compared to comprehensive interactive learning systems, such as LMSs, videogames are still much more sophisticated. They offer many additional ways for fulfilling the requirements of completion logics required to earn badges. While an LMS might be able to track the time a user has logged into the overall system or the overall number of assignments completed, game engines can use the same affordances offered to the player within the virtual world to deliver badges. Any data we can extract from the software constituting the game – such as the physics engine, the collision detection models between various objects, the player's inventory, or even the virtual weather patterns – is fair game for connecting to a badge in some fashion. This flexibility and fine degree of granularity is handy when using badges to redirect behaviors toward specific types of practice.

Consider this scenario: a player is playing a game where she pilots a spaceship through the outer rims of the galaxy. In this game, badges could be awarded for the player's facility with spaceflight controls, the number of alien beings she identifies, or her efficient utilization of propellant as a strategic resource. This is quite different from the palette of available actions delivered in an online LMS, even one that is rich with multimedia videos and animations. The number of interactive options available to the player to earn badges in this science fiction game is significant. There are still universal badge design considerations, though. For instance, why is each badge offered and what is its core purpose within the gameplay experience? Effective designers know how to answer those questions when designing achievements for their games.

The elements of fantasy and failure are equally useful. If this same player plays another game where she takes on the role of a medieval knight in the twelfth century, then the visual representations of badges can be designed to coincide with themes of that time. For instance, graphic embellishments could become more ornate as more complex badges are earned, mirroring the player character's progression from a lowly squire up to a full-fledged knight of the realm. Here, badges are explicitly linked to the player's performance while also staying true to the fantasy-based environment.

With regard to failure as a strategic tool for shaping play behavior, consider a mountaineering game that offers the player a series of challenging mountains to climb. Gameplay mechanics require the precise placement of belays, pulleys, and ropes before the player attempts each ascent. There might exist within this game a particularly challenging level with a hard to reach upper portion of a treacherous mountain accessible only through many trial-and-error practice runs. A design team might decide to offer a badge both for initial failures as well as for the player who repeatedly risks virtual life and limb to ascend the virtual peak. Rewarding failure and incentivizing future performance is another strength of game-based badging.

Oftentimes, designers will take advantage of a combination of these unique capabilities to create desirable badges for their players. For example, in the game *Dragon Age: Inquisition* (BioWare, 2014), players can earn the *Saddled Up* badge by purchasing or locating at least five different mounts, or rideable animals, within the game. Mounts can include real-world animals such as horses, but also fantastic fictional creatures such as dracolisks and harts (IGN, 2015a; McDaniel, 2016). The design of the *Saddled Up* badge takes advantage of not only the affordances of the game engine used by *Dragon Age: Inquisition* and its ability to track player inventory data precisely, but also the game's fantasy-based environment and its mythical creatures. It also will be likely that the player could face repeated virtual deaths on this quest, particularly when trying to locate and ride the more dangerous creatures in the game. Ultimately, this badge also shapes player behavior by encouraging players who are motivated to earn it to seek out avenues in the game that might lead to the successful acquisition or purchase of new types of mounts.

Given this potential, then, how does one go about taking advantage of flexibility, fantasy, and risk-taking to design effective badges in game-based environments? It turns out that a number of the same principles of good game design in general also apply to the design of digital badges. Because badges are also earned through interactions in the game-based world, many of the same experiential dimensions considered by game designers also apply to badges. In other words, it is not only the completion logic and the reward that are important, but also the psychological and cognitive factors that accompany the player as she experiences the game. Badges can credential specific types of experiences or they can shape behaviors to lead to alternate types of experiences. In the next section, we will move from the broad to the specific in order to better understand some of the tactics for designing effective achievements and trophies in games.

Designing Effective Badges for Videogames

Videogame design at large is a complex subject that has many volumes of work dedicated to it. Titles exploring videogame design and development range from the philosophical and theoretical, such as Bernard Suits' *The Grasshopper* (2005) and Salen and Zimmerman's canonical *Rules of Play* (2004), to highly technical volumes looking specifically at related topics such as artificial intelligence, level design, or modeling and animation techniques. In general, designers tend to agree that digital games are complex and worthy of critical attention because they combine complex engineering systems of rules and logic with the experiential dimension of playing the games and the cultural dimension of how these games influence and are influenced by society at large. A sophisticated bestselling game such as *Portal* (Valve, 2007), for example, cannot be fully explained only through the rules of how *Portal* operates. One must also understand the experiential process of playing the game as well as the many cultural influences surrounding the game. Now that *Portal* is many years old, the historical influences of the game on the broader field must also be considered and recognized.

Gamers who play new games often have expectations based on their experiences with older games.

Game-based achievements and trophies are slightly easier to study than games at large because they often exist as overlays atop existing game engines and can be considered distinctly from other elements of the game (this can also be problematic, as we discuss later in the chapter). While there is not yet a comprehensive book focused specifically on badge design for videogames, there is a useful series on the topic by Blair (2011a, 2011b, 2011c) published on *Gamasutra*, a popular online magazine for game design professionals. Blair (2011a) suggests a number of design principles for developers looking to incorporate badges into videogames. Drawing from his own research exploring the different possible permutations of badges in game-based environments, Blair first developed a taxonomy for considering badges according to their function within games. Most useful in Blair's work is his focus on the types and features of badges and his analysis of which configurations are most useful for specific objectives.

For example, Blair (2011a) considers measurement achievements, which we discussed in Chapter 2, in terms of their utility for game design. The example Blair uses is the star system used in the iOS mobile game *Angry Birds* (Rovio, 2009) in which players earn one to three golden stars based on how well they performed in the level. The goal of *Angry Birds* is essentially to destroy a screen full of virtual pigs by launching various types of cartoonish birds from a slingshot. The player interacts with the game by aiming the slingshot up or down and determining the strength of the shot based on how far they pull back on the slingshot. While the mechanics seem somewhat primitive, there are actually deep gameplay possibilities since the player can launch various types of birds with distinct abilities and the pigs fortify themselves using various materials. Further, each interaction between bird type and fortification material produces interesting variations in gameplay. From a badging perspective, then, even when a player completes a level by destroying all the pigs, her performance can still be evaluated using one to three stars. The ultimate ranking depends on how efficiently she used her available resources to accomplish the objective.

While measurement achievements express information about a player's performance (e.g., one star in *Angry Birds* versus three), completion achievements merely note that a player has completed an objective and do not provide more nuanced information about performance (Blair, 2011a). For example, the *Medic!* badge provided for reviving 25 teammates in the game *Mass Effect: Andromeda* (BioWare, 2017) is awarded to players after they accomplish this objective, but there is no differentiation layer associated with the badge that distinguishes between how quickly or effectively these revivals were performed. In large part due to the additional feedback provided by measurement achievements, Blair recommends using measurement achievements over completion achievements in order to increase players' intrinsic motivation. We discussed intrinsic motivation in more detail in Chapters 3 and 4, but the idea is to encourage the player to continue playing for the enjoyment of the activity rather than for some external reward. Again, this might seem contradictory at first, given that achievements themselves can be seen as external rewards. However, for many gamers, they are an essential component of the gameplay experience rather than some external system layered atop the game. To these gamers, they become part of the holistic experience of the game. Further, when properly designed, these external rewards can fulfill purposes such as goal-setting or providing feedback. These factors can then create the proper conditions for improved intrinsic motivation – in this case, higher levels of competence.

Blair's (2011a) next point of examination is with the degree to which badges are awarded for "interesting" versus "boring" types of activities. He uses the example of trade skills in online role-playing games as an example of a boring game activity, and more strategic activities, such as learning to use units more effectively in the game *Starcraft II* (Blizzard, 2010), as an example of an interesting game activity. Both types of activities can be reinforced through badges. For example, many tasks that are less interesting are still necessary for gameplay, particularly in games of larger scope in which a player must build up skills, abilities, or inventories over sustained periods. For these types of "boring" tasks, Blair suggests rewarding them, but saving feedback for more interesting tasks that demand greater attention or strategic adjustment from players. Using this guideline, then, it might be reasonable to use completion achievements to reward players for less interesting tasks and measurement achievements to reward players for interesting ones.

Another important consideration in the design of badges used in videogames is how difficult the badge is to obtain. There are several ways we can define gameplay difficulty. One way is to consider the amount of time required from the player to earn the badge. Achievements that reward completion percentage, for example, often require tremendous amounts of time from the player. One example is the *My Kung Fu Is Stronger than Yours* achievement from the reboot of the classic videogame *Mortal Kombat* (Warner Bros., 2011). The game requires the player to spend over 600 hours of total playing time, playing each character in the game for a minimum of 24 hours and accomplishing a number of other challenging tasks, in order to earn this badge (IGN, 2015b). This badge is so difficult to earn it has spawned in-depth study guides posted by players to Internet forums which outline the specific actions required by players in order to unlock it (Obie83, 2011).

We can also consider difficulty in relation to the skill required to unlock the achievement. The game *Lost Planet 2* (Capcom, 2010), for example, requires the player to set a world record in training mode in order to earn the *'Til the End* achievement (IGN, 2015b). As opposed to using time on task as a metric, achievements with high skill-based difficulty make no guarantee that a player will earn a badge unless her skills are at a sufficient level. Obviously this becomes easier with the practice that goes along with the additional time playing the game, but a world-record-caliber performance is something that even a dedicated player is not likely to see (unless, perhaps, she plays the game sufficiently early when the records being set are lower and easier to surpass). This notion of being the very best at a particular game is deeply embedded within the hardcore gaming mythos. We see these themes emerge in popular fiction as gamers vie to be the very first person to solve a series of difficult virtual puzzles that leads to an enticing treasure. Two examples of this include virtual gamer Wade Watts (gamer name Parzival) who seeks vast treasure and fortune in Ernest Cline's (2011) novel *Ready Player One* and antagonist hacker/gamer Brian Gragg (gamer name Loki) who maliciously seeks great power and influence in Daniel Suarez's (2009) novel *Daemon*. Developers who devise badges that are very difficult to acquire often exploit dedicated gamers' desire to be the best at a game.

There are other ways that game-based badges can be difficult, too. Perhaps they are scarce – limited in number so that only a certain number of players can obtain them. Maybe they require interactions, such as combinations of players working together or amalgamations of already secured achievements (i.e., metabadges) from other games, in order to be earned. They might depend on random chance or good fortune, in the likes of particular randomly generated battles or randomly generated loot in treasure boxes that are pre-requisites to locating the badges. There are even some achievements and trophies that are so difficult to obtain they have never been earned at all (Brown, 2016). As with most things, the proper degree of difficulty in a game-based achievement is somewhere in between the extremely easy badges that are given seemingly just for booting up a game and the trophies that are so challenging to obtain no one has yet managed to do it. Blair (2011a) suggests that achievements *should* have some modest degree of difficulty, though, if only to require the player to increase her skill level and monitor her performance in order to earn them. He also suggests challenging achievements are more likely to be enjoyable to earn and will require players to increase their self-efficacy as they work toward attempts to earn them.

Another area in which achievements are useful for videogames is in aligning gameplay toward particular objectives and outcomes within the games' interactive environments. These environments often offer multiple ways for gameplay to unfold, so players devise individual goals that dictate how they will operate in this space. Previously, in Chapter 3, we discussed how badges are useful for goal-setting. Blair (2011a) discusses how players' game-based, goal-setting activities relate to the design of achievements. Goal orientation is critical in gaming because games often provide openness in allowing players room to decide how to pursue the missions they are given. Many games provide much flexibility here, particularly those designed as large open-ended or "sandbox" games (Squire, 2008). For example, after a brief tutorial in the game *Fallout 3* (Bethesda Softworks, 2008), a player is released into a giant open world with only a vague suggestion of where she should go next. While there is an obvious second step to follow that leads the player into a nearby town, the player could alternatively choose to completely ignore those clues and instead wander anywhere on the map that is accessible by foot. This opens up many opportunities since the *Fallout 3* map is very large.

Blair's (2011a) work distinguishes between performance orientation, in which players consider other individuals' assessment of their performance, versus mastery orientation, where players work to improve their own mastery. With regard to design, Blair suggests that performance goals and mastery goals can be used to encourage different types of behaviors. For simple, repetitive tasks, performance goals are useful and designers might wish to consider design cues that emphasize time and points, allowing this information to be used as feedback and data for other players to see. For more complex tasks that require a mastery orientation, Blair suggests thinking about badges that recognize creativity, exploration, and risk-taking. Acknowledging the effort it takes to build up skills is an important strategy to improve motivation, particularly when players are still new to the game.

The second and third parts of Blair's series on researching game achievements (2011b, 2011c) study a number of other variables that can be used to manipulate how achievements are displayed, unlocked, and earned in game environments. For example, part two (2011b) considers whether achievements are expected or unexpected (known in advance or unknown and surprising to the player when earned), when achievement notification occurs, how permanent achievements are once earned, and who can see the achievements once they are earned. He makes recommendations for particular types of scenarios in which each of these variables can be manipulated for different outcomes. Part three (2011c) then considers the use of negative achievements (awarded for failures rather than success), the ways achievements can be used as virtual currency (points, coins, and stars that have purchase power in and outside of games), the use of incremental and meta-achievements, competitive achievements, and non-competitive, cooperative achievements. The depth to which each of these variables can be tweaked and configured speaks to the utility of game-based achievements for behavioral and performance tweaking in different contexts.

While a detailed discussion of all of these achievement components could easily make for a book of its own, what is important to understand is the richness of digital badges within game environments and the many different ways these badges can be manipulated, awarded, and monetized for different purposes. In contrast to other forms of media, videogames can embed interactive elements of fantasy and allow players to manipulate virtual instantiations of real-world forces and objects, all for the sake of fun. These are powerful design elements in our toolboxes as we work toward our goal of building more effective digital badges. Even if we are not designing for game-based environments, it is possible to use many of these design tactics in other contexts and mediums.

A Few Cautionary Notes

Although game-based achievements are useful to study and we can learn a lot from the strategies used by game designers, there are also some caveats to consider. For one thing, some consider achievements and badges to be outside the game experience. From this perspective, critics see digital badges as distractions for players – objects that take gamers away from the true artistic experience of the videogame. Sometimes, this is a deliberate move on the part of the game developer. For example, a number of games on the digital distribution platform Steam have taken to creating "achievement spam" which involves "front-loading subpar games with thousands of achievements" (Grayson, 2017, para. 1). This is done to sell more games by reeling in players to play games they would likely otherwise ignore. This is an important trend to be aware of given the exponential growth of achievements in videogames. For example, of the approximately 350,000 achievements available for players to earn on Steam, developers added 125,000 of them in 2017 (Grayson, 2017).

These tactics also speak to the broader commercialization of achievements and the impact of that on the player's experience. While games can and do use achievements to modify player behaviors, as we have argued in Chapter 4, they also serve a branding and marketing purpose for the companies that develop them. For example, Bogost (2010) points out that achievements are essentially loyalty programs for videogames that reward players for repeatedly returning to the games. Much like frequent flyer miles or restaurants' frequent customer punch cards, game achievements may cause players to return to the same product repeatedly. This might reinforce a player's association with the company's brand and the game's intellectual property, but it does not mean the game is a better experience or more fun than other competing titles. Bogost notes similarities in the way social value is assigned to game achievements, allowing earners to brag about accomplishments to other players much as they might compare their frequent flyer status with other regular travelers. Achievements also provide evidence verifying that specific in-game actions have occurred, evidence that can add to this social dynamic in troublesome ways or lead to potentially nefarious strategies for monetizing player histories.

Other researchers have pointed out that videogame achievements and other gamified elements are seemingly useful for training and education, but that their reward structure is problematic, sharing the same sorts of addictive properties that gamblers find appealing. Some even suggest they can be used for the purposes of indoctrination (Owens, 2012). For example, a game like *America's Army* is successful not just because it is an engaging military simulation, but also because it teaches young players about the cultural and operational mindset of the US military and helps to recruit new US soldiers (Owens, 2012). In other words, in addition to the explicit operations reinforced by badges, there are also implicit values and ideas that are conveyed stylistically and procedurally through the visual representations of badges and the specific gameplay activities required to earn them. Whether cultivating brand recognition or indoctrinating players to recognize particular activities as natural to a culture or process, digital badges, like videogames at large, have underlying effects on audiences that we as designers must consider.

One final note speaks to the type of player who is a completionist and seeks to earn every achievement in a game. Gamers of this type are compelled to explore every nook and cranny of a videogame and will try to unlock every digital badge possible. While such behavior can be enjoyable and motivating for players, it can also turn into a compulsion that eventually seems more like work than pleasure. When this happens, it is worth questioning whether the achievements are truly serving a more important purpose in the game's ecosystem or if they are instead encouraging addictive behaviors. These less desirable behaviors might work against what a designer wishes her players to take away from the experience.

Next Up

In our next chapter, we venture into another commonly used domain for badging systems: online learning systems. In contrast to commercial videogames, which primarily use digital badges to shape behavior for the purposes of prolonged interactive entertainment, online learning systems use digital badges to improve learning through processes such as scaffolding, feedback, and personalization of learning.

References

Activision (1982). *Chopper Command*. Atari 2600 video game.
Arent, S. (2007, Oct. 17). Study: 360 games with more achievements get better reviews. *Wired*. Retrieved from www.wired.com/2007/10/study-360-games/.
Bethesda Softworks (2008). *Fallout 3*. Xbox360/PS3/XboxOne/PC video game.
BioWare (2014). *Dragon Age: Inquisition*. Xbox One video game.
BioWare (2017). *Mass Effect: Andromeda*. Xbox One video game.
Blair, L. (2011a, April 27). The cake is not a lie: How to design effective achievements. *Gamasutra Feature*. Retrieved from www.gamasutra.com/view/feature/134729/ the_cake_is_not_a_lie_how_to_.php.
Blair, L. (2011b, May 11). The cake is not a lie: How to design effective achievements, part two. *Gamasutra Feature*. Retrieved from www.gamasutra.com/view/feature/134744/ the_cake_is_not_a_lie_how_to_.php.
Blair, L. (2011c, May 25). The cake is not a lie: How to design effective achievements, part three. *Gamasutra Feature*. Retrieved from www.gamasutra.com/view/feature/134756/ the_cake_is_not_a_lie_how_to_.php.
Blair, L. (2016). What video games can teach us about badges and pathways. In L.Y. Muilenburg & Z. L. Berge (Eds.), *Digital badges in education: Trends, issues, and cases* (pp. 62–70). New York: Routledge.
Blizzard (2010). *Starcraft II*. PC video game.
Bogost, I. (2010, February 10). Persuasive games: check-ins check out. *Gamasutra Feature*. Retrieved from www.gamasutra.com/view/feature/4269/persuasive_games_ checkins_check_.php.
Brown, J. (2016, June 4). PS4: Twelve hardest platinum trophies nobody unlocked. *Whatculture.com*. Retrieved from http://whatculture.com/gaming/ps4-12-hardest-platinum-trophies-nobody-unlocked.

Capcom (2010). *Lost Planet 2*. Xbox360/PS3/PC video game.

Cline, E. (2011). *Ready player one*. NY: Broadway Books.

Cunningham, E., & Gordon, S. (2007). *King of Kong*. United States: Picturehouse.

Davidson, M. (2017, Sept. 11). Nintendo working on achievement/trophy system for Switch, says indie dev. *IGN.com*. Retrieved from www.ign.com/articles/2017/09/11/nintendo-working-on-achievementtrophy-system-for-switch-says-indie-dev.

Deterding, S., Dixon, D., Khaled, R., & Nacke, L. (2011, Sept.). From game design elements to gamefulness: Defining gamification. In *Proceedings of the 15th International Academic MindTrek Conference: Envisioning future media environments* (pp. 9–15). ACM.

Fanfarelli, J. (2014). *The effects of narrative and achievements on learning in a 2d platformer video game* (Unpublished doctoral dissertation). University of Central Florida, Orlando, FL. Retrieved from http://stars.library.ucf.edu/etd/4772/.

Fanfarelli, J. R., & McDaniel, R. (2015, July). Digital badges for deliberate practice: Designing effective badging systems for interactive communication scenarios. In *Proceedings of the 33rd Annual International Conference on the Design of Communication* (p. 49). ACM.

Gee, J. P. (2003). *What video games have to teach us about learning and literacy*. New York: Palgrave Macmillan.

Girl Scouts (2018). Badge explorer. Retrieved from www.girlscouts.org/en/our-program/badges/badge_explorer.html.

Grayson, N. (2017, June 29). 'Achievement spam' games are causing controversy on Steam. *Kotaku*. Retrieved from https://steamed.kotaku.com/achievement-spam-games-are-causing-controversy-on-steam-1796528445.

Hamari, J., & Eranti, V. (2011). Framework for designing and evaluating game achievements. Paper presented at *the DiGRA 2011: Think, Design, Play*. Hilversum, Netherlands.

IGN (2015a). *Mounts*. Retrieved from www.ign.com/wikis/dragon-age-inquisition/Mounts.

IGN (2015b). The eleven hardest achievements in video games. Retrieved from www.ign.com/articles/2015/06/30/the-11-hardest-achievements-in-video-games.

Jakobsson, M. (2011). The achievement machine: Understanding Xbox 360 achievements in gaming practices. *Game Studies*, *11*(1), 1–22.

Kent, S. (2001). *The ultimate history of video games: From Pong to Pokemon—The story behind the craze that touched our lives and changed our world*. New York: Three Rivers Press. [Kindle version]. Retrieved from Amazon.com.

Kominers, S. D. (2009). Sticky content and the structure of the commercial web. In *2009 Workshop on the Economics of Networks*.

McDaniel, R. (2016). What we can learn about badges from video games. In D. Ifenthaler, D. Mah, & N. Bellin-Mularski (Eds.), *Foundations of digital badges and micro-credentials: Demonstrating and recognizing knowledge and competencies* (pp. 325–342). Switzerland: Springer International Publishing.

Nintendo (1981). *Donkey Kong*. Arcade video game.

Nintendo (1989). *Tetris*. Game boy video game.

Obie83 (2011, August 17). My Kung-Fu Is Stronger in depth trophy guide. Playstationtrophies.org. Retrieved from www.playstationtrophies.org/forum/mortal-kombat/120840-my-kung-fu-stronger-depth-guide.html.

Owens Jr, M. D. (2012). It's all in the game: Gamification, games, and gambling. *Gaming Law Review and Economics*, *16*(3), 114–118.

PlayStation Trophies (2018). *Trophies.* Retrieved from https://www.playstationtrophies. org/trophies/.

Qualls, E. (2018, February 1). What is an Xbox Gamerscore? *Lifewire.* Retrieved from www.lifewire.com/what-is-a-gamerscore-3563172.

Realtime Worlds (2007). *Crackdown.* Xbox360 video game.

Rovio (2009). *Angry Birds.* iOS mobile video game.

Salen, K., & Zimmerman, E. (2004). *Rules of play: Game design fundamentals.* Cambridge, MA: MIT Press.

Schwarz, S. J. (2016). *Digital badge adoption: Earner's perceived educational value.* Iowa State University.

Squire, K. (2008). Open-ended video games: A model for developing learning for the interactive age. In K. Salen (Ed.), *The John D. and Catherine T. MacArthur Foundation Series on Digital Media and Learning: The ecology of learning: Connecting youth, games, and learning* (pp. 167–198). Cambridge, MA: MIT Press.

Suarez, D. (2009) *Daemon.* New York: Dutton.

Suits, B. (2005). *The grasshopper: Games, life, and utopia.* Orchard Park, NY: Broadview Press.

Valve (2007). *Portal.* PC/Xbox360/PS3/OSX video game.

Warner Bros. (2011). *Mortal Kombat.* Xbox360/PS3/PS Vita/PC video game.

Xbox Achievements (2018). *Achievements.* Retrieved from www.xboxachievements. com/achievements/.

Yandoli, K. (2013, April 22). Girl scouts create video game developer badge to push young women into science and technology. *Huffpost.* Retrieved from www.huffingtonpost.com/2013/04/22/ girl-scouts-create-video-_n_3133482.html.

CHAPTER 6

Using Badges in Online Learning Systems

Overview

The prevalence of online learning has long been on the rise, especially in higher education where approximately 30% of all students are enrolled in at least one online course and nearly half of those students are exclusively enrolled online (Allen & Seaman, 2017). With this large share of web-based learners comes a need to enhance the practices that improve online learning processes and outcomes. Luckily, we are off to a good start, as there is some evidence that students in online learning conditions tend to perform better than those who receive face-to-face instruction (U.S. Department of Education, 2010). Of course, there is more to online learning than higher education; sites such as Khan Academy, Coursera, Codecademy, and Lynda offer courses infused with tutorials and practice exercises that allow their users to learn topics on a flexible schedule and from a distance. This sort of learning is becoming increasingly prominent as the Internet continues to offer a greater variety of ways to learn.

As we take note of modern trends in virtual and online learning, we should examine how badges fit within these environments. Many of these less formalized learning environments have already begun to incorporate digital badges. For example, sites such as Codecademy and Khan Academy use badges as credentials to signify course completion and as rewards for consistent practice. However, we also see badges emerging in online university courses, either through home-grown badging systems or through the usage of pre-existing systems that allow for custom badge creation and development (e.g., Badgr, Credly).

In this chapter, we consider online learning in its broadest definition to account for any type of learning that occurs in a web-based environment. We describe how badges can be used for a variety of roles and applications in online learning environments so that designers can create badges that align with the goals in their courses or applications. While this chapter primarily emphasizes higher education-based practices, these practices can be similarly applied to other online learning environments. Further, this chapter emphasizes the design and creation of new badges, but these same design aspects can be applied to home-brew badging systems or external badging sites administered by outside organizations.

Badging in Learning Systems

Recognition of academic achievement has been commonplace in education for quite some time. In fact, most educational institutions depend on such recognitions for their final deliverables. Grades, certificates, diplomas, and transcripts are all physical forms of recognition for academic achievement. While digital badges are a relatively new addition, the use of certificates, medals, and various other physical indicators of accomplishment is quite familiar to current and former students. Now, digital badges are finding their way into the education realm and research about their use and effectiveness is evolving in tandem.

While educational badges have not always been effective, the idea that badges *can* be effective in education is well supported. Haug, Wodzicki, Cress, and Moskaliuk (2014) examined the effect of badges on investment within a Massive Open Online Course (MOOC), where investment is a term that refers to the level of student involvement in course activities. While student investment decreased over time, students who aimed to obtain a badge experienced a smaller decrease in investment compared to those who did not aim to obtain a badge. Another study revealed a greater quantity of student contributions in a badged classroom without a decrease in quality of those assignments, indicating additional student effort and motivation (Denny, 2013). Likewise, a study by the same author and colleagues found that badges increased student self-testing, leading to higher test scores (Denny, McDonald, Empson, Kelly, & Petersen, 2018). However, badging is not a magic bullet that will always increase student output. Although one study did find an increase in student interaction in a badged online course, there was no increase in student participation in general (Chientzu & He, 2017).

As we argue throughout this book, the specific design of the badging system is important to its success. However, additional factors may also be at play in educational badges. For example, Hickey, Willis, and Quick (2015) found a link between the success of introducing digital badging systems into educational settings and the extent to which members of the learning community value them. If the community does not consider them valuable, the badges are less likely to positively influence learning. In another study where students were motivated to earn badges, Hakulinen, Auvinen, and Korhonen (2015) found that students in a badging group engaged in more beneficial study practices, such as spending more time on assignments and completing exercises multiple times, than students in a control group without badges. They also reported a positive motivational effect of badges, indicating that this particular sample valued the badges. A number of factors could affect whether or not a badge is valued, and more research is needed on the topic. However, we do know that the *type* of badge matters. Badges awarded for skill-based accomplishments are valued more than badges awarded for participation (Carey & Stefaniak, 2018).

Special Characteristics of Online Learning

In addition to difficulties related to promoting value, online learning presents other unique challenges, too. Here, we detail two specific issues. First, we examine the challenges of fitting badging systems into pre-existing learning structures (e.g., learning management systems (LMSs)) that have become commonplace in online learning. We then proceed to examine how badges can be useful for managing instructor workload in large courses, which have also become quite common in online learning.

In LMSs there are well-established and longstanding structures already in place and it is important to consider how badges can work with them. For instance, letter grades and points are foundational in most formal learning scenarios. A certain number of earned points translates to a certain grade on an assignment. Likewise, a certain number of earned points across all assignments translates to a certain final letter grade in the course. These grades, to an extent, serve as rudimentary rewards, feedback, and credentials – all roles that badges can fill. When we receive an A, it feels good, we know we performed well, and it is added on our transcript so that future employers or graduate schools can better judge our strengths. It is thus important to consider how your specific badging system fits within the pre-existing structure. We should identify which roles are being filled adequately by other subsystems (e.g., grading, assignments, and exercises), which are not being filled satisfactorily and require some attention, and which roles are not being filled at all. In Chapter 3, we identified a number of different functions that badges *can* perform, but it is important to identify which functions badges *need* to perform in the current system, too. Instructors who design badges to complement or enhance their existing course feedback systems rather than to perform redundant activities will leverage badges more effectively and will avoid duplicating roles and effort.

Let us return to the example of letter grades as feedback. We can say that the letter grade is already fulfilling the feedback role, but is it doing a satisfactory job? Although grading is a longstanding tradition in academia, the answer is likely not. After all, it is rare to have a course where no additional feedback is given beyond the letter grade. Typically, an explanation of the grade is given so that the student can learn what they did well or how to improve. In small classes, doing this verbally or through detailed written feedback might be the path of least resistance, but in larger courses, where hundreds or thousands of students could require feedback, an instructor might be physically incapable of fulfilling this role. Here, an automated badging system can provide feedback in a useful and engaging way that allows the instructor to focus more on course development and helping students who really need the personal attention.

To aid in developing effective badges for different learning situations, instructors can make a table or chart that articulates the different roles of the instructor and identifies the pre-existing structures within the course that fulfill each role. For example, consider Table 6.1.

Table 6.1 Instructor roles and associated structures

Role	Tool
Feedback on exams	Letter grade
Feedback on major projects	Letter grade, written feedback
Feedback on practice exercises	None. Unable to provide written feedback three times a week for each student.

Here, we see a gap regarding feedback for practice exercises. Badges might be useful for these if the badging can be automated and save the instructor time while providing consistent feedback for students. With this sort of a list, shortcomings can be assessed and badges (and other tools) can be considered for each gap in the table. Badges are useful when they are the *best* choice and should not be used simply because they exist and are *a* choice. Time and effort are required to prepare and deploy a badging system, so an instructor needs to decide if the benefits of badging particular course elements will outweigh the time and effort required to implement them.

Badges can be particularly useful for large enrollment courses. These large courses are becoming increasingly common in online learning. Online instruction is often offered as a way to increase the number of students that can be taught in a single course, especially when physical classroom capacity is not large enough to handle enrollment. While this solves the physical space issue, online courses can also place a burden on the instructor who must spend additional time grading, providing feedback, and communicating with each additional student. With this in mind, it is important to consider how badging systems impact instructor workload; while initial design of a badge system is likely to temporarily increase workload, the specific design of the system will dictate whether there is a long-term gain or loss of time spent on these activities.

For example, consider the badge issuing process. Badges that are manually awarded require the instructor to spend time issuing each badge. For a small class, this might not be a substantial amount of time, but for a large 1,000-student MOOC, this certainly adds up. Even one second spent issuing a badge that will eventually be issued to every student adds up to 16 minutes and 40 seconds. Of course, after considering the time spent examining the badging evidence for compliance with the completion logic, one might realize that the time to issue will be far more than one second per student. Even a fairly quick to assess assignment will likely require a minimum of 30 seconds per student, adding up to a little over eight hours spent for that one particular badge, or a full working day.

If a badge is automatically awarded, there may be no direct strain placed on the instructor as a function of assessing students' activities or issuing badges. However, indirect effects could result. Suspend the thought of badging for a moment and consider a normal classroom setting where an instructor is teaching a particular course for the first time. The instructor does her best to create clear learning modules and assignments, but her perspective is singular and does not account for the variety of prior experiences and directions in which the students will approach these learning objects. Thus, the students will likely not find the content to be as clear as the instructor hoped and the instructor will need to field questions in order to clarify the content and her expectations surrounding assignments. During her second time teaching the course, she can modify assignment descriptions and learning content in order to provide information before it is requested, providing clearer communication to the students without her having to spend time directly answering questions. This ultimately lowers her workload for the second offering of the course.

Badges can be refined in a parallel fashion. When they are automatically awarded the initial description might be imprecise or not fully developed due to the way the badging system implements them. Initial descriptions might be similar to the assignment descriptions automatically provided via a web-based LMS. Even if badge descriptions and logics are clear, there could be unforeseen circumstances due to the badge designer's singular perspective. In both cases, developing effective badges might require more instructor–student communication or other similar demands on instructor time until they can be refined and polished. While it is unlikely that a badging system will be perfected before initial release with the population of interest, badging designers should do their best to test their system with a subgroup before releasing the live version. This does not always mean that an entire course needs to be taught. Some preliminary usability testing with a small sample of testers can be used to confirm that users understand what each badge is for, how it can be earned, and what it means to earn that badge. For example, before rolling out badges to a MOOC, it might be worth piloting the same badges with a research group or asking some colleagues to look them over to help work out the kinks.

This all sounds like a lot of extra work and might reduce the appeal of using badges due to all of the time it will take. However, we should remember the potential benefits to using badges that have been discussed throughout this book. Additionally, once the badging system has been refined, automated badge awarding could be a low-effort method to help students set goals and subsequently provide specific and tailored feedback to students exactly when they need it.

Build Your Own or Use a Pre-existing Badging System?

Whatever the reason for deciding to use badges, the designer must decide between creating a brand new badging system from scratch and using a pre-existing system. Such a decision is not superfluous – the decision should be made with special consideration of the needs and desires of all stakeholders as well as the technical ability of the badging system designer.

First, consider the merits of fully designing and developing an original badging system. Developing a system from the ground up allows for the design of a system that is tailor-made to specification and need; since there are practically no limitations to what can be built, the designed system can be made to cater to every whim and desire of the designer, resulting in a system that is perfectly built to align with her goals. There is no need for the badges to be constrained to the limitations of a pre-existing system. Additionally, such a system can be reprogrammed to accommodate any unforeseen risks or issues found in the previous design or to extend the system when future capabilities are required.

Conversely, a pre-existing badging system lacks the flexibility of a home-built original system. Pre-existing commercial solutions (e.g., Credly, Badgr, OpenBadges.me) are ready-built, but limited. These systems allow users to create badges with certain customizable options (e.g., changing the name, design, and metadata of each badge), but limit the ways in which a badge can be created and manipulated. Many of these pre-built systems do not allow modifications to the underlying badging system. Of course, those who do not have the technical capability to create their own systems will find themselves with no other choice but to use a pre-existing solution.

That said, even those who do have advanced technical ability might choose to forgo the creation of their own badging system in lieu of something that is developed and ready to go. Being able to create and deploy a badging system within a day can be quite an attractive prospect and might be worth sacrificing the ability to fully control the badging system. Additionally, these pre-built systems will fully meet the needs of many, in which case the instructor can have the best of both worlds, quickly deploying a badging system that perfectly aligns with her goals.

The choice of whether to create your own badging system from scratch or to leverage a pre-existing system is ultimately up to you and your needs. We have previously given this decision a thorough discussion in *Digital Badges in Education: Trends, Issues, and Cases*, and we refer you there if you would like an extended discussion on the topic (McDaniel & Fanfarelli, 2016). Regardless of which choice you make, the recommendations found in this chapter can be applied; however, modifications might need to be made to accommodate the limitations preventing deep customization of pre-existing badging systems.

Designing Effective Badges for Online Learning

Now that we understand a bit about the history of educational badging research, the specific characteristics of online learning, and the decision about how to choose an appropriate system, we can move deeper into the details of badging design. First, building on Chapters 3 and 4 from the first section of the book, we discuss a few uses for badging that are relevant to the educational realm. These include designing badges for goal-setting and scaffolding, feedback, and to create personalized learning pathways. We conclude this section by examining the role students might have in creating and issuing badges to their peers.

Goal-Setting and Scaffolding

In online environments, successful students tend to apply more self-regulated learning strategies than their counterparts (Yukselturk & Bulut, 2007). Self-regulated learning refers to the process of planning, monitoring, and evaluating one's own learning (Cucchiara, Giglio, Persico, & Raffaghelli, 2014). In the absence of self-regulated learning, the learner is guided by the instructor or material, but might not know why they are doing what they are doing, what their goals are, or how much progress they are making. In contrast, a self-regulated learner regularly sets goals, develops methodologies to achieve those goals, tracks progress, and adjusts course if progress is not being made. Being able to set useful goals is important to this process.

Goal-setting is a critical factor in learning in general, but becomes especially important in an online environment where asynchronous communication is the norm and real-time student–instructor communication is rare. Students in this environment, consequently, might not receive the same level of structured guidance that is found in a face-to-face class. This is problematic because novices receive greater benefit when learning is structured (Kirschner, Sweller, & Clark, 2006). Structure and scaffolding enable learners to see clear paths forward and help them exert their effort in ways that are meaningful to their learning. Consider students who are told to complete a major group project. With no direction, the students will probably manage, but fumble around and produce an inferior project in an inefficient manner due to lack of team-based skills. Contrast this to a group of students who received a series of lectures on team dynamics, work allocation practices, creating effective milestones and schedules, and so on. This second group of students has received the structure needed to engage in the next challenge, and will likely produce a better project in less time.

Badges can incorporate more guidance and structure into a course by facilitating student goal-setting. As a result, students can better identify paths toward success and forecast potential obstacles along the way, improving their self-efficacy, or their confidence in their ability to succeed at the task in front of them (Zimmerman & Kitsantas, 2005). When we described goal-setting in Chapter 3, we mentioned a few qualities that good goals should have in order to foster intrinsic motivation. Creating goals that are of moderate difficulty is one of those qualities (Locke & Latham, 2002).

Difficulty can be tough to modify in a course of students with varying skill levels. While some instructors teach to the mean skill level of the course, badges offer an opportunity to create dynamic difficulty levels that cater to students of varying skill levels. This strategy not only tailors goals to individual ability, but it also scaffolds goals so that lower-skilled students have a clear pathway to catch up to their classmates. Consider a scaffolding example in an algebra course that incorporates a pre-test at the beginning of the semester. The pre-test might be designed as follows:

- The pre-test contains not only the information that will be taught throughout the present semester, but also contains a couple of questions for each foundational competency that is considered pre-requisite for the course (e.g., addition, multiplication).
- Each one of these competencies is tied to a badge.
- Students can see the list of badges for all competencies.

After the pre-test is complete, students are awarded badges for all competencies they have successfully demonstrated on the test, allowing them to see which competencies they hold and which they must strive to acquire. Additionally, a metabadge might be available once all pre-requisite badges are earned. When a student sees that she did not obtain the metabadge, she can identify which badges remain and can take the appropriate measures to get herself up to speed. Perhaps the instructor has created modules or linked to tutorial videos for the pre-requisite skills. Likewise, each competency badge's name might begin with a number so that students can see the order in which they should obtain each badge and thus the order in which they should establish each competency.

For example, the following might be the titles and descriptions for a pre-requisite competency badge and a metabadge that could be given once all pre-requisite badges have been earned:

- Competency Badge 2 – Multiplication: You've successfully demonstrated your ability to multiply numbers. Now, review "Module 3: Division" and try for the third competency badge.
- (Metabadge) I'm Ready – You've earned all pre-requisite badges. You're ready for Algebra. Hop into module 5 and get started. (Figure 6.1)

Through this method, the learner can see what has been accomplished and what she should do next. This allows her to avoid, for example, solving for y in equations before she understands the meaning of variables. Here, badges provide a scaffolded structure for learning advanced concepts within a course. In a similar fashion, badges can be used to help students set appropriately difficult goals. In Chapter 2 we discussed several different types of badges. One of these types was the incremental badge, which can be a single badge that can be repeatedly upgraded based on performance, or several badges with similar but increasingly difficult completion logics. The key to using these badges to set appropriately difficult goals is to design them so they offer goals at a range of difficulties. This allows learners to identify an appropriate level of challenge and then work through the incrementally more difficult badges as their skills improve. Each badge in this progressive sequence corresponds to pre-requisite knowledge and skills needed to obtain the next badge.

Figure 6.1 "I'm Ready" badge

Consider an online English course with a game that requires players to correct the punctuation in as many sentences as possible within one minute. While the highest level badge might require the learner to correct 12 sentences within the one-minute time frame, five seconds per sentence might be too fast for less advanced students. Others might find it challenging, but achievable. To better suit a variety of skill levels, the first level of the badge could be given for correcting four sentences, the second at eight, and the third at 12, enabling learners to set and achieve goals that are challenging but within their grasp. Ideally, this also improves their motivation and sense of self-efficacy so that they are better prepared to handle tougher challenges in the future. Of course, not all goals need to be about speed; badges might also be given for solving a set of easy, medium, and hard sentences, where difficulty level is defined by the quantity and variety of errors in each sentence. As these types of badges are considered, the designers should identify the correct sequence of skills based on skill progression and foundational knowledge.

Feedback

As a learner attempts to achieve their goals, the instructor or system provides information that helps a learner understand their successes and shortcomings, and how they should adjust or proceed to better progress toward the goal. This feedback is quite important to the learning process in general, and extends into the realm of badging. Jermann, Bocquet, Raimond, & Dillenbourg (2014) gave feedback in a MOOC via badges by awarding a bronze, silver, or gold badge for completion of blog posts, tasks, or comments. Each was accompanied by verbal feedback to explain the instructor's reasoning. While this implementation shows one way in which badges can be used to provide feedback, the implementation is quite simple. By awarding bronze, silver, and gold badges, the feedback is similar to awarding an A, B, or C letter grade. We could extend the feedback capabilities of these badges by considering how badges can be combined with personalized and timely feedback, and how feedback can be given by the badges themselves. This type of feedback is important for facilitating self-regulated learning in students, which is associated with higher achievement in online learning environments (Nicol & MacFarlane-Dick, 2006; Yukselturk & Bulut, 2007).

In badges, feedback can be provided through careful design of completion logic and description. While we just discussed using incremental badges for setting appropriately difficult goals, we can use the same incremental badges to provide feedback as students attempt to achieve these goals (Fanfarelli, Vie, & McDaniel, 2015). Badges awarded as a learner moves closer to the goal signals improvement since the last badge was earned and can build upon earlier feedback. This is important, as feedback is most effective when it builds upon feedback given in earlier trials and is given with a specific focus on recognizing correct responses (Kluger & DeNisi, 1996).

Feedback given via badges should include carefully designed descriptions in order to ensure that useful and specific information is given when the badge is awarded. Such a system might also include multiple badges for each increment so that a student could be awarded the badge that best fits her specific learning situation at the particular increment or learning milestone. Consider the case of reading comprehension, where comprehension is higher in students who engage in metacognition. Metacognition in reading is defined as the students' ability to actively maintain awareness and exert control over their strategies and processes for comprehending the text (Coiro & Dobler, 2007). To assess metacognition, a standard reading comprehension quiz might be given to a student along with a list of questions that assess the student's metacognitive activity on a number of levels. For example, one question might ask the student to reply true or false to the statements:

- "I thought about the writer's purpose for writing the article."
- "I considered how this article related to the one we read yesterday."

Badges can also be useful here. A student who meets a milestone criterion (e.g., 80% on the quiz) could be awarded a badge for their success that includes a description accounting for the accompanying metacognitive test responses:

- 80% – You scored an 80% on your comprehension quiz. It looks like you're doing a great job of considering how your reading compares to other text you have read. *Now, try reading the article again, but think about the author's purpose in writing the text*, and I bet you'll do even better.

Depending on the badging system's capabilities, there could be multiple badges for the 80% milestone that all slightly vary the latter portion of the description. The correct one could be awarded based on the student's answers on the metacognitive portion of the quiz. Or, if sufficiently complex, the badging system might simply replace the feedback portion of the description to include an appropriate message.

The use of badges for this purpose is useful, because it allows the feedback to come along with a positive stimulus. As earners feel recognized for and satisfied with their accomplishments, they are also learning how they could do even better on future trials. Badges are also useful in this regard because of their ability to be awarded *just in time*. Automated badging systems, such as one that might be connected with our reading comprehension example, can (1) generate specific feedback, (2) fit it within the pre-designed badging framework, and (3) award it to the student immediately following quiz submission. In this manner, badges communicate complex information "just in time"; the feedback is given exactly when a student needs it and before they lose interest (Fanfarelli & McDaniel, 2015). The automated nature of feedback badges used here could also reduce instructor workload by removing the need to assess and recommend to each student individually. At the same time, the badges help students acquire the required knowledge before moving forward and making further errors (Bottino & Robotti, 2007).

Personalized Learning

In the academic realm, each course typically has a set of foundational requirements that absolutely must be learned before the student passes and moves on to the next course. After this, there is usually some room left in the course that is filled with other instruction; here, instructors choose information that they believe would be most useful or relevant and infuse it into the course. Instructors are beginning to do this more frequently by leveraging the use of online learning to create personalized learning experiences through the use of pre-designed modules, videos, and other content. In these instances, learners are able to choose from a variety of pathways to customize their learning to better suit their interests and developmental goals. This is helpful for students because autonomy and choice are key components of intrinsic motivation, potentially motivating learners through these personalized learning objects (Ryan, 1982; Deci, Koestner, & Ryan, 1999).

Some courses may even infuse this customizability into the entirety of their course. For example, McDaniel, Lindgren, and Friskics (2012) created a course that was taken by a mix of students with varying digital media-related majors. Each week, students chose one module from a group of three to four modules. For example, one week covered the history of emerging media and students were able to choose from courses such as "history of videogames," "history of the Internet," "history of animation," and "history of interactive entertainment," depending on their specific focus area.

While this course did use a badging system, it was not tightly tied to the course's choose your own adventure style of structure, in the sense that the badges did not interact with topic choice. Instead, it recognized user effort for exhibiting proactive behaviors, such as creating thought-provoking projects or working ahead of schedule. This sort of system could be expanded to directly support the customizable learning pathways we previously discussed. Consider an introductory digital photography course that has aims to teach students how to operate image editing software. After this objective is achieved, students are free to choose one or more modules from a variety of learning pathways that examine different topics (e.g., photo repair, marketing materials, concept art, or website mockups).

Here, badges might be used to motivate users to go deeper into their chosen pathway. Or, they might encourage users to pursue multiple pathways, even though only one is required, in order to broaden their perspectives and learning. A relevant badge might recognize learners who have completed more than one pathway in a given week. Or, even better, badges might be given out to students who complete the entirety of a learning pathway to a certain degree of success. Here is an example:

- Image Repair Expert – You have completed all modules and exercises within the image repair pathway to exception, but there are many paths to success. Do you choose just one?

Such a badge could take the form of an Open Badge that would be transferable to badging backpacks. It could then be shared on ePortfolios or other places where potential employers might view it. This credentialing incentivizes successful completion of one pathway. Completion of multiple pathways might also be incentivized through the inclusion of an incremental metabadge for students who complete multiple learning pathways. Consider the following badge that upgrades through each subsequent pathway completion, providing students with additional incentive to go above and beyond the minimum required effort in the class (Figure 6.2).

- Bronze Expertise – You have completed one pathway to exception. Do you stop here?

Figure 6.2 Expertise incremental badges

- Silver Expertise – You have completed two pathways to exception. You're really setting yourself up for success. Can you go for the gold?

- Gold Expertise – You have completed all three pathways to exception. Very few will earn this badge. You should be proud of your efforts. Be sure to think about all of the skills you've gained.

Figure 6.2 (continued)

The learning pathways approach to badges is not yet common in academic courses, but has been used in other learning situations. For example, consider Khan Academy (2018), a website where users can sign up for an account and learn a variety of different skills while earning badges along the way. For example, users who learn HTML and JavaScript (JS) web coding through the HTML/JS course will earn a relevant badge:

- HTML/JS: Making webpages interactive – Complete all the "HTML/JS: Making webpages interactive" challenges.

Similar to the academic example provided earlier, Khan Academy also incorporates a large number of badges and metabadges. These range from mastering one skill all the way up to 500 skills. Here are two examples:

- Just Getting Started – Achieve mastery in 3 unique skills.
- Da Vinci – Achieve mastery in 500 unique skills.

The variety of badges is important, as it allows for a steady stream of goal-setting and recognition from the very beginning of a user's experience on the site, through the common user's longer term experiences, and yet also encompasses those super users who will engage in long-term learning across a number of domains from within the site.

Of course, as this sort of system is created, it is important to remember the goals of the system while designing. The customizable learning pathways model is meant to motivate users by increasing user autonomy through the use of choice, so the badging system should give users a sense of freedom, not prescription. Consider, also, how this system might affect high-achieving (i.e., highly motivated) and low-achieving users. While the system should be designed to encourage low-achieving users to put forth greater effort, it should also provide ample opportunity to recognize high-achievers, push them to even higher levels of achievement, and further provide them with enough opportunity to exert their energy in a positive direction. Khan Academy does this well by recognizing smaller and larger accomplishments that account for both types of users.

Peer-created Badges

While this chapter has primarily discussed badges awarded by the instructor or an automated system maintained by an instructor, there is another source of badging that should be considered: the learner's peers. When examining student outcomes in online learning, learners who engage in collaborative work tend to have better outcomes than those who work independently (Means, Toyama, Murphy, Bakia, & Jones, 2010). Further, peer assessment and feedback can be a useful learning tool when learners perform preliminary checks for satisfaction of the assignment criteria, deliver feedback related to the assignments' strengths and weaknesses, and provide tips for improvement (Falchikov, 1995). Collectively, this research suggests that peers can perform a number of useful functions in the learning process. Likewise, allowing students to help design their learning systems (i.e., participatory design) can lead to the creation of learning systems that better suit the needs and desires of their users.

Participatory design might also be useful in helping students engage in meta-cognition and other reflective processes related to learning (Könings, Seidel, & van Merriënboer, 2014). This is likely to be true when it comes to participatory design of badges and some preliminary evidence supports this (Bell & Davis, 2016). If each badge has a completion logic that must be satisfied before it is earned, then the badge designer who creates that completion logic must think about goals that are worthy of earning a badge. In other words, students who create badges will have to think about what goals their peers (and, by proxy, themselves) should have to accomplish in order to be successful on an assignment, in the course, or in some other aspect related to the course. This process necessitates reflection on the course, its goals, and the necessary pathways to accomplish them. While some of this could be misconstrued by students, an instructor–student discussion or class-wide discussion board discussion can help to expose these misconceptions held by students so that they can be corrected.

Since peer-to-peer interaction can enhance the online learning experience, it makes sense to consider how these interactions can take place within the realm of digital badges, where peers can be involved in both the creation and issuing processes. During the issuing process, peers can be given the power to directly issue badges created by the instructor, or they can recommend to the instructor that the badge be issued (i.e., a nomination system). Giving students the ability to directly award badges empowers them and might give them greater feelings of autonomy over their own learning and the classroom setting. However, it also provides them with a level of power that must be closely monitored, as it can be abused intentionally (e.g., students only issuing to their friends) or unintentionally (e.g., giving badges that are actually demotivational, or making non-earners feel left out). Badge issuing should be closely monitored and regulated to mitigate these risks and ensure that the peer issuing dynamic remains productive.

If this is not possible or is likely to be abused by a potentially less mature group, the recommending process might be a good substitute. Here, students can nominate a peer for a badge. The instructor might choose to directly award the badge or wait for further validation. For example, the instructor could specify that a certain number of peers must nominate before the badge is issued, or a voting process may ensue. Once the threshold is reached, the instructor can assess the situation and issue the badge if she feels it has been earned by the nominated student, or she also has the right to veto a nomination. Such a process might fit especially well within a government or law course.

While issuing is one potential level of peer-badging, badges may also be *created* by one or more students and then issued either by those students or by the instructor. In other words, peers can be both badge creators and issuers. This is both a new potential advantage that can be added to a course and a new potential pitfall. As this book has described, creating and giving badges should only be done with careful thought and design, so it might seem counterintuitive to ask novice designers to suddenly slap some badges together and hand them out without proper training. Students should not simply be told to create badges and sent off on their own. First and foremost, students should be given some guidelines on badge creation, helping them understand what makes a good badge and what pitfalls to avoid, so that they can start off on the right foot. Going over some of the badges you have created and explaining your design choices can help students to think more deeply about badging design and ultimately make better decisions. Inevitably, some of the student-created badges might not be useful. For this reason, badges should undergo some sort of validation procedure by the instructor before being added to the course's badging system. During this process, instructors can help students to maintain the spirit of their badge while making and explaining the adjustments required to make the badge a productive part of the class's badging system. With care, forethought, and monitoring, implementation of peer-created badges can add an exciting new dynamic to the course.

A Few Cautionary Notes

Badges can produce a number of benefits when properly designed, but there are some risks that are associated with badging systems that should be considered and worked around. When introduced into a classroom setting, digital badging systems can create a sense of competition between students. For example, some students might feel a need to be the first to earn particular badges. For some learners, competition might be motivational (Lister, 2015), encouraging them to push harder to earn the badge, thereby completing the learning objectives faster and to a greater degree of perfection. However, others might feel unable to compete due to low self-efficacy (i.e., reduced competence), feel forced to compete (i.e., reduced autonomy), or be intimidated by the competition because of the potential for reduced social status (i.e., reduced relatedness) (Ryan, 1982; Deci, Koestner, & Ryan, 1999).

This sort of competition can be encouraged or discouraged. For example, a badging system that keeps badges private to the earner will limit student-to-student sharing and likely limit feelings of competition due to reduced access to comparative performance information. Alternatively, some teachers might choose to go in an entirely different direction and use a leaderboard. Such a leaderboard might display badge quantity for each student or focus more on badge difficulty by assigning higher values to badges that are more difficult. A leaderboard is quite likely to increase feelings of competition, which could lower the motivation of those who do not enjoy competition (Hanus & Fox, 2015) or who might find themselves embarrassed by being at the bottom of the leaderboard. However, even here, careful design can lessen potential disadvantages. The negative effects of such an inclusion would likely be mitigated by a leaderboard that only shows the top students, thereby recognizing the highest achievers while avoiding shaming those who have not been as successful. Such a tradeoff may be worthwhile, as leaderboards can incentivize learners to maintain performance longer than they would have in the absence of a leaderboard (Mekler, Brühlmann, Opwis, & Tuch, 2013). In the same vein, students should not be actively embarrassed or shamed through negative badges; teachers should be aware of how badges might make their students feel, and how public badges make a student look to peers and other stakeholders, such as instructors and parents. Badge design can affect social status in either direction, with corresponding motivational ramifications.

One last caveat of information sharing and competitiveness relates to student privacy. In the United States, the Family Educational Rights and Privacy Act (FERPA) prohibits the disclosure of identifiable student information to third parties without the student's formal consent (Family Educational Rights and Privacy Act, 1974). This has important implications for designing badging systems. For example, when badges are made public or shared with classmates, they should not contain grading information. Thus, visibility and transferability of badges should be designed in consideration with the type of information being shared in those badges. Giving students ability to selectively hide or share badges, as they please, might be useful to this end.

Next Up

Next, we will examine how badging systems can be designed for mobile applications. Just as visual and interaction design-related fields have had to adapt to the ubiquity of mobile technologies, badges must also be adapted. The next chapter examines the specific challenges and considerations faced when designing and deploying badging systems for these unique applications.

References

Allen, I. E., & Seaman, J. (2017). Digital learning compass: Digital education enrollment report 2017. Retrieved from https://onlinelearningsurvey.com/reports/digtiallearning compassenrollment2017.pdf

Bell, A., & Davis, K. (2016). Learning through participatory design: Designing digital badges for and with teens. Proceedings from *The 15th International Conference on Interaction Design and Children* (pp. 218–229). Machester, UK: ACM.

Bottino, R. M., & Robotti, E. (2007). Transforming classroom teaching and learning through technology: Analysis of a case study. *Journal of Educational Technology & Society*, 10(4), 174–186.

Carey, K. L., & Stefaniak, J. E. (2018). An exploration of the utility of digital badging in higher education settings. *Educational Technology Research and Development*, 66(5), 1211–1229.

Chientzu, C. C., & He, S. (2017). The effectiveness of digital badges on student online contributions. *Journal of Educational Computing*, 54(8), 1092–1116.

Coiro, J., & Dobler, E. (2007). Exploring the online reading comprehension strategies used by sixth-grade skilled readers to search for and locate information on the internet. *Reading Research Quarterly, 42*(2), 214–257.

Cucchiara, S., Giglio, A., Persico, D., & Raffaghelli, J. E. (2014). Supporting self-regulated learning through digital badges: A case study. In Y. Cao, T. Väljataga, J. Tang, H. Leung, & M. Laanpere (Eds.), *Proceedings from the International Conference on Web-Based Learning* (pp. 133–142). Tallinn, Estonia: Springer.

Deci, E. L., Koestner, R., & Ryan, R. M. (1999). A meta-analytic review of experiments examining the effects of extrinsic rewards on intrinsic motivation. *Psychological Bulletin, 125*(6), 627–668.

Denny, P. (2013). The effect of virtual achievements on student engagement. *Proceedings from the SIGCHI Conference on Human Factors in Computing Systems* (pp. 763–772).

Denny, P., McDonald, F., Empson, R., Kelly, P., & Petersen, A. (2018). Empirical support for a causal relationship between gamification and learning outcomes. *Proceedings of CHI 2018* (pp. 1–13). Montreal QC, Canada: ACM.

Falchikov, N. (1995). Improving feedback to and from students. In P. Knight (Ed.), *Assessment for learning in higher education* (pp. 157–166). London: Kogan.

Family Educational Rights and Privacy Act, 20 U.S.C. § 1232g (1974).

Fanfarelli, J. R., & McDaniel, R. (2015). Digital badges for deliberate practice: Designing effective badging systems for interactive communication scenarios. *Proceedings from The 33rd Annual International Conference on the Design of Communication.* Limerick, Ireland: ACM.

Fanfarelli, J. R., Vie, S., & McDaniel, R. (2015). Understanding digital badges through feedback, reward, and narrative: A multidisciplinary approach to building better badges in social environments. *Communication Design Quarterly Review, 3*(3), 56–60.

Hakulinen, L., Auvinen, T., & Korhonen, A. (2015). The effect of achievement badges on students' behavior: An empirical study in a university-level computer science course. *International Journal of Emerging Technologies in Learning, 10*(1), 18–29.

Hanus, M., & Fox, J. (2015). Assessing the effects of gamification in the classroom: A longitudinal study on intrinsic motivation, social comparison, satisfaction, effort, and academic performance. *Computers & Education, 80*, 152–161.

Haug, S., Wodzicki, K., Cress, U., & Moskaliuk, J. (2014). Self-regulated learning in MOOCs: Do open badges and certificates of attendance motivate learners to invest more? *Proceedings from The European MOOCs Stakeholders Summit* (pp. 66–72). Lausanne, Switzerland: École Polytechnique Federale de Lausanne.

Hickey, D., Willis, J., & Quick, J. (2015). Where badges work better. *Educause Learning Initiative.* Available: https://library.educause.edu/resources/2015/6/where-badges-work-better

Jermann, P., Bocquet, G., Raimond, G., & Dillenbourg, P. (2014). The EFPL MOOC factory. *Proceedings from The European MOOCs Stakeholders Summit* (pp. 228–233). Lausanne, Switzerland: École Polytechnique Federale de Lausanne.

Khan Academy (2018). *Khan Academy | Free Online Courses, Lessons, and Practice.* Retrieved from: www.khanacademy.org/

Kirschner, P. A., Sweller, J., & Clark, R. E. (2006). Why minimal guidance during instruction does not work: An analysis of the failure of constructivist, discovery, problem-based, experiential, and inquiry-based teaching. *Educational Psychologist, 41*(2), 75–86.

Kluger, A. N., & DeNisi, A. (1996). The effects of feedback interventions on performance: A historical review, a meta-analysis, and a preliminary feedback intervention theory. *Psychological Bulletin, 119*(2), 254–284.

Könings, K. D., Seidel, T., & van Merriënboer, J. J. G. (2014). Participatory design of learning environments: Integrating perspectives of students, teachers, and designers. *Instructional Science, 42*, 1–9.

Lister, M. (2015). Gamification: The effect on student motivation and performance at the post-secondary level. *Issues and Trends in Educational Technology, 3*(2), 1–22.

Locke, E. A., & Latham, G. P. (2002). Building a practically useful theory of goal setting and task motivation: A 35-year odyssey. *American Psychologist, 57*(9), 705–717.

McDaniel, R., & Fanfarelli, J. R. (2016). Evaluating design frameworks for badges. In L. Y. Muilenberg & Z. L. Berge (Eds.), *Digital badges in education: Trends, issues, and cases* (pp. 176–188). New York: Routledge.

McDaniel, R., Lindgren, R., & Friskics, J. (2012). Using badges for shaping interactions in online learning environments. *Proceedings from International Professional Communication Conference* (pp. 1–4). Orlando, FL: IEEE.

Means, B., Toyama, Y., Murphy, R., Bakia, M., & Jones, K. (2010). Online learning: A meta-analysis and review of online learning studies. Retrieved from www2.ed.gov/rschstat/eval/tech/evidence-based-practices/finalreport.pdf

Mekler, E., Brühlmann, F., Opwis, K., & Tuch, A. (2013). Disassembling gamification: The effects of points and meaning on user motivation and performance. *Proceedings from the SIGCHI Conference on Human Factors in Computing Systems (CHI EA'13)* (pp. 1137–1142).

Nicol, D. J., & Macfarlane-Dick, D. (2006). Formative assessment and self-regulated learning: A model and seven principles of good feedback practice. *Studies in Higher Education, 31*(2), 199–216.

Ryan, R. M. (1982). Control and information in the intrapersonal sphere: An extension of cognitive evaluation theory. *Journal of Personality and Social Psychology, 43*, 450–461.

U.S. Department of Education (2010). Evaluation of Evidence-Based Practices in Online Learning: A Meta-Analysis and Review of Online Learning Studies. Retrieved from www2.ed.gov/rschstat/eval/tech/evidence-based-practices/finalreport.pdf.

Yukselturk, E., & Bulut, S. (2007). Predictors for student success in an online course. *Educational Technology & Society, 10*(2), 71–83.

Zimmerman, B. J., & Kitsantas, A. (2005). Homework practices and academic achievement: The mediating role of self-efficacy and perceived responsibility beliefs. *Contemporary Educational Psychology, 30*(4), 397–417.

CHAPTER 7

Using Badges in Mobile Applications

Overview

Mobile devices are portable personal technologies that we can take with us on the go. Mobile applications are software programs that run on these devices. Common examples of mobile devices include smartphones, tablets, smart watches, and other devices with the ability to roam freely with their users in physical space. As compared to their desktop cousins, mobile devices have special design constraints that badge designers should recognize and consider when devising badges for these platforms. For example, their screens are much smaller, they run different types of software that require specialized forms of user interaction, and they have batteries that will eventually deplete. Similarly, there are unique opportunities and possibilities for mobile badges that take advantage of the special abilities of computers that can follow users into spaces previously unavailable to computers. Using mobile devices, we can now explore possibilities for digital badging that move through the world with us rather than badges that our users can earn only by using a computer in a central physical location. For these reasons, it is worthwhile to consider digital badges in mobile environments as we think about the contexts and applications of badging.

An Emerging Market

These days, it is near impossible to go very far into civilization without seeing a human interacting with a mobile device. So-called "smart devices" are everywhere and have augmented the ability of humans to interact with their environment. Information feeds into smart devices from networked sources that can be downloaded on the go. This provides users with the ability to read restaurant reviews, stay in touch with friends and family, and read news articles while sitting on the train, walking through a city, or relaxing by the beach. The devices can also provide directions to motorists and pedestrians, allowing instantaneous communication through text messaging and multimedia messaging services. They entertain us with music, video, and games, and serve as emergency contact devices for older adults. Their sensing and automation capabilities are even changing the way information is acquired during emergencies. Their various sensors can collect and distribute critical information following natural disasters or other significant environmental events (Gahran, 2011).

Mobile technologies are also transforming the practices of specialized professions, such as medicine, by serving as sophisticated databases for storing records, communicating with caregivers and physicians, gathering information, monitoring patients, and making clinical decisions (West, 2012; Ventola, 2014). Mobile health, or mHealth, is a growing area of research and commerce with initiatives under way throughout the world (West, 2012). In educational and legal settings, many use their devices as study aids or notetaking tools to combine formerly analog systems (such as tablets and writing instruments) with their new electronic counterparts. In addition to written notes, other multimedia assets such as photographs and audio recordings can be appended to these records. Tablets and smartphones in particular are used to entertain children, but also increasingly to educate them, as education applications are projected to grow at a rate of almost 30% between 2016 and 2020 (Chang, 2017). To many, mobile devices have become as connected to their daily routines as the wristwatches, wallets, or purses of the pre-mobile period. In other words, to think about digital badging and not consider the mobile implications would be a very large oversight.

In his book *Constant Touch: A Global History of the Mobile Phone* (2013), Jon Agar notes that there are three different concentric rings of what he terms "personal" technologies. Outer ring technologies are owned technologies that do not move around with the user. An example is a desktop computer that remains in one central location, such as a home office, when it is used. Middle ring technologies are portable, but more cumbersome than one might like. A laptop computer is an example. The device is transportable from one place to another, but many models require a large carrying case, a power cable, and a number of accessories. However, the inner ring of what Agar describes as "intimate" technologies are both portable and convenient. We bring them with us from place to place because they travel so easily and are incredibly useful. As Agar (2013) describes:

> These are portable but carried without exertion. They are kept close to the body. They are so useful or important or engaging that we don't register their weight. Very few technologies make it through to the inner ring, and some of those that do date from the earliest periods of human existence. Right now my intimate technologies are clothes (Paleolithic), shoes (ditto), glasses (a medical innovation) and my intimate general-purpose computer, my little chip of modernity – a smartphone.
>
> (pp. 177–180)

Indeed, the original iPhone, released in January of 2007, began a new era for mobile computing. When the device was introduced by Steve Jobs during his now famous keynote demonstration (Kroon, 2017), it transformed the way consumers conceptualized not only mobile devices, but also computers in general. Up until this point, clunky keyboards and small screens with slimmed down versions of desktop software were the best options consumers had for their mobile devices, while computers were generally confined to single rooms. Laptops existed, but transporting them was difficult and required cables and accessories. Developing mobile phone systems had also proven to be tremendously challenging; almost every phone ran its own separate software and the large telecommunications companies exerted ironclad control over what they allowed to run over their networks (Vogelstein, 2013). Jobs' new device was impressive not only because of its hardware and software capabilities, but also because he managed to convince one of these telecommunication giants, AT&T, to cede some of this control in exchange for initial exclusive rights to carry the device (Cohan, 2013). Additionally, the sleek and aesthetic look of the new device was well ahead of the previous models we had seen up until that point.

Nearly all modern smartphones now run software from iOS or Android, the Google-owned competitor to Apple. Together, they own 99.6% of the market share, with 352 million of the 432 million total smartphone devices sold last quarter (81.7%) running Android software and 77 million devices (17.9%) running Apple software (Vincent, 2017). This data shows that in the years since the iPhone's release and the subsequent competition from Android and other smartphone manufacturers, people have become acclimated to the idea of having these intimate mobile computing devices accompany them into all areas of their lives. The smaller form factors of mobile devices combined with the growing ubiquity of cellular networks and public Wi-Fi hubs has opened up opportunities for mobile devices that were previously off limits or unavailable to desktop computers. Staying true to Moore's Law, processing power also increased dramatically over the years, making these devices not only ultra-portable, but also ultra-powerful.

This new revolution for personal mobile devices also brought with it a new suite of versatile applications that were designed to take advantage of these more powerful processors. Many of our modern mobile devices are capable of doing more, and more quickly, than our desktop computers of the past. As an example, the amount of computing power available in a modern iPad tablet computer would have cost $100 trillion in the 1950s (Floridi, 2014, p. 7). Modern smartphones are millions of times more powerful than the computers that sent early NASA astronauts to the moon (Sinicki, 2017). Vastly more capable than traditional cellular phones, individuals now have the ability to use these portable computing devices as multimedia studios, sophisticated cameras, portable gaming devices, GPS devices, e-readers, scanners, reporter's notebooks, voice recorders, business cards, payment systems, business note-taking and measurement tools, and for other purposes that previously had required a separate device (Mims, 2012). As the functionality of these devices expanded, so did the range of behaviors individuals exhibited when interacting with them. Competition also spawned new features. For example, Google's

Android platform initially borrowed from early advances made by the iPhone, but then later began to develop market-leading features that the iOS software eventually adopted, such as multitasking, cross-application sharing, and an application switcher (Amadeo, 2016).

Market facts bear witness to the growth and impact of mobile devices. By the end of 2016, there were 10 billion mobile devices in use worldwide (West, 2012) and by 2017, 65% of people worldwide owned mobile phones (Rosling, Rönnlund, & Rosling, 2018). According to the aggregator website Statista (2018), mobile applications are projected to generate approximately 189 billion dollars in revenue by the year 2020. The number of global users accessing the Internet using mobile devices surpassed those surfing the web from desktop computers in 2014 and the gap between the two groups has widened even further since then (Chaffey, 2018). People are also spending more time than ever on their mobile devices, with one study estimating the average American adult spends nearly three hours on their smartphone every day (Lipsman, 2017) and another suggesting an even higher four hours a day (eMarketer, 2018). It is clear that for those individuals who own these devices, they tend to use them for significant portions of their daily routines.

Given that these devices are more powerful and portable than ever before, it is no surprise that they are so heavily used by so many individuals in multiple areas of their personal and professional lives. Communication is a central function of organized society. As the sources of data in our lives become richer and more diverse, it makes sense that we depend more heavily on these small computers capable of operating and communicating in such data-rich environments. Before delving too deeply into the specific features and functions of these mobile devices, and before exploring the implications of those characteristics on mobile badges, it is useful to discuss some of the historical precursors to our modern mobile computing devices. These technological advancements can help us to better understand the evolution of mobile technology and speculate about the badge-based features that might be coming next as these devices continue to evolve.

A Brief History of Mobile Devices and Mobile Badges

The historical timeline of mobile computing reveals a number of interesting gadgets and design features that eventually evolved into our modern sophisticated mobile devices. During the First World War, German soldiers used field telephones, which pioneered a number of technological innovations that later matured into the technologies we see today (Washington Post Staff, 2014). These wireless field telephones were used in 1941 to help coordinate military movements. By the early 1970s, later prototypes were being used in vehicles as devices for spy patrol cars. They continued to evolve into the large blocky devices we associate with the earliest mobile phones, such as the Motorola DynaTAC (Washington Post Staff, 2014), although only Wall Street executives could seemingly afford them at the time. Indeed, in 1980 only .0003% of individuals owned a cellphone and that percentage did not begin to significantly climb until the late-1990s and early 2000s (Rosling, Rönnlund, & Rosling, 2018). In terms of our more modern and versatile digital mobile devices, Paul (2011) presents a number of additional historical precursors that did not focus solely on telecommunication. Notable entries include the first *Handy-LE* portable calculator in 1971, the first *Merlin* computer toy in 1978, the *Osborne* personal computer in 1981, and the original *Palm Pilot* in 1996. In 1999, Apple Computer introduced the iBook G3, the first consumer laptop to carry a Wi-Fi card, which started a new category of devices that could connect to the Internet without a hard line connecting them to an Ethernet port.

However, it was not until the release of the iPhone in 2007 that we began to see digital badges as heavily used design features for shaping user behavior. This was in large part due to the importance of touch as a central interaction mechanic for the device. The simplicity of the devices opened up new possibilities for mobile computing and made the device accessible for new types of audiences, including older adults and younger children. Soon, designers recognized that there needed to be a way of signaling importance when software required attention. We explore some of the deeper implications of this ecosystem in the next section of the chapter, but before we do that, we will describe some of the notable badging applications in the relatively short history of mobile badging.

Aside from the core operating systems themselves, which use limited versions of badges in various ways to signal and provide information to their operators, a number of applications use digital badges in different ways to provide users with information about functionality, data, and relationships. Health and fitness applications, for example, use mobile platforms for delivering badges when their users complete real-world physical activities. The social possibilities for comparing and sharing badges are especially interesting from a health and wellness perspective. Users can share the badges they earn for completing challenges and the hope is they will also be inspired or motivated by the badges earned by their online friends. The *Nike* + application, for example, allows users to challenge friends to races and awards virtual gold medals to the winner (Fanfarelli, Vie, & McDaniel, 2015).

Mozilla's Open Badge movement, which began in 2010 and continued gaining momentum through 2016, also created a number of possibilities for mobile badging (Mozilla, 2016). The Mozilla Open Badges program was notable because it opened up the source code for the badges to developers and designers (Goligoski, 2012). The idea behind the program was to enable a number of different badge issuers – which might include after-school programs, online learning providers, or job training centers – to issue badges to learners. These badges would then reside in a virtual backpack that integrates with students' personal websites, social media accounts, and professional résumés. Specific products could then be certified by a third party to be open-badges compliant, meaning that they work with Mozilla backpack and adhere to the open badges standard, which we presented in Chapter 2. A full list of these current products can be found in IMS Global's database (IMS Global, 2018).

Although increased mobility presents excellent possibilities for informal learning that may occur in classrooms, museums, library, and field sites, badges are also used for educational purposes in formal learning environments. For example, in 2012, Purdue University created Passport, a system for demonstrating competencies through badges on a mobile learning platform (Passport, 2018). The system includes mobile applications for both iOS and Android users. The Passport system has been used for various courses including learning systems design and courses on science, engineering, and nanotechnology (Croom, 2014).

Modern devices continue to explore possibilities for mobile badges. Some of these possibilities extend beyond the idea of badges as objects earned for performance or accomplishment. For example, the additional hardware capabilities of portable devices enable new types of interactions with security systems and door locks, extending the credentialing possibilities for mobile badges. Close-range networking technologies such as Near Field Communication (NFC) or Bluetooth Low Energy (BLE) allow mobile phones to be used as access cards to enter restricted areas unavailable to those without the proper credentials (Access Security Corp., 2016). This means that there is a wide range of possibilities for mobile badges – from entertainment devices that signal accomplishments in gaming or virtual worlds to robust, secure systems for credentialing that can accompany users into privileged virtual and physical locations.

Mobile Environments: A Badge-Driven Ecosystem

The modern mobile experience is dominated by the use of badges, notifications, and banners. Notification badges inform users of when new e-mail messages arrive, of tasks that need to be attended to within mobile applications, and of comments or "likes" on social media posts. These badges are often limited and simplified versions of their more complicated cousins. For example, in the iOS operating system that powers Apple's portable devices, badges appear as superimposed white numbers surrounded by red backgrounds that indicate a number of unread messages, voicemails, or application notifications. Android devices use a dot mechanic that similarly indicates to users when applications have information or notifications to provide that users have not yet received (Birch, 2017).

While the badges or dots used for notification purposes are not exactly like the digital badges we have been discussing throughout the book, they do share notable similarities. They use small visual form factors to display information, they provide a reward of sorts to the user who engages with them, and they provide feedback that shapes user behaviors. The reward of seeing how many individuals "liked" a particular post on Facebook has been described by the co-inventor of this feature, Justin Rosenstein, as a "bright ding of pseudopleasure" (Herrman, 2018, para. 1). Mobile applications report an increase in usage simply by using these features; the mobile language learning application *Duolingo*, for example, reported a 6% increase in daily active users (DAUs) by implementing a simple badging strategy within their software (Centofante, 2017).

Other software applications have extended traditional ideas about digital badges' functionality in order to use them as connective devices in collaborative settings. For example, the popular file sharing and synchronization software *Dropbox* debuted a feature called the Dropbox Badge that appears within Microsoft Office applications when files are edited by single or multiple users. Rather than awarding users for activities that have already been completed, the badge instead provides a more robust set of information that conveys the current status of the file, when it was last updated by another user, and who is currently viewing or editing that file (Dropbox, 2018). In contrast to a single badge that can be earned and displayed in a repository, the Dropbox Badge is constantly changing in state throughout the lifespan of a document. It is not "earned" in the sense of the badges we have been discussing throughout this book. In this sense, like the notification badges and dots used by iOS and Android operating systems, the feature works more as a software accessibility aid and notification system than as the type of digital badge or microcredential we have been discussing. Nonetheless, it is an interesting example of how the traditional notion of a digital badge can be broadened by including more robust information display and functional capabilities.

Special Characteristics of Mobility

In this section, Table 7.1 outlines some of the special characteristics of mobile devices and their implications for badging. We then discuss a few of these properties in more detail. This table is not exhaustive, but rather shows some of the most salient features of mobile devices that pose exciting possibilities and challenges for digital badges. As this is a rather new space that has not yet been heavily studied, mobile computing is an area in which new research is necessary to better understand the precise implications of these features on digital badging.

As with other emerging technologies, the features and capabilities of mobile devices are constantly expanding, so it is likely that this table will need to be updated sooner rather than later. However, the idea here is to show how mobile devices offer unique opportunities for deploying badges that might not be possible with other types of computing infrastructure. Each feature is noted with a key adjective that describes the feature along with a brief description. The current status of that feature (mature and established, emerging but in use, or future and under development) is also provided. The final column then discusses the impact of that feature on digital badging.

Many of the features shown in Table 7.1 have deeper implications for badging as well. For example, one primary characteristic of mobile devices is portability, or their ability to bring networking computing capacity to remote areas. Although one benefit of this is simple convenience and utility, there are also broader economic implications. For example, some of these remote locations might have little infrastructure in place. Using only cellular networks and relatively affordable mobile phones provides such areas with access to

Table 7.1 Ten key features of mobile devices and their implications for badging

Feature	Description	Status	Implications for Badging
Portable	Mobile devices can be taken places where other computers cannot go.	Mature	Badges can be awarded for activities completed in diverse environments. Badges can be provided to users while they travel from place to place. An example is a badge that unlocks and deploys when a certain number of national landmarks are visited.
Locatable	Mobile devices can use location awareness to track activity within geographical coordinates. They are context aware and can help route network transmissions or phone calls to specific physical locations depending on a user's location (Chen, Chang & Wang, 2008).	Mature	Badges can be triggered by geographic coordinates, such as when a user enters a certain area of the physical world. Badges that encourage effort for exploration, as are often awarded in virtual worlds such as videogames, can now be easily applied to the physical world as well.
Extensible	Mobile devices can use cloud-based computing technologies to provide a continuous user experience across devices.	Mature	Badges can be used to credential continuous transactions, such as in the case where a user starts an educational experience on a desktop computer and continues that experience on a mobile device. Or vice-versa.
Simple	Mobile devices use intuitive, touch-based controls to simplify the user experience. Deeper functionality can be layered within interactions that begin with a single touch.	Mature	Badges can be deployed to a wide range of audiences including some that were previously inaccessible due to interface complexity. These audiences include young children or older adults with cognitive impairment. Consumers age 55 and above are now a leading category for mobile device and mobile service purchases (Deloitte, 2017), suggesting that mobile-based badges might be an opportunity to connect with these demographics using technologies they are comfortable with.

Automatic	Since mobile devices are highly configurable and customizable with notifications and can accompany users into all areas of their lives, they also have great potential for automation. Traveling alarm clocks can be extended into systems for reminding and notifying that can extend into all areas of one's life.	Emerging	Badges can be used to provide visual indicators of important information on a daily or monthly cycle. For example, West (2012) notes how mobile devices are increasingly used in healthcare to remind people to take their medication at the proper time. A progressive badging system would provide an easy to visualize representation of this and remind individuals at the proper intervals.
Intimate	As Agar (2013) describes, mobile devices are "intimate," meaning they are personal devices that are close to the body and nearly always at hand for those who use them.	Emerging	The intimate nature of mobile devices opens up a number of possibilities for badging. One possibility is the use of physiological data as triggers to unlock badges (heart rate, sleeping patterns, etc.)
Secure	Using advanced biometrics such as fingerprint authentication or facial recognition, mobile devices can be used as portable identity authenticators.	Emerging	Badges can be used not only to recognize performance or achievement, but also as secure credentials to provide access to virtual or physical resources in restricted locations.
Mutable	Different views and layers of information, which can combine real-world with virtual data, can be used to create new types of virtual and augmented reality experiences. Strong processing power combined with advanced camera features allow for continuously changing display possibilities that blend the real with the virtual.	Emerging	Badges can be used in scenarios that blend real-time data from the camera with digital information, such as the display of virtual badges in real-world environments. A gamer could walk through a forest and then arrive at a predetermined point where they can see a virtual version of their badge superimposed over the real-world landscape.

(continued)

Table 7.1 (continued)

Feature	Description	Status	Implications for Badging
Intelligent	As early AI systems such as Cortana and Siri continue to evolve, virtual private assistants (VPAs) might become sophisticated enough to provide more advanced interventions to users in need of information or training.	Future	Smart agents and intelligent devices could become the author and distributor of special badges. Just-in-time badging becomes a possibility for shaping human behaviors in particular directions at a machine learning algorithm's discretion.
Porous	As technologies continue to evolve, mobile technologies will continue to play a role in connecting and integrating digital and physical environments. For example, real-world items can potentially be photographed then automatically rendered into 3d objects for use in virtual worlds. Similarly, virtual objects can be used to provide overlays or additional contextual information about real-world environments. 3d printing technologies and improved processing and graphical rendering capabilities will continue to push boundaries in this direction.	Future	There are already applications that exist today that allow mobile devices to capture information from real-world identity badges in order to gather contact information and other details. These are in use at large events such as conferences and tradeshows (IDScan.net, 2018). However, there is also the potential for virtual accomplishments to be awarded with physical badges. One can imagine a system where virtual feats unlock trophies that can be printed using a 3d printer, for example, and proudly displayed in a trophy case in a real-world location.

the World Wide Web and electronic mail, for example, through the use of temporary, ad hoc networks (Johnson & Maltz, 1996). This means that the portability of mobile devices opens up not only the potential for new types of badges deployed according to geographical functions, but also the potential to distribute badges to new audiences that did not previously have access to the Internet. The temporary nature of these networks, however, can make the administration of such a system challenging.

Another deeper example relevant to learning is found in the extensible nature of mobile computers. Extensible here refers to the transaction itself in that a single experience, such as a learning investigation or project, can be extended across multiple types of technology. Using this extensible model in which transactions can begin on one device and end on another, mobile technologies can support "seamless mobile learning" (Boticki, Baksa, Seow, & Looi, 2015). This learning strategy uses the geographical freedom of mobile technology to allow learners to shift from devices or contexts to continue learning in different environments. For example, a college student might begin a science report document on a tethered PC in a classroom or at home, then switch to a mobile device to take notes in the field and continue editing the document. Or, a middle school student might follow through a PowerPoint lecture about space exploration while sitting in a classroom (formal learning environment), then visit a space science center with a virtual tour delivered through an iPad (informal learning environment). Badges can be used throughout these types of seamless transactions to reinforce a consistent experience and shape behaviors in productive ways.

While these characteristics speak to the exciting possibilities for mobile badges, we still need to design them effectively in order for them to have maximum impact. As with other types of badges, poorly designed objects could do more harm than good, particularly when the other software designed for our smartphones, tables, and smart watches is so carefully designed to be intuitive and usable. Fortunately, many of the general strategies for effective design we review in the next section will be familiar to the reader by this point in the book. There are, however, some special caveats to consider with regard to mobile design.

Designing Effective Badges for Mobile Use

There are many principles that carry forward from other applications and inform best practices for designing effective badges. As always, badges should be used thoughtfully, with specific user behaviors and outcomes in mind. Several of the effective design techniques we discussed in the previous chapters, dealing with videogames and online learning systems, will also be relevant to badges designed for mobile systems. This is because today's mobile systems can also run learning management system (LMS) applications and videogames. In fact, so-called casual mobile videogames remain some of the biggest sellers that take up the most of mobile users' time when on their devices (Agar, 2013). Early examples included games such as *Angry Birds* (Rovio, 2009) and *Fruit*

Ninja (Halfbrick Studios, 2010). However, there are also some specific characteristics of mobile devices we should consider when thinking about how to best deploy badges on this type of hardware.

One primary factor in mobile design is properly accounting for the hardware limitations of mobile devices. Although even LMSs, games, and simulations often include mobile components, these large-scale software systems are often designed and tested on large computer monitors or through consoles connected to large, high-definition televisions. Many smartphone devices, however, run software that must adapt to much smaller screen sizes. Mobile applications also need to consume less power to prolong battery life. This means that in mobile software, good design is often just as much about what you *do not* include in the software interface as well as what you *do* include (Hoekman, 2011). Extra features that would work just fine in desktop PC environments might take up too much screen real estate or consume too much power in these smaller form factors.

Smart watches, for example, are severely limited in the amount of screen real estate they have to work with, as are certain fitness applications that are designed to provide only the bare minimum of visual feedback. Apple's human interface guidelines for their watchOS software, for example, require developers to build applications that are "glanceable, actionable, and responsive" (Apple, 2018b). Key information should be conveyed on the watch face that communicates clearly and concisely. As much as possible, a user's intent should be anticipated so that the watch can display information accordingly. Finally, interactions should load quickly and minimize the time necessary to provide more information as the watch's screen changes. With these diminutive pieces of hardware, it might be better to provide only a limited visual accompanied by a haptic or auditory notification that a badge has been earned. The device can then upload the credential to a network. This allows the user to later access more visually sophisticated information about their badges using a connected device such as a smartphone, tablet, or desktop computer.

Other mobile application designers use strategies that nest badges within other areas of the software. For example, the *Audible* audiobook application offers a total of 15 different incremental badges that can be obtained at silver, gold, and platinum levels (Macbride, 2017). Badges can be earned for activities such as adding bookmarks, sharing achievements with other users, and listening to books during certain times of the day or for certain amounts of time. However, rather than prominently displaying a user's badges in the main interface of the program, the user needs to navigate first to her profile page, then to an additional link that will take her to the collection of earned badges. When a badge has already been earned and is clicked, the actions taken to earn it are displayed to the user. When a badge is still blank, a poem is displayed with hints on how to earn it (Macbride, 2017). The *Audible* mobile applications successfully use these features to make users curious about how to earn additional badges without overwhelming them with persistent visual information on their limited visual display areas.

Another design consideration for creating effective badges in mobile environments is to think about how users will interact with the badges when they are earned. The badges will exist within an application designed to run on a mobile operating system. It will be important to work with the application developers to ensure that appropriately accessible features are designed for viewing earned badges and for conveying feedback about progress to users in an appropriate way. In many of these devices, users' sense of touch will be their primary method of operating the devices.

Since touch is so central to the experience of mobile interaction, it deserves some scrutiny in the design planning stages. It will be important to think about how users will interact with badges using press, swipe, and tap mechanics. For example, rather than using a keyboard or other complicated peripheral to interact with devices, users instead use their fingers to touch screens, interact with virtual controls such as zoom-in and zoom-out, and play or pause media. Many contemporary users of smart devices are now quite adept with touch as a primary mode of interaction and can manipulate complex features within sophisticated applications. They can play online games and multimedia without any problem at all.

The complexity of touch-based mechanics is also expanding as technologies evolve. Rather than simply registering and responding to a single keypress, modern mobile devices are now using technologies capable of registering multiple touches at different points on a display surface (multi-touch) as well as differentiating between different levels of touch (e.g., a light tap versus a strong press). As such, badges must be designed to operate smoothly and seamlessly within applications alongside these other features. Appropriate visual and haptic notifications should accompany badges deployed in those environments. It is possible, for instance, that a visual badge indicator be shown on screen during a particular moment of activity. Then, a user can "long press" the visual icon to see a popup display detailing how the badge was earned and other details associated with the badge.

For those designing a badging system running on iOS devices, it will be important to familiarize oneself with Apple's Human Interface Guidelines such as the iOS Design Themes (Apple, 2018a). These guidelines suggest that iOS differs from other platforms in areas of clarity, deference, and depth. Clarity deals with legibility and focus as well as aesthetically pleasing graphic design. Deference focuses on fluid motion with appropriate design cues that show when content can be minimized or expanded. And depth deals with the use of distinct visual layers to provide a sense of hierarchy and order within nested windows. Each of these areas helps a system optimized by touch to have a distinct sense of design and a familiar user interface.

Last, it is necessary to consider the overall reason for including badges within a mobile application. Given the limitations of screen real estate, it is worth asking whether badges are truly necessary. The best argument for including badges within mobile applications is probably the reason we discussed at length in

Chapter 4: they are excellent design cues to help modify behavior. For example, the *Lose It!* weight loss application is a mobile software program that users can install on their smartphones and tablets. It functions by providing a daily calendar of separated meal headings (breakfast, lunch, dinner, and snacks) through which a user can apply different foods to track overall calorie and nutrient information. Because the application is mobile and portable, users can bring it with them to the grocery store and to restaurants and diners in order to make healthy choices while ordering food and beverages. The core idea is that by paying closer attention to what – and how much – they are eating, users will be able to better track their food intake and lose weight.

Lose It! strategically employs badges to direct users to do things that allow them to experience the full range of what is possible with the software. For example, *Lose It!* users earn the "Hello My Name Is" badge for completing their profile, the "Keep It Up" badge for logging food and activities for at least three days in a row after signing up, and the "Losin' It" badge for logging their first weight loss in the application. Each potential badge that can be earned here directs the user toward specific behaviors using the software: completing a profile, logging meals repetitively, and entering their weight, at least twice, into the Goals section of the application. Over time, these badges guide users toward the types of interactions necessary to sustain the application's use. Further, by providing the user with rewards when weight loss milestones are met, the badges provide additional motivation to continue logging calories and food data.

Another example of badge design is found in the *Runkeeper* exercise application for iOS and Android mobile devices (Runkeeper, 2008). *Runkeeper* is a mobile software program that users employ to keep track of their jogging data. It operates in the background while individuals are running, allowing the tracking of data such as the amount of time spent jogging, the pace, the GPS coordinates of the run, and additional performance relating to specialized training programs, such as intervals. For example, a jogger might alternate pace throughout the course of the run, which the program can track. *Runkeeper* uses a series of badged challenges (see Figure 7.1) to encourage its users to participate in special events such as 5-kilometer races and other specialized achievements, such as logging runs over a certain interval of time or for a certain number of repetitions. Using touch-based interaction, users can scroll through the list of challenges and easily see which ones have been personally completed. These are noted by a checkmark in the lower right-hand corner of each badge. They can also see which challenges have been completed by other users of the software, indicated by the numbers below each description. Finally, they can see a title and abbreviated description for each challenge.

Within the detailed list view, *Runkeeper* users can select an individual challenge by touching it. This then opens a secondary view that contains additional detail about the challenge as personalized to the user's account and exercise activity. As shown in Figure 7.2, for example, the user has

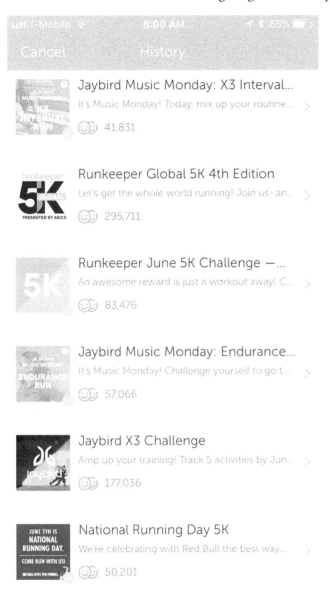

Figure 7.1 Runkeeper list of challenges (iOS version)

selected the challenge "Runkeeper June 5k Challenge – 2017" in order to view more detail about the badge. The detailed view provides additional information about the user's progress toward earning the badge and the time limit in which they have to earn it. In this case, the badge has been unlocked,

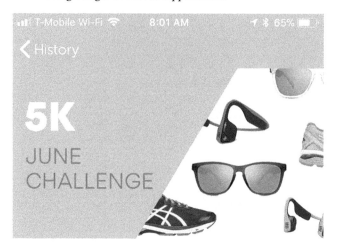

Figure 7.2 Runkeeper challenge detail view (iOS version)

as indicated by the progress bar stretched to 100%. Additionally, information about the challenge and reward are provided in the bottom half of the
display. For completing this challenge, the exerciser was awarded with not
only the virtual badge itself, but also a coupon for 10% off a future purchase
in the *Runkeeper* online store.

As *Runkeeper, Lose It!, Nike+,* and other application developers have shown, it is possible to create effective digital badges in mobile environments. As with other, non-mobile applications, these badges are useful for a variety of purposes such as motivating users, shaping behaviors, encouraging exploration, and credentialing. While the particular design features will vary according to the badges' use and purpose, it is clear that certain design decisions, such as minimizing extraneous information and building touch-sensitive controls, are universally necessary for this type of hardware. In addition, the specific affordances and capabilities of mobile devices, such as geolocation, built-in audio/video recording capabilities, and biometric sensors, might present new possibilities for future design and development. Using these features, it is easy to imagine a future for mobile digital badges in which they are extended in a number of novel, creative, and interesting directions. This is a fertile area of research for badge designers.

A Few Cautionary Notes

As with the other technologies we have been discussing throughout this book, there are some areas in which we must exercise caution when designing badges for mobile applications. One area relates to privacy and security, which can both be at odds with the desire to use contextual information from real-world environments (Naismith, Lonsdale, Vavoula, & Sharples, 2004). For example, a mobile application that awards digital credentials based on landmarks visited within a city also provides a historical map of geographical activity derived from the users that earned those badges. Similarly, a badge system designed to reward fitness habits or weight loss milestones also makes protected health information available to the general public. As a result, security and privacy concerns should be carefully considered when designing badging systems that take advantage of the affordances of mobile media.

Other concerns deal with the perceptions of badging systems in public settings, such as those systems designed to bridge both formal and informal learning environments. A case study written in 2014 chronicles some of the challenges in implementing a badging system at scale within an existing curriculum (Mozilla, 2014). The study, which reports on a badging system developed for the Sustainable Agriculture & Food Systems major at UC Davis, is indicative of the types of challenges faced by developers of these systems. An interview with Joanna Normoyle, learning coordinator for experiential and digital media learning, indicated that despite their receiving one of Mozilla's Badges for Lifelong Learning Competition awards, they still encountered delays with using the badging system and there were worries about how the badges would be perceived by student learners (as "lame" or not worthy of their attention). With mobile devices, students might be even more reluctant to interact with digital badges if they are regarded in this fashion. This is because the mobile devices are more intimate and immediate than other devices they might use for learning. Other students are not likely to see individuals earning badges on a PC in their dormitory room, for example, but earning virtual badges on a cell phone while out in the field is more visible and more public.

Even if we acknowledge these cautionary notes, however, it could still be that the potential benefits of mobile badging outweigh the potential risks. Most interesting in the UC Davis case study, for example, was the focus on student *experiences* rather than the badges themselves. Central to the design of the UC Davis system is an acknowledgment that the experiences students in the agriculture program undergo – washing and planting vegetables, planting new crops, running reports and building research around new sustainability initiatives, and so forth – are the critical components of this educational experience. Although not explicitly acknowledged in the case study, the principle of mobility, of allowing students to learn seamlessly both in formal classroom environments as well as in outdoor field study environments, is important to the design goals of the program. It could be that mobile badges help the designers to produce the types of student learning behaviors to help support these goals.

Ultimately, as with any technology, these cautionary points are worth acknowledging, but should not discourage the use of mobile digital badges altogether. The balance between security/privacy and usability/accessibility is a longstanding challenge in technology development and it is not surprising that this dynamic is also potentially problematic in mobile contexts. However, the intimacy of these technologies and the ways in which these technologies are perceived by their users do suggest challenges that we should be aware of when designing and developing with these digital objects.

Next Up

In our next and final chapter on the contexts and practices of digital badges, we focus on military and training simulations. As with the digital badges used in videogames, learning systems, and mobile applications, there are special considerations to be aware of when designers use games in these types of scenarios. There are also some special opportunities for using badges effectively in simulations.

References

Access Security Corp. (2016, May 6). Mobile phones can now replace ID badges. Retrieved from www.accesssecurity.com/2016/05/06/mobile-phones-can-now-replace-id-badges/.

Agar, J. (2013). *Constant touch: A global history of the mobile phone*. London: Icon Books.

Amadeo, R. (2016, Oct. 31). The (updated) history of Android. *Ars Technica*. Retrieved from https://arstechnica.com/gadgets/2016/10/building-android-a-40000-word-history-of-googles-mobile-os/.

Apple Inc. (2018a). iOS design themes. Human interface guidelines. Retrieved from https://developer.apple.com/ios/human-interface-guidelines/overview/themes/.

Apple Inc. (2018b). watchOS design themes. Human interface guidelines. Retrieved from https://developer.apple.com/watchos/human-interface-guidelines/overview/themes/.

Birch, J. (2017, June 14). Exploring Android O: Notification badges. *Medium*. Retrieved from https://medium.com/exploring-android/exploring-android-o-notification-badges-32e1152eb1a0.

Boticki, I., Baksa, J., Seow, P., & Looi, C. K. (2015). Usage of a mobile social learning platform with virtual badges in a primary school. *Computers & Education*, 86, 120–136.

Centofante, P. (2017, Sept 6). Best practices for driving engagement with iOS app notification badges. *Willowtree*. Retrieved from https://willowtreeapps.com/ideas/best-practices-for-driving-engagement-with-ios-app-notification-badges.

Chaffey, D. (2018, Jan. 30). Mobile marketing statistics compilation. *Smart Insights*. Retrieved from www.smartinsights.com/mobile-marketing/mobile-marketing-analytics/mobile-marketing-statistics/.

Chen, G. D., Chang, C. K., & Wang, C. Y. (2008). Ubiquitous learning website: Scaffold learners by mobile devices with information-aware techniques. *Computers & Education*, 50(1), 77–90.

Chang, R. (2017, Jan. 26). U.S. Education apps market to grow 28.15% in 2016–2020. *T/H/E Journal*. Retrieved from https://thejournal.com/articles/2017/01/26/u.s.-education-apps-market-to-grow-28.15-percent-in-2016-to-2020.aspx.

Cohan, P. (2013, Sept. 10). Project vogue: Inside Apple's iPhone deal with AT&T. *Forbes*. Retrieved from www.forbes.com/sites/petercohan/2013/09/10/project-vogue-inside-apples-iphone-deal-with-att/#60c62a504d3c.

Croom, A. (2014, April 22). A brief history of digital badges in higher ed. *Adam Croom's blog*. Retrieved from http://adamcroom.com/2014/04/a-brief-history-of-digital-badges-in-higher-ed/.

Deloitte (2017). 2017 Global mobile consumer survey: US edition: The dawn of the next era in mobile. Retrieved from www2.deloitte.com/us/en/pages/technology-media-and-telecommunications/articles/global-mobile-consumer-survey-us-edition.html.

Dropbox (2018). What is the Dropbox badge? Dropbox.com. Retrieved from www.dropbox.com/help/business/badge-overview.

eMarketer (2018). Top 5 stats to know about US mobile usage. Retrieved from www.emarketer.com/corporate/coverage/be-prepared-mobile.

Fanfarelli, J., Vie, S., & McDaniel, R. (2015). Understanding digital badges through feedback, reward, and narrative: A multidisciplinary approach to building better badges in social environments. *Communication Design Quarterly Review*, 3(3), 56–60.

Floridi, L. (2014). *The 4th revolution: How the infosphere is reshaping human reality*. Oxford: Oxford University Press.

Gahran, A. (2011, July 21). Mobile devices save lives in emergencies. *CNN*. Retrieved from www.cnn.com/2011/TECH/mobile/07/21/mobile.emergency.response.gahran/index.html.

Goligoski, E. (2012). Motivating the learner: Mozilla's open badges program. *Access to Knowledge: A Course Journal*, 4(1), 1–8.

Halfbrick Studios (2010). *Fruit Ninja*. iOS mobile video game.

Herrman, J. (2018, Feb. 27). How tiny red dots took over your life. *The New York Times*. Retrieved from www.nytimes.com/2018/02/27/magazine/red-dots-badge-phones-notification.html.

Hoekman, Jr., R. (2011). *Designing the obvious: A common sense approach to web and mobile application design*, 2nd ed. Berkeley: New Riders.

IDScan.net (2018). BadgeScan. iOS Application. Retrieved from https://idscan.net/solutions/mobile/badgescan/.

IMS Global (2018). IMS certified product directory. IMS Global learning consortium. Retrieved from www.imsglobal.org/openbadges-certified-products.

Johnson, D. B., & Maltz, D. A. (1996). Truly seamless wireless and mobile host networking: Protocols for adaptive wireless and mobile networking. *IEEE Personal Communications*, 3(1), 34–42.

Kroon, T. (2017). Steve Jobs introduces iPhone1. 2017 Keynote address. Retrieved from www.youtube.com/watch?v=G8d7E26WLsY.

Lipsman, A. (2017, March 17). Mobile matures as the cross-platform era emerges. *ComScore*. Retrieved from www.comscore.com/Insights/Blog/Mobile-Matures-as-the-Cross-Platform-Era-Emerges.

Macbride, K. (2017, August 24). Audible badges decoded! *BookRiot*. Retrieved from https://bookriot.com/2017/08/24/audible-badges-decoded/.

Mims, C. (2012, July 23). A surprisingly long list of everything smartphones replaced. *MIT Technology Review*. Retrieved from www.technologyreview.com/s/428579/a-surprisingly-long-list-of-everything-smartphones-replaced/.

Mozilla (2014, Feb.). University of California, Davis Sustainable Agriculture & Food Systems (SA&FS) learner driven badges. Open badges case study. Retrieved from www.reconnectlearning.org/wp-content/uploads/2014/01/UC-Davis_case_study_final.pdf.

Mozilla (2016). OpenBadges. About Open Badges. Retrieved from https://openbadges.org/about/#history.

Naismith, L., Lonsdale, P., Vavoula, G., & Sharples, M. (2004). *Literature review in mobile technologies and learning* (Futurelab Series Report 11). Bristol: Futurelab.

Passport (2018). Passport: Show what you know. Retrieved from www.openpassport.org.

Paul, I. (2011, Mar. 25). Cutting the cord: Milestones of mobile computing. *PCWorld*. Retrieved from www.pcworld.com/article/222762/mobile_computing_over_the_decades.html.

Ravilabs (2008). *Runkeeper*. iOS/Android mobile application.

Rosling, H., Rönnlund, A. R., & Rosling, O. (2018). *Factfulness: Ten reasons we're wrong about the World—and why things are better than you think*. New York: Flatiron Books.

Rovio (2009). *Angry Birds*. iOS mobile video game.

Sinicki, A. (2017, Sept. 22). Are smartphones still getting faster? Does Moore's Law still apply? *Android Authority*. Retrieved from www.androidauthority.com/smartphone-speed-moores-law-801776/.

Statista (2018). Mobile app usage – statistics & facts. Retrieved from www.statista.com/topics/1002/mobile-app-usage/.

Ventola, C. L. (2014). Mobile devices and apps for health care professionals: Uses and benefits. *Pharmacy and Therapeutics*, 39(5), 356.

Vincent, J. (2017, Feb. 16). 99.6 percent of new smartphones run Android or iOS. *The Verge*. Retrieved from www.theverge.com/2017/2/16/14634656/android-ios-market-share-blackberry-2016.

Vogelstein, F. (2013, Dec. 18). The day Google had to 'start over' on Android. *The Atlantic*. Retrieved from www.theatlantic.com/technology/archive/2013/12/the-day-google-had-to-start-over-on-android/282479/.

Washington Post Staff (2014, Sept. 9). The history of the mobile phone. *The Washington Post*. Retrieved from www.washingtonpost.com/news/the-switch/wp/2014/09/09/the-history-of-the-mobile-phone/.

West, D. (2012). How mobile devices are transforming healthcare. *Issues in Technology Innovation*, 18(1), 1–11.

CHAPTER 8

Using Badges in Military Applications

Overview

In the United States and abroad, defense organizations are frequently on the lookout for new techniques to improve their operations. From the invention of radar to helicopters, the military has a long history of pioneering new technologies that change the way the world works. Technologies originally designed for military purposes often end up in public and commercial spheres, sometimes fundamentally changing the ways in which we live our lives. The digital space is no exception; ARPANET was a U.S. Department of Defense funded project that was the precursor to the modern Internet. Likewise, simulations (live, virtual, and constructive) have been implemented for a number of different training applications and have become integral methods for preparing Soldiers and civilians alike for complex scenarios.

In recent years, the U.S. Army and other branches and defense organizations have turned their attention toward gamification. Just as badges have found a variety of applications in civilian spaces, so too can they be useful in a variety of ways within the corresponding defense spaces. The hope is that these badges can improve engagement and learning to better support the training of Soldiers and other service members who might be enduring long hours of training and have difficulty fully attending to training material that could be interpreted as dry or mundane.

In this chapter, we discuss the design of digital badges for military use, with a strong emphasis on training applications. We begin by assessing the importance of digital badging in the military, citing its long history of physical badging and considering why and how digital badges might expand upon the pre-existing system. We then describe a number of specific applications for digital badging. We conclude with some cautionary notes on using digital badges in the defense space, specifically raising concerns associated with cybersecurity and with leveraging playfulness to train users who will often continue into very serious, and sometimes perilous, environments.

Why Use Badges in Military Applications?

One reason badges are well suited for military applications is due to the organic and evolving nature of personnel assignments. For example, badges can be quite useful when an individual is reassigned to a new unit, which can happen often due to touring, reenlistment, compassionate or family reassignment, or other reasons. When an Airman, for example, is reassigned, she will be surrounded by a group of new people, including peers, superiors, and subordinates who must become familiar with her skillsets and abilities – her credentials. Formal records will inform command about some of the Airman's capabilities, but not always at the desired granularity. A conversation with the Airman could yield more information, but there is always a risk of details being omitted or exaggerated.

A clear understanding of a person's learned skills, abilities, and accomplishments support assignment and promotion efforts. Digital badges are one way of aiding this understanding (Higashi, Schunn, Nguyen, & Ososky, 2017). Credentialing badges can be tied to evidence of the accomplishment as well as the name of the issuer. These accompanying pieces of information create accountability and leave little room for error or exaggeration. They provide a name of someone who can be contacted to provide further details of the accomplishment and what it truly tells about the Airman's skillset. In other words, credentialing badges aid in providing command with an honest understanding of the new individual's capabilities.

Additionally, badges can be unit specific. Many formal traditional records and adornments provide standardized meanings and communication across the entirety of the service branch, which is useful for creating shared understandings among service members. However, different branches of the military or different units within those branches might have different subcultures and operations that yield varying skills or accomplishments that they find important. In this Air Force scenario, it would be useful for the Airman's former unit to be able to communicate that information to her new unit, to help provide a more holistic understanding of the Airman's history. It might be quite tedious for someone to use formal records to try to not only communicate these accomplishments, but also describe their requirements, evidence, and meaning. Badges can be designed to encapsulate all of this into a neat package that is easily created, issued, and shared.

Digital badges are also already familiar to many service members. Mirroring the upward trend in civilian players, service members tend to play and enjoy videogames (Chang, 2009). With the ubiquity of badges in videogames, such as Sony Playstation's Trophies or the achievements systems on Microsoft's Xbox or Valve's Steam platforms, service members will likely either be familiar with how badges work or have a peer who understands them. This is important, because familiarity is an important factor for whether or not someone believes a technology will be valuable and useful (Peek, Wouters, van Hoof, Luijkx, Boeije, & Vrijhoef, 2014).

Badging in Military Applications

Just as digital badges are familiar to modern service members, analog badging has also been a longstanding part of military history. While badges have been used in military forces for centuries, the first badge, in the form of a medal, entered the U.S. military during the American Civil War. In 1861, Abraham Lincoln approved the creation of a Medal of Honor, which Marines and Navy Sailors could earn for exceptionalism in the line of duty (Wright, 2014; Yildirim, Kaban, Yildirim, & Celik, 2016). Around the same time period, in England, the Duke of Newcastle described military ribbons as capable of reducing the negative feelings associated with dangerous situations or resource deprivation (Maxfield, 1981).

In modern times, the military has shown support of digital badging by putting forth funding for research and development. In 2011, the U.S. Department of Veterans Affairs Innovation Initiative offered a $25,000 USD prize for the badging concept that best helped military veterans acquire high paying jobs (Duncan, 2011). We briefly discussed this in the Introduction and explained this initiative sought to identify and credential the useful and transferrable skills veterans learned in the military so that they could be recognized and employable after their service ended. Just as we have discussed the importance of transferring knowledge about a service member's skillset when they change units, the Department of Veterans Affairs has recognized a need to transfer this knowledge, even after discharge.

Digital badges have also been considered for other purposes. For example, Shahriar, Peletsverger Zafar, Bailey, and Johnston (2016) suggested that digital badges might be useful for cybersecurity training, a subfield that has boomed in popularity within the defense sector in recent years due to the increased prevalence of Internet operations (e.g., infiltration, espionage, data theft) and cyberattacks (e.g., distributed denial of service). The U.S. Army Research Laboratory (ARL) and The Advanced Distributed Learning (ADL) initiative have discussed the possibility of using digital badges and open badging backpacks in synergy with intelligent tutoring systems to credential learners in a more organized manner (Regan, Raybourn, & Durlach, 2013). While there has been much discussion about possibilities, the U.S. Department of Defense has already begun implementing digital badges. For example, their Intelligence and Security Professional Certification is accompanied by a credentialing badge that includes relevant metadata and is shareable via the Internet (Department of Defense, 2018).

Special Characteristics of Military Applications

Perhaps the most important special characteristic of military applications, as it relates to digital badge design considerations, is the existing awards system. When it comes to digital badging in military training simulations, one might wonder why digital badges would be necessary if most military organizations already have a well-established recognition and credentialing system with ribbons, ranks, and medals. After all, these awards perform many of the same functions as digital badges, are recognizable by those in the military, and are probably even preferred over digital awards due to their long and prestigious history. However, there are some key differences that make a digital badging system an interesting *addition* to this system.

While physical awards are typically used to recognize major achievements, digital badges might be useful for recognizing smaller achievements or milestones toward major achievements. Earlier in this book, we discussed the relationship between motivation and competence; when a person believes she is competent enough to achieve something, she is more motivated to achieve it. When a prestigious ribbon seems out of reach, digital badges might be useful to scaffold the task, helping the trainee set smaller manageable goals (i.e., goal-setting) that will eventually lead her to the award. Thus, digital badges might be especially useful for those awards that are desirable, but harder to achieve.

Additionally, consider the rigor, effort, and difficulty involved in approving a new ribbon or medal for use across an entire military organization. This is not something that is done lightly. It can take time and, potentially, political standing and prowess to achieve. On the other hand, if a particular division recognizes a need to acknowledge a particular skill development in their Sailors, but this need is not shared by the entirety of the service branch, digital badges might pose a solution. Likewise, when a new technology is introduced that must be learned by Soldiers (e.g., new unmanned ground vehicle software), there might be little justification to put forth the effort to approve and manufacture new ribbons. The technology competency is a minor achievement and the technology will likely be replaced in the near future, anyway. Nevertheless, if it is important to learn, a quick and dirty scaffolding or recognition system might be developed through the use of digital badges. In military applications, digital badges are best used when they fill gaps left by the more traditional credentials.

Designing Effective Badges for Military Applications

Now that we have examined the history, relevance, and importance of badging in the military, we will progress to identify specific applications of digital badging. Digital badges, like the longstanding physical badges present in their history, can be used for a large variety of purposes. They are certainly not limited to those presented here. However, we hope the examples below will provide a better understanding of which roles they might fill in military training and provide some ideas for future badging purposes and design.

Combat Medic Specialist Training

In the U.S. Army, Combat Medic Specialist training (68W) is a rigorous process that includes basic combat training (e.g., weapons training, clearing buildings), civilian-like medical training (i.e., basic medical procedures), and combat-specific medical training (e.g., carrying the wounded to safety, establishing field hospitals) that happen both in the classroom and on the field. There are a large number of skills to learn and training can take up to 68 weeks.

Currently, medics can earn two physical badges. The Combat Medical Badge is awarded to Soldiers of rank Colonel or below who provide medical support during a ground combat engagement. The Expert Field Medical Badge is awarded after successful completion of a rigorous two-week test of field medical skills; only a very small percentage of Soldiers pass this test. While these two badges are prestigious, they leave quite a bit of room for other recognitions and credentials. Likewise, they are not necessarily meant to enhance the learning process, but rather to function primarily as credentialing mechanisms.

While the Expert Field Medical Badge might motivate some to prepare for and participate in the two-week test, this is a fairly rudimentary addition to the learning process. These badges provide little support for goal-setting, feedback, and other boosters of instructional effectiveness. Digital badges can be used in this scenario to target these specific purposes, with special consideration for how completion logic and description can be designed to acknowledge, motivate, and provide feedback on training tasks. Consider the *Combat Medic* virtual simulator, which trains combat medics on three major causes of casualty on the battlefield – hemorrhage, airway management, and tension pneumothorax (Brown, McIlwain, Willson, & Hackett, 2016; Virtual Heroes, 2014). Soldiers who train in *Combat Medic* will be faced with multiple difficulty levels, coupled with environmental distractions, which gradually help the trainee find their way up to a focused state of concentration while they perform their tasks.

Let us consider how digital badges might be integrated into the *Combat Medic* simulator as it simulates real-world training exercises. The badges used here can be applied to other training situations. In the simulation scenarios, the trainee must choose from a number of different supplies such as syringes, bandages, and gloves, to include in the limited space in their aid bags. They are asked to bring only what is necessary. If an important supply is forgotten, the trainee will not be capable of success. Thus, the first badge might acknowledge successful completion of the first step:

- Prepared: You have packed all the necessary supplies for the training scenario.

This badge, and any of the badges discussed here, could easily become incremental badges by improving as the trainee passes each difficulty level. Likewise, they could be tailored to specific training scenarios (e.g., "You have packed . . . for the *airway management* training scenario").

During a mass casualty scenario, there might be many lives that must be saved in a short amount of time, so medics must move quickly while avoiding costly mistakes. Here, medics might move too slowly and inefficiently, resulting in lives lost. Or, they might move too quickly and make mistakes, also resulting in lives lost due

Figure 8.1 Efficiency badge

to poor technique or medic fatigue. A proper balance must be found. Goal-setting badges might be used to facilitate this process (Figure 8.1).

- Efficiency I: You have saved three lives in the mass casualty scenario without making a mistake. This is a good start, but you must move faster. Reflect on your performance and identify where you could improve.
- Efficiency II: You have saved five lives in the mass casualty scenario without making a mistake. You are improving, but there are still more lives to save. Continue to identify shortcomings and improve.
- . . . and so on.

In this way, the trainee is encouraged to engage in metacognition to become increasingly efficient and proficient. Likewise, trainees might receive badges for making good decisions. For example, training materials indicate it is generally not advisable to treat a wounded Soldier in the open during a firefight. Instead, the medic should drag the person to cover in order to safely treat the patient:

- Safety First: You dragged the patient behind cover during a firefight, protecting yourself and the patient from further injury.

While physical actions are useful, so too are communication skills. The medic must not only be able to communicate with other medics in order to efficiently collaborate and assign duties, but must also communicate appropriately with wounded Soldiers:

- Communication: You communicated clearly, sufficiently, and succinctly during a firefight.

Both the Safety First and Communication badges describe the completion logic, but also provide additional details. The Safety First badge elaborates on the importance of dragging the patient to cover to protect the medic and the patient from further injury. On the other hand, the Communication badge denotes that it can only be earned during a firefight (i.e., during a stressful situation) and describes the components of good communication; it is clear, sufficient, and succinct. Always consider when you can incorporate more information to the trainee so that the badge is not simply a goal or reward, but can also provide feedback, justification, or additional useful information. These badges are some examples of how digital badges can elaborate upon the existing physical badge system. When designing digital badges, remember to think about what needs are being served by existing systems and what needs need to be, and can be, served by the digital badges.

Cybersecurity

Cybersecurity experts are trained to preserve information confidentiality, integrity, and availability in a virtual networked environment (Gheorghica & Croitoru, 2016). They defend against digital acts of infiltration, espionage, theft, and destruction that might result from several different types of attacks including injection, cross-site scripting, phishing, and others. By integrating firewalls and encryption, carefully designing networks, observing network traffic, and a range of other processes, cybersecurity experts defend against cyberattacks while also conducting offensive operations.

While the technological components might more immediately come to mind when considering cybersecurity, there are several human aspects to security threats. In fact, humans are often considered the weakest link in an organization's security infrastructure (Furnell & Clarke, 2012). For example, consider the person who uses their spouse's name as their password in a secure system. This is information that might be easily accessible through a social media search. Another human security threat could be someone who clicks email attachments from unknown senders. While these are likely unintentional vulnerabilities where the person does not mean to create the vulnerability, some human aspects are less benign. An example is found in the individual who does not belong in the office, who might be carrying a USB drive containing malware. There are a number of ways in which humans might conduct unsafe practices that create vulnerabilities within the cyber infrastructure. Identifying and addressing these human aspects is therefore a necessary part of cybersecurity training.

A practice scenario addressing these aspects might require the trainee to walk through a virtual office and attempt to identify different types of human threats. While some trainees will be ready to move through training and might easily identify other security risks, others will not be quite as successful. Perhaps some trainees will flawlessly identify one type of security risk, but entirely miss another type. For example, consider the trainee who identifies all agents who leave their password

Figure 8.2 Secured badge

written on a sticky note near their computer, but does not identify unsecured mobile devices. These are also threats since a stolen mobile phone could contain security information or be used as a tool for two-factor authentication. In instances like these, it might be worthwhile to recognize the trainee's achievements, but also to point to the shortcomings so that they can be addressed. Appending feedback to the end of the badge description, or having multiple versions of the badge available to give appropriate feedback would allow this sort of scenario. Consider the following versions of a badge named "Secured" (Figure 8.2).

- V1 – Secured: You've successful identified all *password* vulnerabilities. Now, consider other types of threats you might have missed. *Are there any unsecured devices that could pose a vulnerability?*
- V2 – Secured: You've successfully identified all *unsecured* device vulnerabilities. Now, consider other types of threats you might have missed. *Has anybody left their passwords unsecured?*

By having multiple versions of the same badge, the credentialing, goal-setting, and other positive mechanisms associated with badges can be utilized while also providing adaptive feedback to educate the trainee and point her in the right direction. In addition to these digital and human considerations just discussed, there are physical aspects related to cybersecurity. Examples include locks, safes, and alarms. Ultimately, cybersecurity is a multi-pronged approach. A complete badging system to address cybersecurity would need to have badges for each major facet of cybersecurity, with metabadges encompassing them. Recall that a metabadge is a badge that is awarded after earning a series of other badges. These metabadges might take the following form:

- Physical Security: You've demonstrated your ability to maintain physical security by completing the following five badges: *badge1, badge2 . . .*
- Human Security: You've demonstrated your ability to maintain human security by completing the following five badges: *badge1, badge2 . . .*

In this way, the trainee can gradually practice and improve her skills, working toward one badge at a time in order to develop her abilities in each facet of cybersecurity. Additionally, by having each facet contained in a metabadge, the trainee can begin to frame cybersecurity in terms of those facets. This process considers the holistic picture of cybersecurity and moves beyond the urge to define this problem space purely by digital means.

Finally, it is worth noting that when using badges in cybersecurity training, you might consider communicating how to maintain the security of digital badges. After all, a warfighter's badge set could provide information to enemy forces that could compromise operations by exposing strengths and weaknesses. We will discuss this topic in more depth a bit later in the chapter. For now, we will explore how badges might fit within unmanned systems training.

Robotics – Unmanned Ground Vehicles

Robotics have become ubiquitous in a number of applications, but especially within the military. As early adopters and supporters of robotics research, defense organizations and industry partners have found many uses for unmanned systems, from reconnaissance to explosive ordnance disposal. Properly using these systems is difficult. Consider the unmanned ground systems (UGV) used for explosive ordnance disposal (EOD). EOD often requires that a skilled operator maneuver a robot on a short-range reconnaissance mission to detect explosive devices. Once detected, the device must be either disarmed or remotely detonated to ensure that it is no longer a threat to allied warfighters or civilians.

The UGV operator must learn each control's function on a controller that might have many inputs without clear and explicit descriptions. She must also learn how to maneuver the robot through sometimes tight spaces and over terrain that has the potential to trap the robot, using 2D cameras to judge which paths are safe to traverse. Upon finding the explosive, the operator must get close enough to it, without disturbing it unnecessarily, so that it does not detonate. Then, she must maneuver a robotic arm, with multiple joints, to perform the necessary work involved in defusing or disposal. The claw on the arm can exert enough pressure to damage what it is grabbing, so the operator must learn to gauge how much pressure is being applied to avoid crushing parts of the explosive. If the operator fails, it could result in the loss of a robot that costs hundreds of thousands of dollars, or, even worse, it could lead to the loss of human lives. It is a procedure that must be done with the utmost care and expertise, as calmly as possible, yet with the urgency necessary to rectify a dangerous situation in a timely manner.

Training for these systems is conducted in different ways and for different lengths of time depending on the particular branch of service. One way trainees learn to use these robots is by completing familiar tasks that require the same knowledge and skills of finesse and judgment. For example, trainees might be asked to locate a pitcher of water, lift it without crushing it, maneuver it to a flower vase, and fill the vase with water, all without spilling a drop. Another training scenario, found in the Air Force, infuses competition into training by asking multiple operators to race their robots to pick up balls and put them into goals. The operator of the fastest robot wins.

While simulation-based trainings are not yet ubiquitous, robotics simulator scenarios are far from unheard of; this is where digital badges might benefit training. After all, these robots are expensive to buy and repair and simulation-based training offers a way to train large numbers of people without the associated wear and tear on the equipment. Let us return to the ball and goal training scenario and consider it within a simulation. In some ways, this could be considered to be a type of competitive game, where each operator is trying to make more goals than the others. Here, badges can be used to reward the top competitors, recognizing them just as runners might be recognized via medals in a race. Simple badges that are awarded for finishing first might be useful motivators.

- Robotball Champion – Finish first in a Robotball competition.

By using incremental badges, the first place badge might upgrade, beginning at bronze and upgrading to silver, gold, and so on, for successive wins. The ability to upgrade the badge creates a set of tiered goals for trainees, where higher level badges might also serve as status symbols, helping trainees keep track of who is most adept at maneuvering the robots. Ranking badges could be used to take this a step further, where users' badges can be upgraded or downgraded based on competitive performance. Such a system might use a subset of ranks in the particular service branch to enhance familiarity and tap into cultural norms. For example, if a South Korean Air Force trainee has attained the Captain badge and continues to win, his badge will eventually be upgraded to the Major badge. However, if she continues to lose, her badge will downgrade to the Lieutenant badge. The completion logic (requirements for earning the badge) for such a system could be designed in a number of ways. Consider the Captain badge. The following are a few different options for how the completion logic could be designed:

- Win five games while holding the Lieutenant ranking (upgrade to Captain) or lose five games while holding the Major ranking (downgrade to Captain).
- Achieve and maintain a win percentage of 45–55%, beginning after your first 10 games.
- Place in the 50th percentile of trainees by win percentage.

Whichever logic is chosen could be applied to the other ranking badges, with values adjusted appropriately. While trainees would likely be motivated to improve their badge, there is a risk of demotivation for those who end up in the lower ranks, especially if trainees can see the ranks of others. To combat this, the system might be designed to only make the badge public if the trainee holds one of the top badges. With this design, before a particular threshold is met, all trainees would simply appear to be unbadged, mitigating problems that might arise from being seen as lesser or unskilled. At the same time, highly skilled operators would be more visible and recognized. Not only would this likely serve as a motivator, but these individuals could be sought after by their lesser-skilled peers who would like advice on how to improve. Such design supports not only motivation, but also mentoring.

Marksmanship

In military applications, marksmanship is the ability to land precision shots with firearms. Firearms are a major part of training in the various military branches; in the U.S. Army, every Soldier must become a competent marksman in order to be considered combat ready (James & Dyer, 2011). One or more ribbons already exist for marksmanship in service branches. For example, in order to earn the Marksmanship Ribbon in the U.S. Army, Soldiers must hit 23 of 40 targets, with higher level ribbons earned at 30 (Sharpshooter) and 36 (Expert) hits.

While these feats must be accomplished in the real world in order to gain the ribbon, marksmanship simulators have become quite common in military training. These simulators have been shown to be effective trainers, sometimes even surpassing traditional real-world, or *dry fire*, exercises (Getty, 2014). These marksmanship trainers take many forms, but might simply be a simulation of a gun range, where the trainee holds a modified pistol and aims at a large display of range and targets. In this sort of simulation, digital badges can be used to indicate progress toward attaining expert marksmanship. They might emulate the physical ribbons by providing badges at 23, 30, and 36 hits. However, further scaffolding might also be useful, such as by enhancing this incremental badging system by badging lower numbers of hits. This might motivate those trainees starting out at a lower skill level.

Digital badges can also be used to extend the range of activities that are recognized. While basic marksmanship simulators might be quite simple, other, more dynamic activities could be incorporated to further improve marksmanship skill. These might include elements such as moving targets or dynamic combat scenarios that require appropriate use of cover while demonstrating marksmanship ability against simulated insurgent agents. Currently, ribbons are not used for these sorts of scenarios, providing a gap that can be filled by digital badges. For example, within a dynamic situation, the following badges might be used to encourage trainees to develop their skills in ways beyond accuracy on simple static targets:

- Make it Quick – Hit five moving targets within 10 seconds.
- Danger . . . Watch Yourself! – Hit 20 targets while in cover during the fire-fight training scenario.

Marksmanship is not quite as simple as pointing a weapon at a target and shooting. It is a complex task that requires using several skills in combination. The marksman must master the four fundamentals: steady position, aiming, breath control, and trigger squeeze (Goris & Brawner, 2016). In order to learn these fundamentals, each requires both understanding and application of related practical knowledge. Metabadges are typically useful in applications, such as these, where one complex skill is composed of many simpler skills. Thus, we might consider a marksmanship metabadge, that is only unlocked once the trainee demonstrates the four fundamentals (earning a badge for each):

- Steady Position – Describe and demonstrate, to the trainer, how to assume a steady position, providing a solid foundation for your shot.
- Aim – Describe and demonstrate, to the trainer, the alignment of the body, eye, weapon, and target to properly aim down the sight.
- Breath Control – Describe and demonstrate, to the trainer, the two types of breath control, and when each should be used.
- Trigger Squeeze – Describe and demonstrate, to the trainer, how to execute a proper trigger squeeze, without twisting, tensing, or other issues.
- (Metabadge) Marksmanship Fundamentals – Earn the Steady Position, Aim, Breath Control, and Trigger Squeeze badges to show that you understand the fundamentals of marksmanship.

When considering badging for marksmanship and other complex or difficult skills, it is important to consider how badges can be used to chunk difficult tasks into smaller simpler tasks that can be achieved as stepping stones toward the larger goal. This chunking makes the process more manageable for the trainee by enhancing training and building confidence through repeated success as she accomplishes each chunked goal (Bandura, 1997).

Training the Trainer

In many defense organizations, train-the-trainer courses are an integral part of the training structure (e.g., Barnieu, Morath, Bryson, Hyland, Tucker, & Burnett, 2016; Reivich, Seligman, & McBride, 2011). Train-the-trainer refers to the education and training that a trainer must go through in order to be an effective leader and trainer of others in her organization. Just as teachers benefit from the pedagogical, psychological, and other strategies learned in formal training, so too can military trainers. While some train-the-trainer programs focus on simultaneous training of the subject and the teaching of the subject, many are teaching experts how to train others in their craft. These experts might know their craft inside and out and be able to perform at a very high level, but they do not necessarily know how to transmit that knowledge to others. In order to do this, they must, at a minimum, study learning theory and training techniques (Williams, 2001). Additionally, experts often know so much information that they might transmit too much and risk overloading the trainee with unnecessary details (Trautman & Klein, 1993; Clark, 1994).

Designers of badging systems for train-the-trainer applications will likely benefit from many of the more general suggestions from Chapter 6, where we discuss badging in online learning, especially those related to proper pedagogy. However, there are considerations that extend beyond basic pedagogy that must be considered. While it might seem obvious, it is worth stating that the focus of the badging system should be on the assimilation and demonstration of training skills and not on skills related to the subject matter. Thus, a badge that recognizes a Sailor's ability to put out a ship fire is not quite as useful in this scenario.

Instead, consider badges that are awarded for the specific skills you want the trainer to learn. For example, trainers tend to be more effective when they give clear, succinct, and timely feedback to their trainees (Hattie & Timperley, 2007). A badge that recognizes good feedback and clearly states why it was good will be a useful addition to the badging system. Consider the following badge:

- Feedback about Your Feedback: You provided helpful feedback to a trainee. Reflect on the feedback you gave to earn this badge and think about how it was clear, succinct, and given in a timely manner.

Note the directive to reflect. Reflection is a useful learning technique and a form of metacognitive activity, where metacognition can be defined as the monitoring and regulation of one's own thinking or cognitive processes (Hennessey, 1999). While this is a useful learning technique for most students, incorporating metacognitive strategies like these might be especially useful for trainers; after having trainers engage in metacognition, they can later be taught what it is and how it works, citing the instances when they unknowingly performed metacognition. Later, a badge might even be given out for helping a learner successfully engage in metacognition:

- Metacognitive: You have created a training exercise that helps a trainee engage in metacognition to improve their learning.

Ultimately, just like badging systems for other subjects, badges in train-the-trainer applications should align themselves with the training objectives. In this way they help to identify the knowledge, skills, and attitudes that must be learned in order for the trainee to become an effective trainer.

A Few Cautionary Notes

Digital badging can be a fantastic tool for military applications, but should be used mindfully. Ultimately, digital badges, like other formal recognition systems, do leave a footprint of sorts. Just as when a Marine earns a medal, when she earns a digital badge there is likely to be a record kept somewhere. These records should be adequately protected using standardized security protocols so that they are not accessed by unauthorized users. There would certainly be a security issue if opposing forces were to identify the particular and detailed skillsets of a group of Marines. Fortunately, this is not a new issue, but is one that has been faced by the military since record-keeping practices began. Once records were kept digitally, especially simulation and training records, new cybersecurity practices were developed to protect these records. The same standard practices should be applied with care to digital badging systems to ensure appropriate levels of protection. Strategies include reducing access through systems that are not connected to the Internet and using advanced encryption methods. Always consult a cybersecurity expert before deploying a digital badging system for defense purposes.

Additionally, playfulness is a tool that should be used carefully. In many types of badging systems, we have a tendency to infuse playfulness to reduce the seriousness of the situation and improve users' comfort and sense of ease. Badges can be used in the same way in military applications, but perhaps not in all situations. Sometimes the gravity of the situation should be felt, and stress and seriousness are a strong part of the training. Similarly, the sensitive nature of content might not be compatible with a playful tone. As with all badging applications, the goal of the badges and the activities being badged should be thoroughly considered before badging design. If the activity needs to feel serious in order to be effective, the badge names and descriptions should reflect that need. On the other hand, there are times when playfulness is acceptable and other times when it is highly desirable. After all, we know that there is a particular level of stress that increases productivity; if exceeded, the stress quickly becomes crippling and reduces focus and performance. As with all things, balance is important, and a bit of playfulness might help to lower excessive stress or worry if the levels are unmanageable.

Finally, keep in mind that different service branches have differences in cultures and customs. Badge designers who are service members are likely quite familiar with these differences and will have less difficulty navigating them. However, those without service experience should work closely with service members in order to ensure that mistakes are not being made, or, equally important, opportunities are not being missed. Ultimately, good user-centered research and design practices should be implemented for digital badging in military applications just the same as they would for designing software in any other application.

While the pre-existing military award system is an effective and longstanding tradition that recognizes outstanding achievement, badges can be used to help service members work toward these existing recognitions or otherwise recognize acts that are not currently recognized by pre-existing awards. With careful thought and design, digital badging systems can be designed for a number of military applications and purposes in ways that synergize with existing awards, fill gaps, and enhance learning processes of warfighters and other service members.

Next Up

At this point, we have covered four specific contexts surrounding the design of digital badging systems. These four contexts were chosen because of their dissimilarity. Even if you are not designing for one of these applications, you are likely to be able to translate some of the design principles and considerations to your own unique context and for your own specific purposes. Be sure to critically think about the broader application of the ideas described in this chapter. As we progress to the next chapter, we will examine how to test and evaluate badging systems. We will describe how to ensure your badging system meets all functional requirements and positively impacts users. We will also review a variety of different testing methodologies and special considerations for testing badging systems.

References

Bandura, A. (1997). *Self efficacy: The exercise of control.* New York: W.H. Freeman.

Barnieu, J., Morath, R., Bryson, J., Hyland, J., Tucker, J. S., & Burnett, S. (2016). *Using technology to support the army learning model* (U.S. Army Research Institute Report 1990). US Army Research Institute. Retrieved from www.dtic.mil/docs/citations/AD1007667

Brown, R., McIlwain, S., Willson, B., & Hackett, M. (2016). Enhancing combat medic training with 3D virtual environments. In *Proceedings of the 2016 IEEE International Conference on Serious Games and Applications for Health* (pp. 1–8). Orlando, FL: IEEE.

Chang, H. (2009). Simulators always valuable in military training. U.S. Army Website. Retrieved from www.army.mil/article/19599/simulators_always_valuable_in_military_training

Clark, R. (1994). *Developing technical training.* Phoenix, AZ: Buzzards Bay Press.

Department of Defense (2018). Conferral. DoD Intelligence and Security Professional Certification. Retrieved from https://dodcertpmo.defense.gov/Intelligence-Fundamentals/Conferral/

Duncan, A. (2011). Digital badges for learning. MacArthur Foundation. Retrieved from https://www.ed.gov/news/speeches/digital-badges-learning

Furnell, S., & Clarke, C. (2012). Power to the people? The evolving recognition of human aspects of security. *Computers & Security, 31,* 983–988.

Getty, T. J. (2014). *A comparison of current naval marksmanship training vs simulation-based marksmanship training with the use of indoor simulated marksmanship trainer* (Master's thesis). Retrieved from the Institutional Archive of the Naval Postgraduate School.

Gheorghica, D., & Croitoru, V. (2016). A new framework for enhanced measurable cybersecurity in computer networks. In *Proceedings of the IEEE 2016 International Conference on Communications.* Bucharest, Romania: IEEE.

Goris, T., & Brawner, K. (2016). *Examining the influence of heartbeat on expert marksman performance* (Report No. ARL-TN-0754). US Army Research Laboratory. Retrieved from www.dtic.mil/dtic/tr/fulltext/u2/1008572.pdf.

Hattie, J., & Timperley, H. (2007). The power of feedback. *Review of Educational Research*, *77*(1), 81–112.

Hennessey, M. G. (1999). *Probing the dimensions of metacognition: Implications for conceptual change teaching-learning*. Paper presented at the Annual Meeting of the National Association for Research in Science Teaching, Boston, MA.

Higashi, R., Schunn, C., Nguyen, V., & Ososky, S. J. (2017). Coordinating evidence across learning modules using digital badges. In R. A. Sottilare, A. Graesser, X. Hu, & H. Holden (Eds.), *Design recommendations for intelligent tutoring systems* (pp. 53–67). Orlando, FL: U.S. Army Research Laboratory.

James, D. R., & Dyer, J. L. (2011). *Rifle marksmanship diagnostic and training guide*. Fort Benning, GA: Army Research Institute for the Behavioral and Social Sciences.

Maxfield, V. (1981). *The military decorations of the Roman army*. Berkeley, CA: University of California Press.

Peek, S. T. M., Wouters, E. J. M., van Hoof, J., Luijkx, K. G., Boeije, H. R., & Vrijhoef, J. M. (2014). Factors influencing acceptance of technology for aging in place: A systematic review. *International Journal of Medical Informatics*, *83*(4), 235–248.

Regan, D., Raybourn, E. M., & Durlach, P. J. (2013). Learner modeling considerations for a personalized assistant for learning. In R. A. Sottilare, A. Graesser, X. Hu, & H. Holden (Eds.), *Design recommendations for intelligent tutoring systems* (pp. 217–225). Orlando, FL: U.S. Army Research Laboratory.

Reivich, K. J., Seligman, M. E. P., & McBride, S. (2011). Master resilience training in the U.S. Army. *American Psychologist*, *66*(1), 25–34.

Shahriar, H., Peletsverger, S., Zafar, H., Bailey, B., & Johnston, L. (2016). Digital badges to enhance skills and preparation for a career in cybersecurity. *Proceedings of the IEEE 40th Annual Computer Software and Applications Conference* (pp. 622–623). Atlanta, GA: IEEE.

Trautman, S., & Klein, K. (1993). Ask an expert. *Training and Development*, *48*, 45–48.

Virtual Heroes. (2014). *Combat Medic* [Computer Software]. Orlando, FL.

Williams, S. W. (2001). The effectiveness of subject matter experts as technical trainers. *Human Resource Development Quarterly*, *12*(1), 91–97.

Wright, S. E. (2014). *Air Force officer's guide*. Mechanicsburg, PA: Stakepole Books.

Yildirim, S., Kaban, A., Yildirim, G., & Celik, E. (2016). The effect of digital badges specialization level of the subject on the achievement satisfaction and motivation levels of students. *The Turkish Online Journal of Educational Technology*, *15*(3), 169–182.

PART III
Evaluation and Evolution

CHAPTER 9

Badging System Testing and Evaluation

Overview

Testing and evaluating badging systems is a critical task for ensuring their proper functionality. This allows one to gain a better understanding of how users interact with and feel about the system. Designers are often surprised at the mismatch between the expected and actual ways that users engage with their badging environment, which might justify a reexamination of the system's design. Thus, it is important for testing to occur before system deployment.

In iterative design, testing occurs throughout the development process, and not just directly preceding deployment (Sharp, Rogers, & Preece, 2007). Here, design influences testing results and testing results influence design. To suit the paired nature of these processes, in this chapter we discuss design and testing in tandem. We will examine the major badging subsystems that should be involved in testing, how to test system functionality and user experience, and different methodologies and metrics that might be used for these purposes. While we cannot possibly cover all aspects of testing in a single chapter, through this chapter we provide several ideas and examples that are ready for implementation during your system's development.

Before delving into this chapter, we note that we will provide several examples of design, development, and testing tools and methodologies. We acknowledge that not everyone will need to use these directly. However, regardless of whether or not you will be carrying out testing yourself or will be working with designers, developers, or usability testers, understanding how specifications or specific user testing methods work will allow you to have a clearer understanding of the process and to communicate more effectively during badging projects. With that out of the way, we begin by examining testing considerations for common badging subsystems.

Badging Subsystems of Interest

Before discussing *how* to evaluate your badging system, let us first consider *what* to evaluate. While each badging system is unique, there are a few points of functionality that are relatively constant. Just about every badging system has a showcase where earned badges can be seen, an issuing system for issuers to issue badges, and a notification system for earners to be notified that they have earned a badge. Here, we discuss testing considerations for these subsystems. We additionally examine concerns related to proper system access permissions and restrictions in badging systems.

Showcase

Badging systems will typically have a badge display or showcase area where users can view their earned badges. Within this area, users might also be able to see badges they have yet to earn. As we discussed in earlier chapters, such a design facilitates goal-setting. This showcase must be findable, should show all badges that have been earned, and should clearly delineate between badges that have been earned and those that have not yet been earned. Figure 9.1 shows an example of a showcase within a learning system that designates earned and unearned badges through checkmarks and timestamps. Each of these badges can be clicked to provide more information to the user.

First and foremost, a showcase should be discoverable (Terry, Matthew, & Lafreniere, 2010). Users should be able to discover the different parts of the system so that they do not feel lost when attempting to interact. Users should be brought to the place where most users will originate and then led through a series of tasks in order to expose weaknesses in discoverability. For example, we might provide the following instructions to test users to find shortcomings:

- You would like to see which badges you have earned. Navigate to that place.

When evaluating a showcase area for discoverability, tasks should be clearly stated without giving away the solution. Users given instruction to click the badge showcase link and identify a badge would not provide much insight into whether or not the user could find their badges without being told where to find them. Likewise, it is helpful for testers to have a clear objective. Ask users to identify some end product or perform some task that you can examine for completion. This will provide you with informative data that is likely to point you toward any potential issues.

Figure 9.1 Learning system badging showcase

Once users arrive at the showcase, they should be able to clearly understand which badges have and have not been earned. Simply asking test users which badges appear to be unearned should provide useful data.

- How many badges have you earned so far?
- Which badges have you earned?
- You want to earn a new badge. Figure out which badges have not yet been earned and identify one you would like to pursue.

While the previous concerns are based on user understanding and perception, be sure to also test your badging subsystems to make sure they are working properly. With regard to the showcase, each badge should be issued to a test user to ensure that all earned badges appear as earned in the showcase. This testing should also verify that unearned badges are not displayed. Ideally, this should be done several times and in several configurations to ensure that certain combinations of badges do not promote errors.

Issuing System

The issuing system is the portion of a badging system that gives issuers the power to distribute badges to earners. While some systems, such as videogames, automatically distribute badges, others require a manual issuer. In these systems, the issuer must be able to use some sort of interface to actually give out the badges. This subsystem should be tested to ensure that it allows issuers to issue *specific badges* to *specific users*. Figure 9.2 provides an example of an issuing system for a "High Score" badge.

Here is an example of a testing task requiring the use of an issuing system:

- Issue the Superstar badge to the earner named Shringi Aswani.

While we should strive to reduce the potential for user error through careful interface design, users should be able to correct any errors they make. For example, we should make sure that users are able to retract badges that

Figure 9.2 Issuing system interface

they might have accidentally issued. To assess this functionality, a tester might be given the following instructions:

- A Superstar badge may have accidentally been given to Sam Alcoveda. Identify whether or not the badge was issued in error and retract the badge if it has been issued.

Of course, any good system should not only enable a user to complete the task, but should enable that user to do so easily and efficiently. Just about any issuing system might feel efficient when one issuer is issuing badges to one earner, but what happens when the system scales up to include one issuer issuing badges to several hundred earners? This can be a monotonous task; if a 300-earner system requires five clicks to issue a badge and badges can only be issued one at a time, giving the same badge to all 300 earners would require 1,500 clicks. This is a time-consuming and potentially carpal-tunnel-inducing process if the system has many badges.

Thus, in addition to making sure the system works, it should also be examined for efficiency with regard to scalability. Designers can sometimes be unaware of user workload and should communicate closely with users to see how they use the system. This will help avoid potential problems. In this specific scenario, even being able to reduce the process by one click would be substantial. However, other fixes might be even more useful. If badges will frequently be given out to multiple users at once, testing might reveal cumbersome processes that can be optimized. For instance, rather than issuing badges one at a time per student, selecting students (or premade groups of students) using checkboxes and then choosing the badge(s) to send to all of them might be a useful way to reduce the issuer's workload and improve efficiency. Interface design and testing can be a deciding factor in whether the system is useful and efficient or too burdensome to be worth implementing.

Notification System

The notification system lets earners know that they have earned a badge. Whenever an issuer sends a badge to an earner, the notification system tells the earner that a badge has been earned. However, a good notification system should also make clear which badge was earned and why it was earned. It should do all of this in a relatively unobtrusive, yet timely manner – a balancing act, to be sure. Figure 9.3 provides an example that includes the name of the earner and badge, the badge's image, and a brief description of the badge.

Earlier in this book, we discussed the importance of timely rewards and feedback; to be most effective, badges that reward or provide feedback should follow completion of the task being recognized, as quickly as possible. This seems like a simple consideration to handle until we consider badges that might be earned during fast-paced gameplay, time-based math exercises, threat-detection simulations, or while the earner's phone is in their pocket during a running session. In these situations, how do we handle notifications?

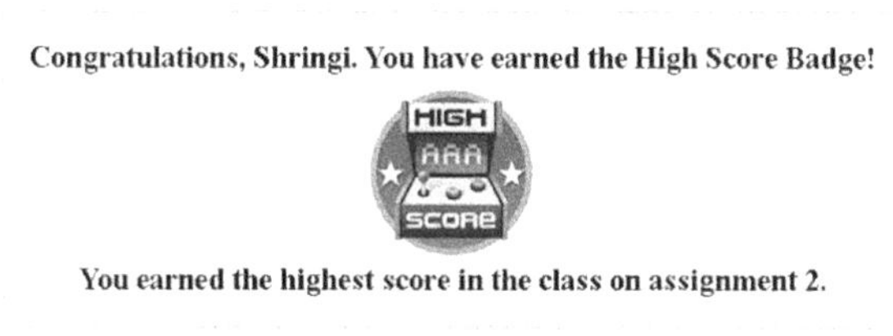

Congratulations, Shringi. You have earned the High Score Badge!

You earned the highest score in the class on assignment 2.

Figure 9.3 Badging notification

Ultimately, the particulars of the usage situation and purpose should dictate design. If we recall that badges communicate information from the issuer and system to the user, we can make decisions based on the importance of the time-liness and saliency of this information to the user. Do players urgently need to know that they defeated their 100th enemy during a difficult boss fight? If not, perhaps the notification can be delayed until the boss fight ends, at which point all notifications for badges earned during that fight can be shown at once. However, maybe it *is* important to receive that information right away. Perhaps the 100th enemy's defeat is when the player unlocks a new ability that must be immediately used, lest they will lose the fight. In this case, location and size of the notification should be intentionally designed to be unobtrusive, taking care to not occlude any important user interface elements or portions of the screen necessary for the actual fight.

These, then, are the considerations for testing. Allow earners to use the system and ensure that notifications are not obstructing important visual ele-ments. Consider the times when users should be shown the entire badge, a simple notification letting the user know they have earned a badge, or when notifications should wait until after the earner finishes their current task. We might ask testers to answer particular questions to learn more about the noti-fication system, such as these:

- Did you receive a notification about a new badge during the previous scenario?
- On a scale of 1 to 5, where 1 is very little and 5 is very much, how much did the badge notification distract you from your task?

System Access: Permissions and Restrictions

System access is a key point of functionality that ensures users have the ability to perform the necessary functions within the system and that per-mission is restricted only to authorized users. Further, certain users should be able to access only certain portions of the system. Issuers need to be able to view the interface that allows them to issue badges, but they might also need to be able to view portions of the earner interface. Perhaps they need to ensure that badges are being properly given, or maybe this access is helpful to aid in troubleshooting for users who are just learning to use the badging system.

While issuer access is necessarily quite open, earner access will typically be restrictive. Earners should have access to their showcase. In addition to seeing their own earned badges, the showcase might also display a list of available badges not yet earned. Depending on the designers' desire to introduce social factors into the badging system, it might also offer the ability to see the showcases of other users. Users should not have access to the issuing interface since the integrity of the badge-issuing process is a central keystone to the ethos and value of badging. A potential third level of system access might be given to an administrator who can oversee the entirety of the system. However, in smaller systems, this role is generally fulfilled by the issuer.

Regardless of the role, each user type should be created and tested for access. While this might seem straightforward, missing the small details can be disastrous for a badging system with value that depends on its credibility. Thus, the tester should methodically attempt to access each portion of the badging system with each account type, noting what they can and cannot access, and comparing this to the list of parts they should and should not be able to access. Of course, testers might not have this ability if they are using a commercial system instead of a homemade badging system. As we noted in Chapter 6, pre-existing badging systems might not offer the flexibility of systems built from the ground up. This is one of those instances.

System Testing

In the previous section, we turned our focus to some of the major badging subsystems that should be tested. Note that these do not compose an exhaustive list of testing points, but some of the major ones that will be present in most badging systems. Ultimately, all system components should be tested thoroughly, since specific elements will vary based on the particular system being used. However, the ones discussed above are common in many systems.

Now, we turn our attention to formally testing the system, including and extending beyond those subsystems. When we refer to formal testing, we mean testing with explicit and rigorous methodologies and associated factors. We begin by defining the requirements specification. This is a formal document that describes the essential components to a system's design. We outline how it can be extended to create a thorough testing plan and proceed to describe testing of badging system functionality. The testing plan relies on the system's specifications, which we will now discuss.

Requirements Specification

Every developed system has requirements that must be fulfilled in order for it to be considered successful. These requirements are critical to the successful development of that system (Yamamoto, 2017). The requirements specification is the document that gathers and lists, in a systematic manner, all of the requirements that the system must fulfill. These requirements are gathered from the various stakeholders in a system (Zowghi & Coulin, 2005). In badging, this might include potential earners, issuers, investors, and anyone else who is or might be affected by the badging system.

A system's requirements should be specified at the beginning of the project in order to ensure development has a clear vision and path. Yet, the particular way in which each requirement is written can influence testing. For this reason, we first examine requirements within a specification document before showing how they can be used to generate a testing plan. The requirements specification examines the desired final qualities of the system. It answers design questions such as "what should it be able to do?" and "how should it look and behave?" When creating a requirements specification for a badging system, it is important to be specific as possible with each requirement. A requirement might state:

- *The system shall allow users to view their badges and share them to their ePortfolio.*

Unfortunately, this is a poorly written requirement as it refers to two different requirements: the system shall allow users to (1) view their badges and (2) share them to their ePortfolio. When requirements are compounded in this manner, it is easy to make mistakes and overlook the latter part of the requirement. This can also lead to misreading or misinterpreting requirements.

Further, it is more difficult to reference them when discussing development. This problem is mitigated by numbering each requirement for easy reference (e.g., requirement 1.1.2). If we consider that all aesthetic requirements are under the number 1 and all functional requirements are under the number 2, we see how these requirements are organized. Subcategories for the functional requirements might also be broken down into sections, where 1 refers to earner functions and 2 refers to issuer functions. Here, we might be able to label and discuss requirements like these:

- *Requirement 2.2.1* – Issuers shall be able to view a list of all earner badges on the "Badge List" page.
- *Requirement 2.2.2* – Issuers shall be able to use a dropdown box to filter the earner badges by each specific earner on the "Badge List" page.

When planning out who develops which portion of the system, developers can be assigned a series of requirement numbers to ensure they know exactly what they are responsible for. Likewise, discussion of requirements, especially via e-mail, is facilitated by referring to requirement numbers. This can avoid the miscommunication of requirements in hastily written e-mail messages. This assumes the requirement itself is clearly written, of course. All developers can have a copy of the requirements specification for easy reference.

Ultimately, this specification document might take the form of a spreadsheet, where columns exist for the requirement's number and description. It might also include further information, such as which stakeholder requested the requirement. While this document enables a team to better communicate and develop, it is also useful for helping the development team understand the features stakeholders request. The development team should strongly consider sharing this document with stakeholders and asking them to sign off on the requirements to ensure that they agree upon the system's qualities before development begins. However, this is with the understanding, of course, that sometimes plans do not go as expected and some flexibility might be required throughout development.

Testing Plan

Since the requirements specification articulates each requirement for the badging system in extreme detail, the document is a useful testing tool to ensure all requirements are met. Each requirement should be systematically tested for completion to ensure that the developed system is ready for release. To do this, the person in charge of testing might choose to modify the requirements specification to incorporate a testing plan. If adopting this approach, you might consider adding the following columns:

- *Testing Method* (e.g., "Think aloud"): designates a specific type of test to each individual requirement so that there is no question about how to test those requirements.
- *Tester* (e.g., "Jorge Ramirez"): assigns responsibility for testing a requirement to a particular person so each person knows what they are responsible for testing.
- *Satisfactory* (e.g., "Yes"): specifies the result of testing for each requirement.
- *Sign Off*: to maintain accountability, the tester can sign when they have completed testing of the requirement.
- *Testing Notes* (e.g., "after trying X, Y happened. Needs further development."): any notes on the testing process. Perhaps testing did not go as planned and needs to be reconsidered, or maybe the requirement was not yet satisfactory. These notes help the developers understand why, and what, needs to be done.

In this way, each badging system requirement can be tracked and tested. At any point, anyone on the project team can check the document and see the status of each individual requirement, understanding what still needs to be done. After the testing plan has been completed, all requirements should have been met. This reduces the risk associated with incomplete testing before release.

Functional Testing

Functional testing is the testing of software to ensure it works properly by meeting all functionality requirements specified throughout the development process (Nidhra & Dondeti, 2012). This is tightly linked to the requirements specification document we discussed earlier. It involves entering a series of inputs into the system and observing the outputs. Inputs can take a number of forms, from issuing a badge to clicking a badge to see its metadata.

While the development team will likely first try out each point of functionality to ensure it is working, this test should be conducted, ideally by an independent tester, before functional testing can be considered successful. Throughout development, the development team will interact with the software in particular ways and gain specific interaction habits. These habits form through consistent, long-term experiences with the software and often do not represent how a new user would interact with the system. This is a common problem in videogame development, for example, where developers play their own games so much they end up with an inaccurate view of the game's difficulty (Rouse III, 2005). Thus, during functional testing, independent testers are needed to ensure the system is functioning even for novice users. Game developers call this process "protecting the noob," as in making sure the "noobs" or "newbie users" are sufficiently protected so that they do not immediately abandon the project (Rouse III, 2005). You can hire these independent testers from a company that performs this type of testing, or, on smaller-scale projects, other team members or associates who did not play a role in the design or development of the system can serve as testers. Regardless of where these users come from, they should understand or be trained in these proper testing procedures.

When testing for satisfaction of the functional requirements, it is important to consider depth of testing. Consider the following requirements:

- After an issuer issues a badge, earners shall receive a notification of badge earning.
- Earning notifications shall contain the badge with its associated title and description.
- Earning notifications shall contain text that indicates the time of earning.
- Earning notifications shall contain text that indicates the reason for earning.
- After earning a badge, the badge will be added to the earner's badging showcase page.

Issuing one badge and ensuring all of these requirements are met might be tempting; however, it would be insufficient. Each badge should be tested for compliance with these requirements, as different badges can behave differently if there are variations in their underlying code. In major badging systems where there are too many badges to test individually, automated testing scripts might be written that produce output logs that highlight any failures. When this is not possible due to technical or other limitations, a sufficiently large sampling of badges might be tested, with hopes that the sample is large enough to be representative of the badging system as a whole. This is obviously not ideal, but might be a necessary limitation when resources are thin.

User Testing

Functional testing is important to ensure that all of the system's functional requirements are being met. However, while a system might be functioning, its users could be frustrated, bored, or distracted. The way a system functions affects the way its users interact with the system, as well as how they feel when using the system. This is where user testing begins. This process examines the impact of the system on the user. More specifically, *usability* examines the extent to which software can be used by users to achieve a specific goal, in a specific context, in an effective, efficient, and satisfactory manner (International Organization for Standardization, 1998). Closely related to usability is *user experience* (UX), which regards the user's thoughts, feelings, and perceptions that emerge from use or anticipated use of the software (Albert & Tullis, 2013; International Organization for Standardization, 2010). For a badging system to be effective, it needs to provide a good user experience for its users. In this section, we examine several factors for measuring how a digital badging system affects its users.

Usability Errors

When we discuss usability errors in user testing, we are discussing how a user succeeds or fails in improving the system's use, which could include system failure, or design shortcomings that lead to user errors. An example might be a user who attempts to click a hyperlink on a web-based badging system but misses. Now, we might say that this is the user's fault, and move on. However, it could be the case that the hyperlink was too small and difficult to accurately click, pointing to a fixable shortcoming in the design that prompted the user error.

So, while one type of usability error is missing the intended target, another error is successfully clicking the intended target, but then realizing that it was not the right target. Consider the scenario where we successfully click a button labeled "Assign," thinking that it will lead us to place where we can assign badges to users. Unfortunately, it leads us to a place where we can assign tasks to our users instead (e.g., assignments). There will always be outlier users that will misclick or misjudge; however, we should pay attention when multiple users begin to make the same mistake and identify if there might be a shortcoming in our badging system. We should always design with errors in mind. This means trying to prevent the emergence of errors or providing paths for recovery once mistakes are made (Abras, Maloney-Krichmar, & Preece, 2004). Prediction and detection are the first steps to being able to do this.

Intrinsic Motivation

Intrinsic motivation (Ryan & Deci, 2000) is the motivation to do some particular thing simply for the rewards inherent in doing that thing, and not for some external reward. This construct has reappeared in several places throughout this book. It makes yet another appearance here because it is also commonly used in badging user research. Typically, it is measured through the interest/enjoyment subscale of the Intrinsic Motivation Inventory, or IMI (SelfDeterminationTheory.org, n.d.). The IMI is a validated scale created by the researchers who first described the construct.

Intrinsic motivation might seem like an odd thing to measure in a badging system. After all, if the user is motivated to complete a task only because they will receive a badge, they are not intrinsically motivated. They are extrinsically motivated by the external reward of badges. However, while a user might initially be motivated solely by the prospect of gaining badges, continued interaction with the system might improve intrinsic motivation in tandem. Recall that intrinsic motivation is enhanced when a person feels competent enough to complete a task. If a learner feels incapable of completing a more complicated task but tries some basic tasks to earn badges, learning along the way, she might inadvertently increase her competence. This, in turn, improves her motivation to interact with more advanced course content. This is why intrinsic motivation can be useful to measure, even when extrinsic rewards such as badges are used.

Engagement

Engagement is another great construct to measure because it indicates the user's willingness to take an active role in the task (McDaniel & Fanfarelli, 2015). Questionnaires are useful tools for measuring engagement. In education, the Classroom Survey of Student Engagement (Ouimet & Smallwood, 2005), or the Student Course Engagement Questionnaire (Handelsman, Briggs, Sullivan, & Towler, 2005) might be useful for this purpose. However, many surveys exist in the educational realm and it is worth taking the time to review the research to see if there are surveys available for the specific type of engagement you wish to examine. When badges in games or simulations are being studied, alternative engagement questionnaires, such as the Game Engagement Questionnaire by Brockmeyer, Fox, McBroom, Curtiss, Burkhart, and Pidruzny (2009), might be more relevant. The Game Engagement Questionnaire is a valid and reliable survey used to measure player engagement, immersion, flow, presence, and absorption. These factors yield plenty of useful data to better understand how the game or simulation is affecting its users.

Other non-questionnaire methods (e.g., McDaniel & Fanfarelli, 2015) might also be useful when additional metrics are desired or users are unavailable for questioning. There might be cases where users have already completed a number of different tasks and adding a questionnaire would be overly burdensome. If engagement describes a user's willingness to actively engage with the system, we might measure frequency of interactions, number of interactions, or time on task to measure engagement. If users are frequently logging in, completing activities, or otherwise browsing content, they are likely highly engaged. On the other hand, users who are minimally engaged probably will not spend much time with the system.

Demographics

As with any system, different users may interact with or benefit from the system in different ways. For example, one's prior experience can influence one's dispositions toward that system. If a user used something similar in the past and had a good experience, it is likely that they will look forward to using the new system, and vice versa for the opposite scenario. For this reason, you should collect demographic data to better understand effective and ineffective design elements for different user backgrounds.

The normal demographic information (e.g., age, gender, and ethnicity) are useful to collect as a starting point. Consider a website that caters to an elderly population. This website might be frequented by two major groups of users – the elderly, to whom this site directly applies, and their younger caregivers. In such an instance, results might reveal confusing results (perhaps a bimodal distribution, for those who are statistically inclined), where one group of users rates the system quite high, and another rates it very low. If the system is primarily designed for one group of users, the other group might find it unintelligible, inefficient, or otherwise hassling. If this result is observed, the data can be cross-referenced with the demographics to identify how the design might be refined to cater to a broader group of users. Ultimately, collecting demographic information improves knowledge regarding the breakdown of system users and their attitudes toward the system, which can enable better decision-making about planned designs, user interactions, and badging features.

Performance Metrics

Depending on the system's purpose, collecting metrics related to earner performance might yield insight into the system's effectiveness. The specific measures chosen will greatly depend upon the system being studied (McDaniel & Fanfarelli, 2015). For example, a running app might use weekly distance as a performance measure, while a military marksmanship simulator might consider shot accuracy. Likewise, in badging systems for formal educational applications, final grade or number of assignments submitted might be appropriate measures to see if the badging system is positively influencing any of these metrics. Ultimately, a decision must be made on what constitutes success and failure.

These results should be considered in combination with other metrics described in this chapter. If students' final grades did not change once the badging system is introduced, we might consider the badging system to be a failure, but what if engagement *did* increase? While the performance measure did not show an increase, students seemed to want to engage with the system more often. Perhaps the ways in which they engaged were not conducive to improving grades. In this case, some slight design changes might take advantage of that increase in engagement to steer student behaviors toward something even more beneficial, like completing more practice problems, engaging in more discussion with their peers, or improving their study skills.

Badges Earned

Regardless of the other metrics you have collected, we argue that you should always collect data on which badges, and how many badges, were actually earned by each user. This data should be compared with the other metrics to see if badge earning behavior made a difference. While this sort of correlational data is currently lacking in the research, some studies have found it to be useful. For example, Fanfarelli & McDaniel (2015) found that student satisfaction, final grades, intrinsic motivation, and productive learning practices increased as students earned more badges.

Consider a practical example. If the data shows that users who used a version of our website with a badging system performed no differently from users who used a version without the badging system, we might conclude that the badging system was ineffective. We would be right, but perhaps we misconstrued the reasons behind this result. If users in the badged system received zero or very few badges, the badging system might never have had a chance to work, and the reasons behind the low number of earned badges should be investigated. Perhaps the badges were too hard to earn and we need to review their completion logics. Alternatively, if users had to manually claim or apply for badges, the process to do so might have been too complex, tedious, or poorly communicated to the users.

Or, consider that a correlation might exist between number of badges earned and another metric. If each badge earned made a user feel more capable, larger numbers of badges earned might have improved constructs such as self-efficacy or motivation, both of which can improve performance in a range of scenarios. If such an effect is found, there might be cause to identify ways in which users can be encouraged to earn more badges from the start. Or, it might be possible to identify why some users earned more badges than others. The direction of causation here is important: did earning more badges increase self-efficacy, or did users with higher self-efficacy earn more badges? Either of these is likely to have design implications.

While knowing the overall number of badges earned is useful, sometimes the earning or non-earning of a single badge can also be telling. In videogames, users who earn a badge for completing the level of a very violent game without killing a single enemy might differ in important ways from users who do not complete this achievement. Whether those who earn the badge desire a challenge or alternate gameplay opportunities, the results might indicate ways in which games can be designed for different user subgroups.

Methodologies

In order to cover all possible methodologies that could be used for testing, it would take a series of books. Thankfully, others have already written these, so we will not attempt to describe them here. Instead, in this section, we include a few easy to implement methodologies that you might find particularly useful in testing your badging system.

Surveys

In its most simplified form, surveying involves administering a list of questions to a user and then interpreting the results. It is a fast, efficient, and potentially effective methodology that can yield results that are also easily interpretable. Pre-existing surveys that have already been validated could be useful if they fit your purposes, but they might also be limited in the constructs they can test. Alternatively, surveys can be crafted by the design team to ask questions specifically about the badging system in question. However, this should be done with care; poorly crafted surveys can yield unreliable data that could mislead redesign efforts. For example, questions could be inadvertently phrased in a leading manner that unintentionally biases the results (Goodman, Kuniavsky, & Moed, 2010). For example, consider two Likert-style questions:

- How much did you enjoy the visual design of the badges? 1 = did not enjoy; 5 = enjoyed very much
- Please rate the visual design of the badges. 1 = low; 5 = high

The first item uses positive framing and could bias the user toward the positive side of the scale. While the scale itself seems reasonable, leading off with "enjoy" might cause problems. Consider if the survey said "How much did you dislike the visual design of the badges?" Here, we would be introducing bias in the negative direction. In contrast, the second item does not put forth an opinion. It is neither positively nor negatively phrased.

A/B Testing

A/B testing involves showing a user two different versions of the same design to see which is better. Specific elements, such as performance or aesthetics, can be targeted (Hanington & Martin, 2012). This type of method is especially useful when the design team splits their opinions between multiple designs. A/B testing can be useful for visual design, but it might also be useful for deciding which version of a feature provides a better user experience. We might consider the following questions when using A/B testing:

- Which issuing system interface is easier for issuers to use?
- Which font is more legible for badging descriptions on the mobile version?
- Which color scheme is the most appealing?

Device Testing

At this point, making digital systems accessible on multiple devices has become standard practice. Websites, for example, are accessible on desktop computers, phones, and tablets. However, the user experience can vary substantially between these devices. When it comes to badges, some specific considerations might include the following:

- Are all badges and associated text viewable and legible on small displays?
- Do badges fit nicely on all displays, or do users have to do an annoying amount of scrolling to see them all?
- Do badge images load efficiently on slower Internet speeds, or do they need to be scaled down, or converted to a more efficient file format?
- Do the issuing and receiving functions work appropriately on all interfaces? While a dropdown box might be useful on a desktop computer, it might be difficult to click on a mobile phone if it is too small.

Think Aloud Testing

Concurrent think aloud testing is a widely used technique that asks participants to verbalize what they are doing and thinking while using the system (Olmsted-Hawala, Murphy, Hawala, & Ashenfelter, 2010). It can be difficult to understand what a user is attempting to do, thinking about, or feeling during interaction, so verbalizing thoughts helps testers understand the user. For example, a user can verbalize that they are trying to find their earned badges, are looking at the upper left of the page, and are feeling frustrated because they do not see it. If many users describe these same things, the design team might consider relocating the badges to that position or otherwise find a way to better lead the user to the current position.

A Note of Caution

There are some caveats to keep in mind when working with direct observation methods. While evaluation methodologies that include behavioral observation often yield valuable data, they can also negatively influence the user and the resultant data. According to the Hawthorne effect, users might purposely or inadvertently adjust their behavior in response to being watched (McCambridge, Witton, & Elbourne, 2014). The precise mechanisms behind why and when this occurs are still being studied. However, we can consider scenarios of when this might occur. For example, a user who is embarrassed by her actions might choose alternate actions during observation, instead of the ones she might have conducted in the privacy of her own home. Or, a user who thinks he is moving too slowly through the testing session might try to rush to finish, especially if he looks at the observers and believes they seem impatient or ready to wrap up and go home for the night – similar to being at a restaurant around closing time. The observer-expectancy effect, which describes the possibility for an observer to subconsciously influence the user, might also be relevant in these situations (Andujar & Brunet, 2015).

Thus, observers should be mindful of their presence and behaviors when looking over the interactions of digital badging users. They might communicate unintentional messages. For example, repeatedly looking at one's watch might communicate impatience and a desire to finish. This is a good general rule for observers as there are a number of ways they can influence users, even beyond communicating unintentional messages. Making too much noise or motion can distract the user, reducing performance, and helping a user through a difficulty might advantage the user, improving their performance. For this reason, it is important to keep interaction to a minimum during experimental sessions. If observer effects seem likely, video/audio and screen capture might be deemed preferable so that behavioral data can be extracted at a later time, without as much intrusiveness to the user during testing.

Next Up

This chapter examined the assessment of badging systems, providing a number of considerations, metrics, and methods that are useful for digital badge studies. The next chapter focuses on novelty of design in badging systems. While badging has received quite a bit of attention in recent years, digital badging is still a relatively new topic of study compared to most and innovation is happening at a rapid pace. Innovation and invention are quite important to emerging digital applications and badging systems are no different. As you read the next chapter, you will begin to consider how to define novelty, relate it to badging system design, and evaluate it.

References

Abras, C., Maloney-Krichmar, D., & Preece, J. (2004). User-centered design. In W. Bainbridge (Ed.), *Encyclopedia of human-computer interaction* (pp. 763–768). Thousand Oaks, CA: Sage Publications.

Albert, W., & Tullis, T. (2013). *Measuring the user experience: Collecting, analyzing, and presenting usability metrics* (2nd ed.). Waltham, MA: Morgan Kaufman.

Andujar, C., & Brunet, P. (2015). A critical analysis of human-subject experiments in virtual reality and 3D user interfaces. In G. Brunnett, S. Coquillart, R. van Liere, G. Welch, & L. Vasa (Eds.), *Virtual realities* (pp. 79–90). Dagstuhl, Germany: Springer.

Brockmeyer, J. B., Fox, C., McBroom, E., Curtiss, K., Burkhart, K., & Pidruzny, J. (2009). The development of the Game Engagement Questionnaire: A measure of levels of engagement in video game-playing. *Journal of Experimental Social Psychology, 49*, 624–634.

Fanfarelli, J. R., & McDaniel, R. (2015). Individual differences in digital badging: Do learner characteristics matter? *Journal of Educational Technology Systems, 43*(4), 403–428.

Goodman, E., Kuniavsky, M., & Moed, A. (2010). *Observing the user experience: A practitioner's guide to user research* (2nd ed.). Waltham, MA: Morgan Kaufman.

Handelsman, M. M., Briggs, W. L., Sullivan, N., & Towler, A. (2005). A measure of college student course engagement. *Journal of Educational Research, 93*(3), 184–191.

Hanington, B., & Martin, B. (2012). *Universal methods of design: 100 ways to research complex problems, develop innovative ideas, and design effective solutions.* Beverly, MA: Rockport Publishers.

International Organization for Standardization (1998). ISO 9241-11: Ergonomic requirements for office work with visual display terminals (VDTs) – Part 11: Guidance on usability.

International Organization for Standardization (2010). ISO 9241-210: Ergonomics of human-system interaction – Part 210: Human-centered design for interactive systems.

McCambridge, J., Witton, J., & Elbourne, D. R. (2014). Systematic review of the Hawthorne effect: New concepts are needed to study research participation effects. *Journal of Clinical Epidemiology, 67*(3), 267–277.

McDaniel, R., & Fanfarelli, J. R. (2015, March). How to design experimental research studies around digital badges. In D. Hickey, J. Jovanovic, S. Lonn, & J. E. Willis III (Eds.), *Proceedings of the Open Badges in Education (OBIE 2015) Workshop* (pp. 1–6). Poughkeepsie, New York.

Nidhra, S., & Dondeti, J. (2012). Black box and white box testing techniques: A literature review. *International Journal of Embedded Systems and Applications, 2*(2), 29–50.

Olmsted-Hawala, E. L., Murphy, E. D., Hawala, S., & Ashenfelter, K. T. (2010). Think-aloud protocols: A comparison of three think-aloud protocols for use in testing data-dissemination web sites for usability. In *Proceedings of CHI 2010* (pp. 2381–2390). Atlanta, GA: ACM.

Ouimet, J. A., & Smallwood, R. A. (2005). Assessment measures: CLASSE – The class learning survey of student engagement. *Assessment Update, 17*(6), 13–15.

Rouse III, R. (2005). *Game design theory and practice* (2nd ed.). Plano, TX: Wordware Publishing.

Ryan, R. M., & Deci, E. L. (2000). Self-determination theory and the facilitation of intrinsic motivation, social development, and well-being. *American Psychologist, 55*(1), 68–78.

SelfDeterminationTheory.org. (n.d.). Intrinsic motivation inventory (IMI). *Self-Determination Theory: An Approach to Human Motivation and Personality*. Retrieved from www.selfdeterminationtheory.org/questionnaires/10-questionnaires/50

Sharp, H., Rogers, Y., & Preece, J. (2007). *Interaction design: Beyond human-computer interaction* (2nd ed.). East Sussex, UK: John Wiley & Sons.

Terry, M., Matthew, K., & Lafreniere, B. (2010). Perceptions and practices of usability in the free/open source software (FOSS) community. In *Proceedings of CHI 2010* (pp. 999–1008). Atlanta, GA: ACM.

Yamamoto, S. (2017). An evaluation of requirements specification capability index. In C. Zanni-Merk, C. Frydman, C. Toro, Y. Hicks, R. J. Howlett, & L. C. Jain (Eds.), *Proceedings of the 20th International Conference on Knowledge Based and Intelligent Information and Engineering Systems* (pp. 998–1006). Marseille, France: Elsevier.

Zowghi, D., & Coulin, C. (2005). Requirements elicitation: A survey of techniques, approaches, and tools. In A. Aurum & C. Wohlin (Eds.), *Engineering and managing software requirements* (pp. 19–46). Berlin, Germany: Springer.

CHAPTER 10

Novelty and Badging

Overview

In this chapter, we acknowledge a central point about digital badges, which is that they are still very new. This means there is much to discover as they evolve into different structures and are used in new ways, for new purposes. Like other modern technologies useful for shaping behavior, trends and developments in hardware and software as well as new strategies for teaching and assessment will influence the ways we use badges in the future. In essence, then, this chapter strives to be predictive. Using two different themes for conceptualizing novelty – recurrence and recombination – we discuss the challenges with properly describing novelty and its attributes and how these two themes are useful for considering novel themes in badging through different perspectives. We first consider recurrence, which analyzes how the past can be remediated into contemporary digital badging systems and explains how technologies and ideas are often cyclical in nature. We then ponder how existing technologies from disparate domains can be combined in new ways to yield exciting new developments in badging technology. We also discuss the role of invention in the creative process and note how the act of invention is often motivated by the need to address prior flaws or deficiencies. The chapter concludes by considering the question of assessment. Given what we already know about badges and about evaluating novelty, how can we be better prepared to assess and evaluate what is on the horizon for these digital objects? What might new badging systems track in terms of learning and performance outcomes, and how can we plan to appropriately measure those outcomes? We consider these questions as we build toward our final chapter: the future of digital badges.

The Trouble with Novelty

In his book *Novelty: A History of the New*, North (2013) outlines a number of problems with scholarly attempts to understand the concept of novelty. For one thing, the word novelty – and its lack of sufficient synonyms – shows that

English as a language is deficient in providing us with a vocabulary to discuss novelty in satisfactory detail and with adequate clarity about the type of novelty we mean. Words like "newness," for example, are synonymous with novelty, but they struggle to sufficiently clarify exactly what it is about an idea or product that pushes it into the category of innovation or originality. The essence of what is meant by novelty is also difficult to conceptualize. Various mental models of novelty might be subjectively different depending on who is observing or evaluating an object or idea. Similarly, the threshold or ratio of new to old is difficult to describe and standardize as a baseline requirement for novelty. All of this means our individual perceptions of novelty can vary greatly.

Another challenge is the cultural baggage associated with novelty. Stylistic movements in fashion, for example, challenge the concept of newness by cyclically reintroducing previous fashions in order to make the old new again. Other cultural and creative works assert the pointlessness of trying to classify things according to their degree of originality or freshness. We see this frequently in the art world. North (2013), for example, quotes Robert Smithson's decree that "Nothing is new, neither is anything old" and writes of the modernist art movement's uneasy relationship with art in the 1960s. North writes:

> In fact, the whole distinction between modernist art and that which followed in the 1960s, a distinction that once seemed so epochal, was based on an apparent disagreement about the very possibility of the new and about the desirability of associated qualities such as originality and autonomy. All of these were blown away like so much dust, it seemed, when Andy Warhol promoted some Campbell's Soup cans from the supermarket to the art gallery.
>
> (p. 1)

Indeed, many contemporary artists reappropriate imagery, language, and symbolism from pop culture or commercial enterprise into their own works to make statements about the commodification of art or fetishism or the relationships between the past and present. Artist Bill Claps' work titled *It's All Derivative: Campbell's Soup, Light Gold*, for example, further extends Warhol's Campbell's Soup imagery by overlaying Morse code atop the iconic image to continue to explore methods of appropriation in art. In this case, the consumerist connotations added by Warhol's famous Campbell's Soup cans are further linked to the past through a layering of technological imagery now rarely used outside of military and emergency training. This is a case in which the work seems new, but its newness is achieved through the inclusion of non-new things.

North (2013) maintains that when these longstanding historical ideas or remixed products can so prominently feature into novel, hip, or fashionable movements, it is difficult to argue that novelty must require the creation of something entirely original. Indeed, as we have discussed in earlier chapters, even though what we are now referring to as digital badges or microcredentials are currently popular in educational technology and instructional design contexts, their core functionality was established many years ago in the military and in scouting organizations. In fact, as we discuss later in this chapter, the roots of some digital badging functions go back even deeper into history into the very beginnings of organized human society. Even though the contemporary technologies that are implanting these features are different, many of the same core ideas about how they work are very similar to prior concepts and techniques used throughout history.

Despite these historical and definitional challenges, North notes that our collective human desire for new things "seems to be a fairly durable human quality, and interest in it persists even now, after its role in the worlds of art and fashion has been exposed and debunked" (2013, p. 1). He cites examples of the computer industry and consumer electronics, where a continuous investigation of new interfaces and features is central to their business models, and of research in biology, where evolutionary novelty is a central issue in arguments between developmental and molecular biologists. Given its usefulness in research and practice combined with its conceptual and definitional difficulty, North acknowledges that novelty is in fact "an indispensable concept and a serious problem, not just in one but in a number of different disciplines" (p. 5). Because of its essential tendency to highlight new and innovative approaches, novelty is useful for highlighting interdisciplinary or multidisciplinary approaches to problem solving. The revolutionary mobile devices discussed at length in Chapter 7, for example, were not novel merely because of their advancements in computer technology. Instead, their newness was striking because these mobile devices paired such advancements in hardware design with new ideas from interface design and new approaches to the integration of hardware, software, and a touch-based user experience.

Ultimately, North articulates two themes that are useful for thinking about novelty. We argue they are similarly useful for discussing novelty as it pertains to digital badging. One theme is recurrence, a phenomenon that appears commonly in nature but does not seem to offer "real" novelty in the sense that something is wholly original. The other is recombination, which seems to offer unlimited possibilities for new things, but only if we allow for new relationships between existing ideas or objects to be considered novel. We acknowledge the philosophical and linguistic challenges with novelty that North has articulated and implement these ideas of recurrence and recombination to use as frames for thinking about novelty in relation to digital badging. Both of these strategies for thinking about novelty are presented in more detail later in this chapter.

What Are Novel Badging Systems?

Before unpacking generative techniques for novel design in more detail, we will begin our treatment of novelty in digital badging with the practical exercise of defining what we mean by novelty within this domain. This allows us to move toward another goal in this chapter, which is to consider how we might evaluate such systems for the purposes of performance or learning assessment. The practical approach also allows us to engage with related concepts, such as invention, as a technique for considering the evolution of digital badging systems as devices constructed to solve problems or address shortcomings.

With this in mind, we define novel badging systems as implementations that approach digital badging in an innovative or unique way. We do not argue that system-wide originality is a prerequisite to novelty, although novel badging systems can certainly exhibit originality in various facets of their design. Novel badging systems might exhibit novelty through new ideas or through old ideas expressed in new configurations. This novelty can stem from the underlying technological layer of digital technologies, such as a system that takes advantage of new hardware or software capabilities to trigger badges in inventive ways, or from their guiding philosophy, such as a system that implements badging for a purpose not yet commonplace. They can also be novel in their approach to the surrounding contexts of digital badging, as in their treatment of the social spheres surrounding badge acquisition and sharing or their approach to assigning value to new types of rewards in badging economies.

Each of these associated areas can be novel. We can use the technological layer as an example. In Chapter 7, we wrote about a number of emerging technologies available to us on mobile devices, including biometric sensors. Biometric sensors are useful for a number of important tasks including recognition and identification (Jain, Ross, & Prabhakar, 2004), but they are also potentially useful for longitudinal tracking of physiological data. A novel badging system could be a new software program for digital badging that awards badges based on various types of biometric feedback that move beyond traditional fingerprint sensing or facial recognition. These types of mobile systems for tracking bodily functions and activities are already being developed and studied in mHealth research contexts (Lupton, 2013). When digital badges can be triggered by personalized biometric data and then tracked in a database for future analysis, many new opportunities for digital badges and their evaluation become viable. Consider a fitness app that awards badges to users when they are able to attain lower heart rates through continued cardiovascular exercise, or a meditation app that awards badges to users who increase alpha or theta brainwave activity through more skilled meditation. These examples suggest that one area of potential for future novel badging systems lies within the domain of biometrics.

The development of such new products such as mHealth-focused digital badging systems is one thing, but how will we know if audiences and users will actually seek them out and use them? Indeed, the ability to predict preferences about competing products is a nontrivial task and is something startup companies and large organizations alike struggle with on a routine basis. Fortunately, there is evidence that suggests humans are inclined to seek out novelty in their selection of products and systems. For instance, Supporting North's (2013) more recent assertion that seeking novelty appears to be a "durable human quality," classic studies that investigated how humans seek out new products provide evidence that humans are wired to seek out novelty in their everyday lives. In one example, Hirschman (1980) reviewed literature that explored novelty seeking in consumerism. Citing Flavell's (1977) work on cognitive development, she noted that when infants are presented with two equally intense visual stimuli, they select the novel stimulus over the familiar one. Hirschman (1980) wrote, "Thus, novelty seeking would seem to represent an innate search for information. However, even if novelty seeking is innate, it is logical to assume that it serves some constructive purpose to the individual" (p. 284). She then continued to consider the different purposes this behavior might fulfill, such as acquiring knowledge that could be useful for later situations or enhancing problem-solving skills that might improve future performance. Digital badges for infants are perhaps improbable, but it does make sense to consider novelty as a positive characteristic for many end users of badging systems. If this is something the users would like to see, then it is also something that badge designers should take into account.

Returning from consumer behaviors to our current domain, we can consider how novelty might be a desirable characteristic for digital badges in specific types of applications. For many purposes, such as motivating learning or encouraging other productive behaviors, badges and other gamification techniques are arguably useful precisely because of their novelty. In other words, they motivate learners by allowing them to experience the material in a new way, or by juxtaposing elements they encounter in entertainment, such as fantasy and reward, with the traditional course materials. When such tactics become more commonplace, though, then that element of originality might wear off and positive psychological benefits might wane. If every learning management system (LMS) uses Mozilla Open Badges, for example, then Mozilla Open Badges simply become another feature found in online learning, similar to discussion threads or chat windows or other essential LMS elements. When this occurs, it is useful to speculate about how badges may evolve to maintain originality and a sense of being outside the normal experiences of content traversal or knowledge acquisition. To brainstorm along these lines, it is useful to think more broadly about the inventive process through which novel systems are designed.

The Role of Invention

As we consider novelty as a probable descriptor for our digital badging systems of the future, then it is also useful to study the generative act that leads to this state of affairs. We can consider a novel technology on its own merits without knowing how it was created, but when we think about evaluation and assessment, we are often trying to consider a problem more broadly. For instance, a badging system designed to motivate users toward particular behaviors might be addressing underlying issues that exist around dry content or unengaging assignments. Understanding not only the system itself, but also the creative act that led to its existence, is useful as we think more holistically about both its implementation and its assessment. Stated another way, sometimes understanding the problem space is valuable because it gives us a clearer picture of the problems a system or technology intends to address. Knowing what these problems are can yield new assessment criteria for us to consider.

Reflecting upon the act of invention is one way of doing this. Invention can be thought of as a brainstorming heuristic, as an activity yielding new products or insights, or as a model for thinking differently. Invention is also one of the five classical canons of rhetoric, along with arrangement, style, memory, and delivery. Invention was widely regarded by Aristotle and other ancient philosophers as a critical device for improving one's memory, communication skills, and argumentation skills. In rhetorical studies, the term did not imply an ability to develop an original argument from scratch, but rather the ability for rhetoricians to "discover appropriate arguments in their research, in the course of their training, in reports of research by others, in other speeches or essays, and in cultural ideas" (Campbell, 1996, p. 212). Invention, then, was not drawing forth wholly original ideas from the ether, untethered to anything else. Rather, it was a method for appropriating concepts from one domain to another in a rhetorically appropriate way.

While rhetorical studies might initially seem far afield from our discussions about badging and learning, the same general principle is useful for contemplating the role of invention in novel badge design possibilities. It is more than likely, for example, that emerging badge designs will not be radical reinventions of what we have seen in prior implementations. Rather, they are likely to be gradual improvements that remedy some of the challenges and shortcomings identified both in existing systems and in the emerging contexts of use that accompany our changing technologies. As engineer Henry Petroski (1992) writes, "If the shortcomings of things are what drive their evolution, then inventors must be among technology's severest critics" (p. 34). Indeed, many technologies evolved because of the shortcomings of the technologies that preceded them.

History abounds with examples of technologies developed in this fashion. Consider the prolific inventor Jacob Rabinow who is discussed at length in the work of Petroski (1992). Over the course of his career as an engineer and inventor, Rabinow corrected shortcomings with new designs for many different devices and systems. He invented improvements for self-adjusting watches and phonograph needles. He refined the calibration systems for measuring the flow of water and tweaked the automatic letter sorting machines used by the Postal Service. Petroski notes that the core technique that drove Rabinow's prolific output was a simple one: finding the faults with existing things. While initial prototypes or early versions of technology might fully address the problems they were designed to accommodate, changing circumstances and new complications can render them impractical or even obsolete over time. First adopters of new digital technologies, for example, often identify faults with products that are corrected in subsequent releases. Similarly, public betas, or emerging products that are flawed but released early to willing consumers in order to garner additional feedback, are now common with software products.

As we consider the future of digital badging, then, it is natural to think carefully about the problems that we find in existing systems and how digital badges might address those problems. It is likely that future implementations will seek to remedy these issues and this can lend us some insight as to how we might evaluate them. Approaching the task as Petroski does, then, means considering at least two different types of faults. The first relates to the shortcomings that current digital badging systems are designed to address. Why are badges even needed in different types of activities? As we discussed in Part II, digital badges are useful in particular applications such as videogames or LMSs or mobile applications because they can shape behaviors or motivate the types of digital activities that users might not naturally gravitate toward on their own. In games, this might mean encouraging more exploration or inspiring gamers to spend more time building up particular skill attributes they would otherwise ignore. In LMSs, it might mean inciting learners to spend more time analyzing the work of their peers rather than focusing on their own deliverables. In mobile systems, it could involve rewarding learners who participate in seamless learning environments that bridge mobile and desktop devices. Articulating the types of faults we see now and predicting future faults on the horizon is one way of predicting the variations of yet-to-be-invented badging systems.

Another fault we must consider relates to the internal functionality of our existing badging systems. In the first case, we are looking outward to broader problems that badges are designed to address. In this case, we must look inward at the technologies themselves to evaluate the shortcomings of our existing products. We have been discussing a number of these shortcomings throughout the book – there are challenges with digital badges we must consider in psychological, technological, social, and economic dimensions, for example. The "cautionary notes" sections of our chapters in Part II also attest to some of the challenges present with digital badges deployed using specific types of technologies or in specific content domains.

For example, one argument against the digital badges used in videogames, as we discuss in Chapter 5, is that they are sometimes perceived to be a threat to the artistic integrity of the medium. Recall that some videogame critics such as Bogost (2010) characterized achievements in games as akin to the loyalty cards devised to encourage consumers to repeatedly return to a product or service. With this criticism in mind, how might future systems adapt to coexist more comfortably with other gaming elements such as core mechanics, story, and aesthetics? Perhaps more natural-feeling achievements that grow organically out of complex interactive environments might lie within the realm of possibility for future badging systems in game-based worlds. One way of doing this would be to bring badge designers into the design process very early in the development lifecycle rather than tacking them on to the game at the very end of its creation. Such an integrated approach to design might yield more symbiotic possibilities for the integration of digital badges with the essential features of the game. This tighter coupling might help address these criticisms raised by Bogost and other games scholars.

In order to be prepared for these types of evolution within digital technology and practice, it is useful to have a paradigm in mind for how we will evaluate novelty in future badging systems. In the next section, we propose some ideas for how we might approach this task. One method is to formulate a model that focuses on the measurement of outcomes rather than the evaluation of the systems themselves. However, before delving too deeply into specific approaches, we will first consider novelty as seen through the lenses of recurrence and recombination. This theoretical basis then forms a scaffold upon which we can build more precise systems for measurement. We begin with a discussion of recurrence.

Novelty as Recurrence

Recurrence is the first approach to conceptualizing novelty suggested by North (2013). Recurrence speaks to the cyclic nature of the new and the importance of the seemingly paradoxical historical dimension of newness. Many novel ideas are in fact new instantiations of older ideas, perhaps reshaped or newly contextualized by modern sensibilities. They might return to the public consciousness through a renewed interest, through repackaged perceptions, or through fashionable trends. For instance, North notes that when we consider them carefully, even artistically powerful terms such as "renaissance" and "revolution" do not mean starting from nothing. Instead, they suggest a state of innovation that blends the past with the present. In North's words, these concepts "imply return as much as they do advance, and even as metaphors they are repetitions of much older patterns of cyclical revival" (p. 36). North uses the example of evolution. Although it emerged as a major scientific concept and leap forward in our understanding of the universe and how life unfolds within it, and it certainly was, he notes that "it was often received as if it merely repackaged Epicurean ideas of random development" (p. 36). Thus, even when novelty does indeed show originality seemingly without historical precedent, our collective reactions to these novel ideas or concepts are necessarily grounded in the ideas and concepts we are already using to understand the world and our place in it.

While North's critical analysis of recurrence is mostly literary and philosophical, it is also helpful in an applied sense for contemplating the digital badges of the future. This is because his ideas about recurrence can be used as generative tools for helping us to think about where future badging systems might take us in domains such as teaching, entertainment, and training. For example, in an educational context, we might refer to historical approaches to understanding behavior and learning, as we discussed in Chapter 4, and consider how progress with technology might meld with classical behavioralist or cognitivist ideas toward learning and education. Or, we could go back even farther than this and consider the technologies of the Ancient Greeks or even the Babylonians. Are there ideas or techniques from this era that might recur to generate new ideas for digital badging systems?

Figure 10.1 Cylinder seal, Old Babylonian (By Hjaltland Collection [CC BY-SA 3.0 (https://creativecommons.org/licenses/by-sa/3.0)], from Wikimedia Commons)

This type of thinking is more squarely in the domain of our final chapter, which deals with the future of badging. However, we will offer one brief example here to support this argument. Our proof of concept focuses on the case of the cylinder seal (see Figure 10.1). Originating in the Late Neolithic Period (*c*.7600–6000 BCE) in ancient Mesopotamia, cylinder seals were small objects made from semiprecious stone that endured the elements for thousands of years. They remain today as some of the earliest technologies in existence. As antiquities, they are found in museum collections throughout the world (Mark, 2015). Although they might seem small and unimportant when viewed through a modern perspective, these objects were in fact quite useful and important to Mesopotamian daily life. As Mark (2015) notes, they were used as impression stamps to authenticate many types of daily transactions, from business deals to routine correspondence. Their owners would wear them on strings around their neck or pin them to clothing so that they could be accessed easily. When needed, the cylinder seals' owners could use them to add their personal signatures into cuneiform tablets. To do this, they would roll the seals on moist clay to leave an impression along with the other information inscribed on the tablet.

Does this type of technique sound familiar? It should, because it is one of the earliest known methods for credentialing, and it is certainly something that modern digital badge designers still see as a core purpose for this much more modern technology. Rather than credentialing performance, however, the cylinder seal credentialed identity. As the cylinder seal example illustrates, this activity of technology-mediated credentialing has recurred multiple times throughout history. It turns out that the authenticity of information, and the restriction of different types of content to properly vetted audiences, is a core problem that reappears throughout human history. Without some means for verifying the integrity of information and its deployment to the individuals who should have clearance to see it, we can easily imagine how counterfeiting, forgery, and propaganda could eclipse more legitimate functions of information transmission. Thus, as a lens for thinking about core human problems and how technology cyclically reoccurs to address those problems over time, recurrence is a useful theme for clarifying our thinking.

We can also use recurrence as a predictor to anticipate new potential uses for digital badges. For example, what if all users of digital badging systems of the future possessed their own, personalized, unique digital badge that they could add to documents and deliverables to endorse the performance of peers or verify the authenticity of information? Perhaps in addition to recognizing performance or achievement, digital badges could also play a role in new developments for cryptography, interfacing with or extending previously developed ideas about security such as the public/private key model of prior digital security technologies like Pretty Good Privacy (PGP). When directed toward these types of use cases, we can see how thinking about badging through the lens of recurrence might suggest particular directions that novel new designs could gravitate toward.

Recurrence is also useful for thinking about in terms of its implications for design. While software engineering in its early years followed a fairly linear pathway from concept to design to building to testing, modern software engineering for many interactive technologies is more cyclical in nature. Agile development methods incorporate frequent testing and iteration into their design process, meaning that initial ideas for functionality may emerge as rough proofs of concept and then gradually be improved and refined over time. Thus, we can imagine a scenario in which core ideas for new badging systems are established, perhaps through a very general design goal, like "badges should be able to talk to each other." Over time, then, this general goal becomes more concrete as this core idea recurs and becomes more sophisticated in subsequent builds.

Recurrence is one useful technique for thinking about novelty, but it is not the only tactic. In some instances, new ideas will appear that do not appear to have historical ancestors rooted in similar ideas of technologies. In these cases, a second model, recombination, might prove more useful. Rather than relying upon cyclical patterns of reintroduction or remediation, recombination instead acknowledges the powerful potential of combining ideas or techniques from different disciplines, domains, or contexts. By taking even well-established content from one place and combining it with similar content from another, recombination shows how novelty can emerge from new combinations of existing content rather than entirely new content.

Novelty as Recombination

Recombination is the act of combining things to produce new things. The term has roots in genetics where it speaks to the rearrangement of genetic material wherein offspring can be produced without traits found in either parent. Recombination is a second technique for considering novelty, building upon recurrence, and North (2013) notes that it was a significant idea used by Darwin in his thinking about principles of novelty in evolution. He writes:

> Like other models of novelty based on nature, evolution involves cycles of recurrence: the whole process depends on the necessity that species recreate themselves, generation by generation. For Darwin, though, the cycle of generation escapes the circular by incorporating an element of recombination, wherein particular traits and features are selected from a constant and constantly changing pool of variation.
>
> (pp. 71–72)

In genetic terms, then, there is a biological imperative for the use of recombination to keep human evolution novel to an extent by continuously introducing variations into our gene pool. Similarly, there are digital badging products or methods that can evolve novel features or functions by combining two different systems into a single framework. When such disparate systems are combined, this presents an opportunity to think about evaluation from the context of those initial systems and then consider which methods for assessment might carry forward into the new, combined configuration. For example, we mentioned earlier the possibility of biometric badges. Here, the combined domains include biometrics and digital badging. In addition to the assessment measures we have been considering for digital badges throughout this book, there are also additional measures that relate specifically to biometrics. These might include factors such as the accuracy of biometric data, the speed at which data collection occurs, the ability to eliminate false positive data, and so forth. In these types of situations, there might be evaluations to formulate for each independent system as well as a new set of evaluative criteria for the integrated system. In this case, for example, while biometrics and badging would each have their own individual criteria for success, we could also consider the interplay between the two areas. For example, are the most appropriate badges being awarded for the most appropriate biometric inputs? Does the speed at which a badge is delivered correspond appropriately to the speed at which biometric collection occurs? Are biological indicators positively influenced by the awarding of badges? All of these questions are pertinent when we consider the interplay of these combined areas.

A specific example makes this point more clear. Consider a mobile fitness game that uses biometric data to adjust gameplay parameters in real time. In this product, the combined domain is comprised of biometrics and video gaming. The premise of the game is this: due to a chemical contamination or disease outbreak or a mass ingestion of bath salts or some other appropriately zombifying catalyst, the world is overrun with zombies. Like traditional zombies, these creatures are antagonistic toward humans and want to convert as many humans to zombies as possible. Unlike traditional zombies, however, these zombies are capable of moving fast. Also, the zombification process is not limited to bites. Players can also be turned into zombies through airborne transmission, greatly increasing the challenge. Certain physiological conditions make humans more susceptible to the contagion, so it is necessary for all remaining humans to wear a biometric monitor for their own health and safety.

Although this situation sounds dire, there is hope on the horizon because an antidote has been found. However, the base ingredients must be delivered across the city to an undisclosed location before the final ingredient can be added and the antidote becomes viable for mass production and distribution. In order to deliver the antidote, the player must act as a courier, finding the delivery location while also outrunning the many zombies keen to cause him harm. As noted above, though, in addition to the challenge of dealing with faster zombies, one of the side effects of the zombie outbreak is that humans are much more susceptible to becoming zombies themselves. This happens through airborne transmission, if certain physiological conditions are met. One of those conditions occurs when the player's heart rate rises above a certain number. Conveniently, this happens to be the maximum heart rate calculation that is significant and useful for exercise biometrics. Thus, one of the primary gameplay mechanics is for the player to jog through the city without exceeding his personalized heart rate threshold. This must be done while maintaining a sufficiently high heart rate to promote cardiovascular benefit; the zombies are coded to not catch the player as long as the players are exerting enough effort to stay in this zone.

The true purpose of this and other types of "exergames" (Sinclair, Hingston, & Masek, 2007) is to encourage physical activity while incorporating fantasy-based elements from fiction and video gaming. In this game, it is easy to imagine how the combination of video gaming evaluation and biometric evaluation combine to create novel opportunities for digital badges. The game that is produced is not quite the same as either parent – the whole here is greater than the sum of its parts. This creates challenging situations for measurement since many elements from both domains may be working together to shape the experience. For example, one biometric criterion is to keep the player exercising without exceeding his maximum heart rate. One gameplay goal is to keep the player distracted from the real-world discomfort of exercising by focusing his attention on elements within the game and to keep the experience fun and engaging. We could therefore track and evaluate the performance of badging along three separate dimensions. The first would be to create and track badges that focus on biometric data and the system's attempts to stabilize biometric performance within a particular range of values for any relevant inputs. The second would be to design and evaluate badges dealing with gameplay goals such as fun, satisfaction, and level progression. The third and most valuable type of badge would be crafted to deal with goals that intersect both domains: biometrics and video gaming.

For our fictional zombie jogging game, a combined badge like this can be created using incremental badges to reward players for jogging under their maximum heart rates for two, five, and ten minutes of continuous running. After earning the badge at each level, new types of useful items are added into the courier's backpack that open up new gameplay possibilities. This badge is useful and important because it supports the biometric goals necessary to improve exercise achievement, but it also supports gameplay goals to make the game world more interesting, engaging, and fulfilling. The performance of running at the ideal target heart rate for increasingly longer sustained periods of time helps the player build up a proper sense of pace and effort while running. In addition, the rewards provided by the badges also encourage the individuals' roles as players to invest more time exploring the game world by testing out each new virtual item and seeing how they augment their abilities and options as a courier.

This type of game might sound outlandish, but there are in fact games of this nature available and under development. For example, when Google Glass was first emerging on the scene as an augmented reality device, a company developed a game called *Race Yourself* that allowed runners to wear the glasses while jogging. In addition to standard data such as distance traveled, pace, and calories expended, the game also displayed virtual options that include races against other friends. However, they could also race against or run from giant boulders, fires, zombies, and even freight trains. The core idea with such games is that these virtual elements can be used to motivate the runner through fantasy-based graphical environments overlaid atop real-world data (Schwartz, 2014).

This zombie running game provides one example for how recombination might generate new methods for novel badge design derived both from the original products and the new, combined system. In this case, digital badges emerged as tools available to help shape user behaviors in ways that are productive for this new union. However, in other cases, digital badges themselves could be one of the combinatory elements rather than an intervention that can be applied to the intersection of two other elements. In these situations, recombination incorporates digital badges as one of the to-be-combined domains and considers how the digital badging process itself might change based on new variables.

For example, one such example grounded in real-world research is profiled in the work of Mah (2016). Rather than biometrics and video gaming, this research studies the integration of digital badges and learning analytics. We have been discussing the contemporary benefits of digital badges throughout the book, but learning analytics is another area that has been receiving significant attention in modern educational practice. By looking carefully at data found within the different phases of learning and assessment, learning analytics seeks to recommend practices to improve different aspects of the learning process and improve student learning and retention. For example, one subset of learning analytics, predictive analytics, seeks to recommend educational interventions based on students' prior performance in particular courses or units of study. Using sophisticated statistics, the technique can employ recommendations that are grounded in data and checked against the performance patterns of many other users in the database. If all students who earned a low grade in a particular foundational math class then performed poorly in an upper-division elective, a predictive analytics algorithm could recommend particular learning interventions as options for an instructor to consider using in his course.

The intersecting possibility space of learning analytics with digital badges is one area for potential research in digital badging that relies upon recombination. In Mah's (2016) analysis, for example, she notes how learning analytics and digital badging can be interconnected to improve student retention. In Mah's model, digital badges become input sources for a predictive analytics system, allowing the predictions to be strengthened as more granular knowledge about students' performance feeds into the system. For example, as we have argued throughout the book, a primary advantage of digital badging is that it allows us to credential student skills at fine levels of detail. When a badge-based competency becomes an input to a predictive analytics system, we are able to see the particular, component-based competencies that drive a student's performance in the course. Rather than knowing if they passed or failed their pre-algebra course, for example, the predictive analytics algorithm is able to use more specific data that indicates they excelled at removing perfect cubes from cubed roots but that they are still having trouble solving linear equations.

As these examples show, both recurrence and recombination are useful focusing techniques for considering the potential evolutionary possibilities of digital badges. There is no guarantee that digital badging systems will continue to cycle through historical attempts at motivating learning, credentialing users, or shaping behaviors. Nor is there certainty that the next innovative badging system will be the result of combined work from disparate fields. However, there is evidence that both recurrence and recombination have historical precedents in the development of new techniques and technologies. We turn next to another speculative task, which is to consider the next step in this predictive process. The question here is as follows: once new badging systems exist, how do we measure their success?

Evaluating Novelty and Novel Outcomes

Over the years, researchers have developed different strategies for determining how novel something is. One method used by computer scientists is to count the number of new things we see in a system that are not present in other comparable systems. For example, y Pérez et al. (2011) designed a computational system to evaluate the novelty of computer narratives by analyzing dimensions such as the specific types of actions that take place in narratives and the percentages of characters reincorporated into new stories from previous stories. Accordingly, a new story that shared much in common with the actions of a previous story might be classified as standard, while a story with a significant amount of original action could be classified as novel. With this technique, novelty can be evaluated by comparing the number of unique or original features that emerge as compared to a base set of criteria extracted from existing products.

The work of y Pérez et al. (2011) shows it is possible to develop a quantitative methodology for evaluating novelty. As described, the process essentially works by comparing the number of new elements in a system (in this case, narrative actions and characters) to the number of common elements and then applying an algorithm to a set of baseline data to determine when a novelty threshold is exceeded. A story could be classified as novel, then, because it contains a certain number of new actions and a certain (and countable) combination of character types. We could certainly apply such a model to digital badging systems to determine whether or not they are novel. We might classify features such as visual indicators, mechanics, and rewards into new or common categories and then count the number of items in each group. Once a certain number of new features is counted, perhaps in a digital badging system that implements unique trigger conditions or visual indicators or reward items, then that system could be classified as novel.

While this sounds doable on the surface, this type of method is in fact quite difficult because digital badges are so diverse. As we have been discussing throughout the book, badges appear – among other places – in videogames, military simulations, mobile software, and LMSs. These domains are sometimes quite different from one another and what novelty *means* in each application area will vary. Similarly, a quantitative methodology might not incorporate more subjective dimensions of the user experience that could lead users to classify a system with many common features as novel simply because it is so well-designed and intuitive. Further, it does not quantify the degree of novelty of each new feature; if one system has only one novel feature, but it is groundbreaking, and another system has three novel features, but none could be considered revolutionary, which system is more novel? To put it simply, the quantifiable method is useful in some cases, but not universally ideal for considering novelty in digital badging technologies.

As it turns out, evaluating novelty at large is difficult, if not impossible. This is because novelty itself is, by definition, unusual or unpredictable, making generalizable assessment a continuously moving target. Further, one could argue that if a system or object exhibits sufficient originality to be classifiable as something novel, then that thing is new enough to warrant its own specialized form of evaluation. However, this being said, there are some methods for evaluating novelty that are useful for our current focus on digital badges. One approach, for example, is to focus on outcomes rather than on the intervention itself. This is certainly a more useful approach for much of what we want to do when we are working with digital badges. Learning whether a badging system is novel is perhaps interesting for some researchers to know, but what is ultimately most useful will be knowing whether or not this system actually does what it was designed to do. That discussion was the focus of our previous chapter.

Ultimately, what is most important in evaluating novel badge systems is remembering that even novel systems may reuse existing assessment methods to evaluate the outcomes of the program. While the visual indicators, completion logics, and reward implementations of digital badges will evolve over time, many of the uses and purposes for these systems will still connect intimately to problems we have seen in the past – problems such as motivating learning, credentialing users, encouraging creativity, and catalyzing proactive social behaviors. With a well-developed toolset of time-tested assessment instruments combined with an open-minded approach toward new opportunities in digital badging, researchers and educators alike will be well prepared both for the badges of today and of tomorrow.

Next Up

In this chapter, we spent some time theorizing about why understanding novelty and novel designs can be useful in considering future types of badging systems and how we might evaluate them. In our next and final chapter, we synthesize what we have discussed throughout this book to speculate about the future of digital badges. What new avenues await us for credentialing, motivating, and shaping the behaviors of those who earn these digital objects? We hypothesize about some of the new directions for badges and consider some of the likely avenues for their future development and use. By closing in on the future, we optimistically assert that the future of digital badges is a rich one. We believe their potential will continue to be realized alongside the advancement of our digital devices and our continually evolving patterns of interaction with these technologies.

References

Bogost, I. (2010, Feb. 10). Persuasive games: Check-ins check out. *Gamasutra*. Retrieved from www.gamasutra.com/view/feature/4269/persuasive_games_checkins_check_.php.

Campbell, K. K. (1996). *The rhetorical act* (2nd ed.). Belmont, CA: Wadsworth.

Flavell, J. H. (1977). *Cognitive development*. Englewood Cliffs, NJ: Prentice-Hall.

Hirschman, E. C. (1980). Innovativeness, novelty seeking, and consumer creativity. *Journal of Consumer Research*, *7*(3), 283–295.

Jain, A. K., Ross, A., & Prabhakar, S. (2004). An introduction to biometric recognition. *IEEE Transactions on Circuits and Systems for Video Technology*, *14*(1), 4–20.

Lupton, D. (2013). Quantifying the body: Monitoring and measuring health in the age of mHealth technologies. *Critical Public Health*, *23*(4), 393–403.

Mah, D. K. (2016). Learning analytics and digital badges: Potential impact on student retention in higher education. *Technology, Knowledge and Learning*, *21*(3), 285–305.

Mark, J. J. (2015, Dec. 2). Cylinder seals in ancient Mesopotamia: Their history and significance. *Ancient history encyclopedia*. Retrieved from www.ancient.eu/article/846/cylinder-seals-in-ancient-mesopotamia---their-hist/.

North, M. (2013). *Novelty: A history of the new*. Chicago: University of Chicago Press. Kindle edition.

Petroski, H. (1992). *The evolution of useful things*. New York: Vintage.

Schwartz, A. (2014, Jan. 10). This horrifying fitness game for Google Glass makes you run for your life. *Fast Company*. Retrieved from www.fastcompany.com/3024644/this-horrifying-fitness-game-for-google-glass-makes-you-run-for-your-life.

Sinclair, J., Hingston, P., & Masek, M. (2007, December). Considerations for the design of exergames. In *Proceedings of the 5th International Conference on Computer Graphics and Interactive Techniques in Australia and Southeast Asia* (pp. 289–295). ACM.

y Pérez, R. P., Ortiz, O., Luna, W., Negrete, S., Castellanos-Cerda, V., Peñalosa, E., & Ávila, R. (2011). A system for evaluating novelty in computer generated narratives. In *Proceedings of the 2nd International Conference on Computational Creativity* (pp. 63–68).

CHAPTER 11

Conclusion
The Future of Badging

Overview

What will the future of digital badges bring us? It is fun to speculate. Will we one day witness badge-deploying (or badge-*seeking*) autonomous robots? Maybe an educator or employer will recognize a need for a new class of badging drones, perhaps designed to remotely credential work done by employees in the field. Or, perhaps an organization will see a need for nanotechnologies with the ability to distribute new types of microbadges, deployed without human intervention, for non-human audiences, and based purely on biological data. More likely, we will experience more modest progress, such as new models for self-paced learning that move the needle forward in a positive direction for both motivation and engagement in learning. Ideally, we will also see a critical mass of employers and graduate schools finally begin to acknowledge, en masse, the potential of microcredentials as evidence of employee and student capability at a fine level of detail. It is difficult to know where precisely digital badging will lead us, but our final chapter charts multiple paths for the evolution of digital badges and considers new genres, designs, and purposes for these technologies. As we discussed in the previous chapters, digital badges are still young tools in a young medium and there are many exciting possibilities for their development and use that have not yet become realities. After reviewing research on digital badges, some that is just emerging and other work that is still underexplored, we delve into some of the emerging interdisciplinary possibilities for this technology. By synthesizing these new ideas with the existing research covered throughout this book, we will be well prepared to work with not only today's digital badging systems, but also the digital badges that still lie on the horizon of possibility.

Charting the Future

This chapter looks forward to consider how digital badges of the future might alter our landscape of education, business, and leisure. We argued throughout this book that digital badges are technologies worthy of our attention. They are useful tools for shaping behaviors, modifying perceptions and attitudes toward learning, and assessing competency at a fine level of detail. However, these functions and purposes are only scratching the surface of what is possible using this technology. In this final chapter, we ask a simple question: what more might the badges of tomorrow do for us?

To consider this line of inquiry, we examine the latest research on digital badges and outline some of the possibilities for their evolution. We focused on the assessment of novel badging in the previous chapter, so here we will concentrate more generally on future badging prospects. Aiding our task are four different perspectives through which to consider the future of badges: new designs, new genres, new contexts for use, and what we call speculative badging, or big, out-of-the-box ideas for this medium. We will discuss each of these areas in turn, integrating emerging areas of research when possible. This allows us to explore different potential routes for the progression of digital badging systems and to consider different purposes and stakeholder outcomes.

New Badge Designs

One immediate area in which we will see exciting new progress in upcoming years is in badge design and development. As we discussed in Chapter 2, the basic construction of a digital badge, as we know it today, is fairly simple: a visual icon, a completion logic, and a reward. However, there are more sophisticated variations of this formula that can yield exciting results for more nuanced forms of teaching and behavioral redirection. Even slightly refining or reconsidering the basic elements of digital badges in new contexts produces new possibilities for these technologies.

Visual Imagery

One component of the basic badging formula that future developers will almost certainly tinker with is the visual icon itself. Other than experimental ideas, we have not yet seen many widely used examples of badging systems that move beyond standard two-dimensional graphical badge images. In general, developers and researchers seem to give little attention to these visual identifiers, choosing instead to focus on the timing, distribution, reward, and triggering of digital badges' completion logics. However, the visual dimension of badging is critical and should not be overlooked. Improved graphical capabilities and modeling techniques continue to surpass users' previous expectations for photorealistic and immersive imagery. We would be remiss in not exploring these enhanced graphics for use in our digital badging systems.

One immediate opportunity in this area is to investigate virtual reality (VR)- and augmented reality (AR)-based signifiers for digital badges. This is a field of inquiry that will bring progress sooner rather than later, particularly since we now have VR and AR devices that are technologically mature and affordable for many consumers. For example, at the time we are writing this chapter in the summer and fall of 2018, the Facebook-owned company Oculus has recently released a portable version of their VR technology, the Oculus Go, priced at a relatively affordable $149. Prior to that in October of 2016, Sony released a console-based VR technology, PlayStation VR, for the PlayStation game console. Consumers could purchase the device for under $300. Such devices are being described, respectively, as "headset(s) that will take VR mainstream" (Fitzsimmons & Lynch, 2018) and "the promised land for virtual reality on consoles" (Pino, 2018).

As these cases of the PlayStation VR and the Oculus Go illustrate, in only a year and a half, the cost of similar VR technology was cut in half (or even more, considering the Oculus Go does not require a separate console device for its operation). Further, the features and capabilities of VR continue to improve rapidly, in parallel with advancements in screen, optics, storage, power, haptic, and peripheral technologies. This type of technology, and the competition that will follow, will surely introduce VR applications to new users and new audiences. That seems to be the point; as Fitzsimmons and Lynch write, "This is VR for the casual gamer, the relaxed consumer of media, the person without the time, money or interest in setting up a PC to power a higher-end headset. This is VR for everyone" (2018, para. 7). As the technology enters the mainstream, so to speak, and finds new audiences, then additional ideas for both entertainment and educational products will continue to find a home in these immersive virtual environments.

We believe digital badges will play a role in these new hardware and software systems. VR-based badges of the future might look similar to their existing cousins, but with the potential for different viewpoints and perspectives. They will allow users to experience digital badges within navigable environments where the virtual graphics are viewable from above, below, or from any side perspective. They will be approachable from multiple angles, examinable in three dimensions, and perhaps carry the ability to be manipulated in virtual space using a controller or remote control device. Similarly new possibilities exist in the technology offered by augmented technology, which blends data from real and virtual worlds into a single perspective. For example, one might look at a restaurant's physical exterior and see online review badges superimposed over the façade in digital markup. AR-based badges such as these have the ability to combine the physical world with virtual information so that a digital badge might, in fact, be some combination of digital and analog, real-world materials. One could imagine a scenario in which digital badges are rendered somewhere on the user's horizon line within a fitness application, for example. This type of application projects a hybrid path, combining a real-world roadway overlaid with a virtually charted path, toward which an exerciser can jog in order to earn digital badges and add them to her virtual inventory. This too presents variations on the visual design of the badges, given that they would need to be observable not only up close, as we traditionally see two-dimensional badges, but also from a distance.

Another area in which visual indicators might become more sophisticated is in culturally personalized imagery. Research tells us that people from different cultural backgrounds react differently to color, imagery, and iconography and vary in their perception and cognition of visual information (Kim & Lee, 2005). This means that digital designers creating globally distributed imagery must design in a way that acknowledges cultural variation and is sensitive to aesthetic elements that are confusing, ineffective, or offensive to different cultures. Organizations acknowledge the business advantage of this process through an investment in localization, or adapting a product developed in one part of the world for usage in others, which is a significant part of the development process for many international companies. If a product is not geared toward the design expectations and values of a particular part of the world, that product risks being outsold by competitive products that *do* localize to account for cross-cultural sensibilities.

Accordingly, to enhance usability across different demographics and cultures, there is a need for badges to vary in their visual representation to different cultures. Cultural semiotics, or the studies of signs and symbols in relation to different cultural contexts, attempts to understand the intersecting communication contexts of these spaces. This raises a number of questions dealing with how signs, processes, and sign systems vary from one culture to another. For example, cultural semiotics research studies might investigate how cultural signs and natural signs differ, how cultural boundaries are determined, and how different cultures that use the same symbolic systems relate to one another (Posner, 2004). These research methodologies are all useful for badges, too. It could be, for example, that icons used for digital badges that make perfect sense in European systems are quite problematic in products designed for usage in Western China. As badges become more predominant and important in digital systems around the world, these types of issues must be considered.

Visual differences in badge iconography are not related just to the specific images chosen, either. Aesthetic preferences can take many different forms, from the differences found in the selection of iconic images to the use of concrete versus abstract imagery for different types of badges. Researchers have already identified differences in preference and performance between different cultural groups using user interfaces. One study found that in a comparison between American and Korean users, Korean users performed much better using concrete icons while American users showed higher performance with abstract imagery (Kim & Lee, 2005). We still know very little about cultural differences in relation to badging graphics, however. There is some research that investigates basic demographics such as age and gender (e.g., Koivisto & Hamari, 2014), but a deeper analysis of badge perceptions and effects along cultural dimensions might spur new types of badges that vary according to cultural norms and expectations.

Trigger Mechanics

Trigger mechanics also have multiple possibilities for variation. A trigger mechanic is a condition that "triggers" a badge's delivery to a user. It is the condition that activates the completion logic of a badge and requires it to be evaluated (Hamari & Eranti, 2011; McDaniel & Fanfarelli, 2016). A digital badge trigger as we know it today is a simple bit of software logic that determines the prerequisite conditions upon which a system releases a badge to a user. Since they are fundamentally governed by algorithms, or repeatable sequences of programmed instructions, these triggers can be manipulated by the same algorithmic techniques used in other areas of computer science. Emerging techniques in machine learning or neural networks, for example, could also be applied to digital badges. Rather than a human programming a one-size-fits-all solution to badge triggers, a machine could instead be programmed to "learn" gradually over time how to best deploy badges that are tailored to the particular cognitive and behavioral characteristics of a given user.

In such a scenario, badge triggers operate within a probability space where different badges can be deployed depending on the events triggered by users. Other data may also be considered here, such as data describing how those events are connected to one another. Connections between potential paths can be weighted, or given more importance within the software system, so that particular instructions are given more consideration in the algorithm over time as other behaviors within the system become clearer. For example, a trigger system might assert that there is a high probability of users performing poorly on a midterm examination if they do not make at least two social connections to other students within the first two weeks. In a machine learning scenario, the logic connections that ultimately lead to the deployment of intervention badges can be strengthened, allowing those badges to be deployed to a sample of test students to test this hypothesis with real data. In the long term, this type of machine learning strategy allows digital badge triggers to adapt to specific users and their idiosyncratic behaviors. This is useful because there might be significant variability between different people using the system. Some users might need to receive initial badges very quickly in order to pique their interest and show them the possibilities for the system, but others might be more patient and see greater impact if this initial badge is delayed a bit more or requires more effort.

As learning algorithms become more sophisticated at customizing content for different types of learners, we will begin to see digital badge systems that cede some of this authorial control to automated algorithms. There is an entire branch of research in computing that seeks to understand how machine learning can be used to form "user models" that consider complex phenomena such as cognition, skill acquisition, behavior, and user characteristics (Webb, Pazzani, & Billsus, 2001). Once these user models exist for sufficiently large data sets, developers can use them to provide deeply personalized and customized learning experiences for users. Imagine some of the scenarios we discussed in Chapter 8, with regard to military training simulations. Machine learning and user modeling would be useful for strategically deploying remedial badges to team members of a struggling squad in a training exercise, enabling them to build additional skills to catch up with their teammates. There might also be opportunities to integrate additional sensory data into the machine learning process so that the algorithms are not just using indirect measures or attitudinal data about the learning process from the individual in question, but also external data from the physical environment or the other individuals working with the learner.

Triggers might also evolve further by strategically integrating additional external information from the outside world into their operation. An example of this is the Smart Kindergarten (SmartKG) initiative, an interdisciplinary project developed at UCLA between electrical engineers and computer scientists. The SmartKG research group developed technologies in wearable computing to mediate learning interactions between young people and their physical world (Park et al., 2002). One of the resulting devices, iBadge, is a lightweight, low-power device that is equipped with sensors to detect what happens in the classroom when children are wearing the device. What is notable about this type of augmented badge is that the triggers used to initiate different actions are expanded by the capabilities of external sensors. For example, rather than just acting upon performance-based data such as the number of correct answers achieved on a math test or the amount of time spent on a project-based activity, these sensors broaden the actionable items that can be processed by technology. The researchers involved with this project speculate about being able to answer more complex social questions such as "'Do students tend to be in a group with the same ethnic background,' and 'Is student C socially isolated?'" (Park et al., 2002, pp. 231–232).

Imagine if our online course badges could move beyond just performance and time-on-task measures and also be triggered by complex social phenomena. This might require us to stretch our conceptualizations of badges slightly – rather than thinking of badges as something external that is earned for completing an action, they might be embedded into wearable computers and activated when necessary to provide aid or support. We might, for example, use sensor-connected badges to determine whether or not Soldiers returning from combat environments are exhibiting signs of post-traumatic stress disorder (PTSD). If such an event triggers, the badge might send signals to support resources, ranging from family members to veterans' networks, in order to provide aid. It is true that the privacy implications of this technology are worrisome and will require careful consideration, but there is always a tradeoff between usability and security. Ethical and legal implications aside, expanding the capabilities of digital badge triggers and implementing additional sensor arrays will certainly make this type of scenario more plausible.

Rewards

Finally, badging rewards too will continue to evolve. Various permutations of reward exist now. In some cases, the digital objects themselves serve as rewards by providing evidence of accomplishment that badge earners can virtually display in online trophy cases or on their profile pages. The potential reward and recognition offered by these technologies are useful within a particular domain such as a videogame or an LMS because of their efficiency, their motivational potential, their ability to be shared with other users, and their meaningfulness within the context of the activities occurring within that domain (Glover, 2016). However, there are also rewards that provide additional real-world value, such as points that can be exchanged for tangible items or discounts on products and services. Like trigger mechanics, these rewards are configurable to compensate different types of individuals in different ways. For example, individuals who place a high value on online reputation could be recognized through virtual accolades, while users who care less about this sort of thing could be rewarded through coupons or currencies with an exchange rate in the physical world. Future badging rewards could also be customized in an incremental fashion so that the amount of reward provided depends upon one's performance when acquiring the badge. A perfect performance might result in a top-tier reward, for example, while a session that just barely met the trigger threshold could generate a lower-tier reward commensurate with that level of performance. This sort of design has been used in non-badging rewards for a very long time, but badging rewards have been slow to catch up.

Other areas in which developers and researchers will continue to tweak digital badge rewards are in their timing, delivery, and permanence. Although we have not addressed permanence much in this book, the lifespan of badges is another dimension that impacts their perceived reward. For example, in one study, researchers devised two types of badges, permanent and temporary (Bista, Nepal, Colineau, & Paris, 2012). The badges were created for an online community developed by the researchers, in collaboration with a government agency partner, and were designed to support welfare workers returning to the workforce. Permanent badges, once earned, remained with members throughout their time in the community. Temporary badges, on the other hand, only remained in place for two weeks at a time. Community members were required to re-earn them by exhibiting the same productive behaviors in order to keep the badges over longer periods of time. When badges were earned more than once in succession, they could be leveled up to show higher levels of mastery and to confer additional status on the badge earners. This study demonstrates that researchers can manipulate the lifespan of digital badges to exert different motivational effects on a population.

With regard to timing and delivery, there is also promising research being done on academic delay of gratification (ADOG) as it pertains to digital badging. The idea here is to investigate the impact of digital badging on students' behavioral choices in pursuing immediately accessible goals versus longer-term academic goals that might have greater overall importance, but fewer opportunities for short-term payoff. In one study detailed in Rughinis and Matei (2016), the researchers designed a badging system for the Cisco Networking Academy Center in Romania. In contrast to cumulative badging systems, they designed their product as a summative badging system that delayed the user-experience of gratification until the end of the course. The software awarded badges for achieving certain quantitative learning goals related to performance in the course, such as attaining a final GPA over a certain number, being involved in a cumulative number of class discussions, or mastering all exams in the course over a certain grade percentage. Their ultimate design rewarded final, rather than intermediary, achievements.

To evaluate the success of this type of reward, Rughinis and Matei interviewed students and instructors who used the system and assessed both the learning experience and the social interactions surrounding the learning experience. Their data suggested that there are both advantages and disadvantages to this type of delayed reward system. On the one hand, some respondents found these types of badges to be useful alternatives to cumulative badging systems in which "badge fatigue" could diminish their motivational usefulness by overwhelming participants with superfluous digital badges. On the other hand, other respondents indicated in their interviews that since the badges were not issued until the end of the course, they were much less useful in guiding students' regular behaviors; they did not provide feedback in a timely and useful manner. In summarizing their study, the researchers noted that "the ADOG principle in badge design supports the guidance function while hindering their self-preservation role, since the delay of allocation creates a time frame when badges are present in discourse, but not as objects that students own" (Rughinis & Matei, 2016, p. 213). Future evolutions of digital badging should continue to explore the implications of this type of delayed gratification and further evaluate the appropriate time to issue badges in different circumstances.

In each of these design components – visual icon, trigger, and reward – we were able to identify future possibilities for expanding these components in new directions. Research shows that this is already starting to occur. This is not the edge limit of future growth for digital badges, of course, because these components are using our existing operational definition for digital badges: signifier, completion logic, and reward. This definition might change as these devices evolve. In the next section, we move beyond the units of design to think more broadly about the contexts and uses of our future digital badges. We will begin by discussing new categories of badging that are likely to form.

New Badge Genres

If we examine our contemporary use cases for digital badging, we see that most digital badges are developed for – and used in – some common categories. Here, we will adopt the term genres, as used in literary and film studies, to frame our discussion of these categories. The idea behind genres is rather simple: by classifying different types of products into different categories, we can analyze the patterns, elements, themes, conventions, and purposes of those products collectively, as a group. We do this by attempting to understand the broader category, or genre, in which they reside. So, for example, we can use genre as an organizing heuristic to discuss dramatic plays and the conventions they use, or to discuss romantic fiction or horror films with some degree of commonality between the artistic deliverables grouped into each. Of course, this is imperfect. There will still be distinction at the individual level, and sometimes work will span multiple genres such as a romantic comedy or a historical musical. However, this genre-based organizational strategy does allow us to make some general observations about what these uses have in common.

We will not delve deeply into the theory of genres in this chapter, but rather borrow some of these ideas to help us think about future genres for badges. Namely, we will adopt the premise that genres are constructed not only of their group's criteria, but also by the specific problems and social practices surrounding those categories. For example, educational badge design as a genre is not only comprised of badges used in educational settings, but also of the problems educators deal with and the social principles that undergird their practices. As Swales (2009) explains, "the work of genre is to mediate between social situations and the texts that respond strategically to the exigencies of those situations" (p. 14). Indeed, thinking of badges as texts, broadly considered, that strategically respond to particular problems and their social connections is useful. It allows us to consider how these texts vary, both developmentally and operationally, in different domains.

We have discussed many common purposes and genres for digital badging in Part II of this book. For convenience's sake, we will revisit a number of them here. First, many digital badges are used in educational genres. These badges operate in learning contexts for purposes such as motivating behavior, evaluating user skills or knowledge at fine degrees of granularity, or changing less useful learner behaviors into more useful behaviors. We discussed online learning systems, another common home for digital badges with educational intent, in Chapter 6. In some educational applications, badge designers hope to encourage additional time on task and promote repeated interactions in virtual environments over time.

A second common genre for digital badges is entertainment. We discussed this type of badging extensively in Chapter 5 when we reviewed the history of achievements in videogames and discussed how digital badges can be designed using game-based strategies. However, we have also alluded to entertainment-based badging in a broader sense throughout the book, in mobile contexts or in other types of informal learning where fantasy or fun can be used to motivate learning in novel or interesting ways. Indeed, like books or novels, badges will sometimes span multiple genres and there is a good deal of interesting work looking into how badges might blend entertainment and learning in productive ways. Chapter 7, which emphasized mobile badging, also featured examples of badging scenarios that fit into both educational and entertainment genres.

A third genre is business and marketing. We have written somewhat less about this area than the other genres mentioned above, but the gamification of business and marketing is still a significant area of use for digital badges. Gamification in industry and commerce is big business. A number of practical uses emerge in this domain, from motivating employees and consumers to training employees and acknowledging exceptional or subpar performance in the workplace (Vinichenko, Melnichuk, Kirillov, Makushkin, & Melnichuk, 2016). Given the intense competition and social scrutiny modern businesses face on a daily basis, many are considering how loyalty programs, behavioral reinforcement, or viral marketing techniques can be integrated with digital badges. Such strategies might reinforce customer loyalty, encourage repeated visits, or make certain aspects of business transactions more fun and enjoyable (e.g., paying for a meal at a restaurant or sharing a review online). Even large companies have invested in gamification tactics: Siemens developed a game called *Plantville* to allow its 23,000 employees to learn operations and management for a simulated plant and IBM developed *CityOne* to explore problems dealing with energy infrastructure and overcrowding (Kappen & Nacke, 2013). Business and marketing will continue to be an area in which gamification and digital badging techniques gain traction.

Finally, we have discussed badges used in military or simulation environments, to finely shape behaviors and encourage habits of deliberate practice necessary for surviving what might ultimately turn out to be life or death situations. Many of these badging scenarios also feature a strong emphasis on education, training, and learning in high-stress scenarios. Like other genres, military badging scenarios carry ethical and psychological considerations that we have addressed in detail in Chapter 8.

While these are all useful and important genres in which to design and use digital badges, are there other areas of practice or domains of study in which we are not yet using digital badges, but could? Many existing genres are quite broad, so we do see variation in the types of digital badges used in courses on information technology versus biology, for example. What we mean to consider here, though, are those genres that remain largely untapped, underdeveloped, or unexplored in relation to digital badges. Sometimes, such areas will require us to rethink our core ideas of what digital badges are. Other applications might require support infrastructure or social/political support systems that are not yet widely adopted. In this section, we will focus on three new genres for digital badges that we see as having great potential, both for digital badges as technologies and for computer-augmented learning in general.

Organic Badges

We will refer to our first new genre as organic badges. We use the term organic to refer to the natural context of a learning environment, meaning that the technologies will be created and manipulated not just by a central authority, but also by the environment's participants. This model for creating things is sometimes referred to as participatory design because the end users participate in the design process. Although this might seem unrealistic, since users' design knowledge and expertise are generally not equal to the development team's abilities, there are some relatively accessible methods for including end users in the design process. For example, early computer hardware designers sometimes used folded cardboard to allow end users to mock up different versions of what computers might look like. These early designs could then be considered and potentially refined by the engineers and developers making the final hardware. A low-cost equivalent for prototyping designs for digital badges might consist of blank playing cards that can be written on using erasable markers. In addition to being participatory, these designs are also organic because they grow out of the specific context where they are being created and are tightly coupled to the environment in which they are designed.

Organic badges might take a number of different forms based on the composition of a learning community. One idea is to allow community members to take ownership of various aspects of the badging process. In previous chapters, we discussed how students might be allowed to construct and issue their own badges, or how different military units might make specific badges for their group. Furthering this idea, community members could design the visual icons associated with badges or they could collectively choose the type and amount of reward associated with particular badges. Such a strategy is similar to a class voting on the final exam parameters or collectively deciding upon the final project a class undertakes in a traditional classroom environment. Even more interesting is when the community decides upon the triggers and completion logics for unlocking certain badges. Here, the design parameters and value of digital badges are not decided upon by a single individual who controls the learning experience, but rather the entire social group. Because these factors cannot be fully predicted at the onset of a given semester or learning cycle, the badges must be designed in such a way that they can evolve organically based on both individual and group dynamics.

Smart Badges

We alluded to this category of badges in our earlier description of evolving trigger mechanics, but another genre of badges of the future will focus on smart badges. These objects will be capable of learning and will not rely purely upon the design and reward parameters previously decided upon by a researcher or instructor. Instead, they will be released into a system with the capability of adapting to different types of user behaviors. They will have the ability to shape the badges' forms, triggers, completion logics, and rewards based upon what is happening in the environment. In other words, the design and function of these badges will be malleable and extensible over time. In contrast to organic badges, however, these types of badges will be capable of changing by themselves, without external validation by a central authority or community group.

These types of badges will be particularly useful in situations where the population's demographics are not well known. Consider a Massive Open Online Course (MOOC) open to the public across the world. The instructor of such a course will not necessarily know the knowledge bases nor the learning behaviors of the students in the course, particularly if there are thousands of them enrolled. In this type of scenario, smart badges would help instructors maximize learning and motivation in the course. Smart badges might provide different rewards for different students, depending on their prior interactions and stated learning objectives. They could also scale in difficulty, ensuring that more advanced learners and beginning learners alike would both have opportunities to earn badges without them being seen as too easy or too difficult. Of course, ethical and fairness concerns will need to be addressed, but this type of badge will likely be quite useful in the construction of future adaptive learning systems.

Persistent Badges

Our final genre for digital badges is persistent badges, or badges that live on beyond their use in a particular implementation. Persistent badging is one of the grand challenges for this technology and is the idea behind open badging initiatives and technologies such as the Mozilla Backpack (see Figure 11.1). The idea is that a secure, independent virtual location exists so that badges can be stored long term. Organizations or employers that use the Open Badges standard for storage and retrieval can access badges stored this way to evaluate, promote, or assist their users and employees. Better yet, learners can earn badges during different parts of their lives, with badges potentially deployed during formal academic experiences, volunteer experiences, and occupational training programs. In this way, both college entrance admissions committees and career providers alike possess the ability to evaluate the well-roundedness of candidates. They might also provide appropriate support scaffolds for these individuals once they are recruited into the academic program or placed within an organization to begin their career.

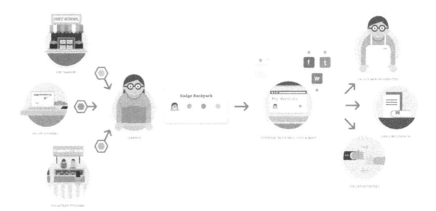

Figure 11.1 Open Badges architecture (Creative Commons BY4.0, Mozilla Foundation, ©2016)

While the technologies to support persistent badges exist, we have yet to see much compelling evidence of long-term success stories in which badges follow users from their formal educational experiences into their ultimate career occupations. However, we believe this genre will continue to gain momentum as technologies and support infrastructures continue to mature. As Rughinis (2013) reminds us, substituting a badge for a course grade can provide a more nuanced look at a learner's performance in a course or educational program. However, he also notes that contrasting grades with *degrees* is also a possibility. Digital badges can enrich a learner's degree credential with additional metadata and information about individual performance as well as evaluations from other community members, such as peer students enrolled in the program.

In this fashion, we can see how persistent badges might be valuable to employers. They could be instrumental for determining who to hire and where to place them within an organizational hierarchy. Two employees hired at a chemical research organization who both earned As in organic chemistry might end up in very different lab environments based on their soft skills, for example. Persistent badges, earned in courses that carry forward into career hiring materials, can tell these soft skill stories. The employee who works well in groups and is sociable may maximize performance in a team-based environment, while another employee's work might be much stronger when produced in an individual office setting with minimal distractions.

As any badge researcher will tell you, these contextual nuances are vitally important in the ultimate success or failure of badging implementations. However, there are some contexts we are not fully considering when we design and distribute badging systems. In our next section, we address context specifically. We discuss some new paradigms for digital badges that might emerge as we work toward building technologies to assist with the grand educational challenges of the 21st century.

New Badge Contexts

While much of the hubbub about digital badging has emerged from studying them in particular contexts such as MOOC management systems, videogames, and simulations, there are many different learning contexts compatible with this technology. Some of these we have seen and some are yet to be designed. Many of these new application areas will be guided by new educational challenges posed by contemporary society. As Sullivan (2013) notes, educators are faced with unique challenges as they continue to educate the students of tomorrow for the modern workplace where knowledge is increasingly distributed, globalized, and networked. Sullivan (2013) writes that these teachers are:

> facing the realities of preparing all students for these complex knowledge environments. In addition to the assessment of concrete content knowledge, post-industrial societies are increasingly demanding that their members

demonstrate their abilities in abstract and soft skills areas such as teamwork, critical thinking and analysis, communication, and personal management of time and resources.

(p. 4)

One challenging aspect of such content is that successful practice is not always limited to a single example. In critical thinking, for example, there are many ways in which a student might successfully reason through a problem. Similarly, multiple types of teamwork can lead to success; in one case, a strong leader who is good at delegating might guide the team's activities, while another team might employ a democratic process with power distributed more equally among team members. Either configuration is capable of getting the job done.

In such situations, it might be difficult to use less precise tools to guide learning and assessment. For example, awarding a simple letter grade or percentage value at the end of a learning exercise will, in ideal circumstances, provide an accurate evaluation of the overall outcome or deliverable. However, such summative assessment does not credential the methods used to get there. A team that has managed to write a successful technical report, for example, might have failed miserably with the subtask of collaborative integration. Perhaps this is due to one team member's propensity for taking charge and ignoring dissent. Another team might have produced a less substantial report, but only because they spent more time allowing each team member to voice ideas. The entire team then needed even more time to process these ideas and consider alternate perspectives. With additional time added to the schedule, that second team might have actually produced the stronger report. Continuing to explore how microcredentialing techniques can more thoroughly evaluate such dynamics is certainly a goal for this technology and one where we are likely to see continued progress.

As this example suggests, new badging contexts often emerge in existing areas of use, but with more substantial integration and more mature techniques. As we learn more about badges, their design, and their evaluation, we will be better equipped to tackle the complex problems that exist on the horizon of education in a digital world. In many cases, we have the technology we need, but we have not yet determined how to use it to maximize student learning outcomes. For example, some digital badge researchers (e.g., Casilli & Hickey, 2016) recognize that some of the "grand challenges" identified for learning in digital environments, as articulated in a National Science Foundation cyberlearning report (Borgman et al., 2008), align nicely with the capabilities of digital badges. Three of these relevant grand challenges noted by Casilli and Hickey (2016) include lifelong digital learning portfolios, interest-profiles that use prior experiences to "help compile additional learning engagement possibilities" (p. 121), and real-time methods for providing instructional support so that learners can build toward certifiable competencies.

Each of these three areas offers development and implementation possibilities for digital badges. In the case of lifelong digital learning portfolios, we can imagine a scenario in which a learner's digital portfolio initiates from her very earliest learning experiences, ultimately housing academic examples spanning her entire formal education. Such a system might also extend beyond formal education and include examples of deliverables pertaining to lifelong learning or occupational skill development. For example, imagine the convenience and utility of being able to see evidence of progress from this student's earliest attempts at writing to her gradual refining of the craft through middle and high school and into college. In later years, as she acclimates to a career in science, this hypothetical student's writing deliverables become even more specialized through the inclusion of language specific to her career and writing formats appropriate to her organization's policies. For example, a scientific lab report might need to be formatted a certain way, using certain headings and fonts, and with certain preferred terminology and voice. A comprehensive portfolio captures and stores example assets from each of these educational and professional contexts. Such a lifelong portfolio system would be immensely useful not only for future educators and employers of that student, but also for the student herself, allowing her to assess her progression as a writer in her discipline. It also allows her to see her growth over time in other academic areas. Although our example here focuses on writing, the portfolio might contain many other categories such as mathematical development, aesthetics, music, design, programming, and so on.

This type of fully integrated product would create compelling new contexts for digital badging. In addition to housing notable deliverables from each period of time, the system would be even more useful if it highlighted salient aspects of performance that accompanied those periods of time. Digital badges could be used for this purpose. For example, perhaps that learner showed a particular aptitude for expository writing, or for scientific report writing, either of which could be credentialed by awarding digital badges. Or, maybe the student possesses a skill that is not easily categorized into a specific domain like writing, but rather crosses over many categories of the digital portfolio system. Leveling up an incremental digital badge for teamwork skills or leadership, for example, would be a useful indicator of progress to the student, to future educators, and to future employers. While existing credentials are important, indicators of growth and potential might be even more important in certain applications. Such a product does not yet exist in a way that makes this possible, although some scaffolding technologies, such as Open Badges and Mozilla Backpack, have the capability to support its development. It could also be that several different products must work together in a more sophisticated way in order to enable this longitudinal scenario.

The second grand challenge called to our attention by Casilli and Hickey in the NSF report deals with the implications of personalized learning. As we develop ubiquitous technologies and interactive systems that we can configure to our liking, our educators and learners will seek out additional ways to personalize our educational experiences. This will allow educational experiences to adapt to our preferences in the same ways we personalize our digital entertainment. Imagine the equivalent of a Spotify music playlist or a Netflix movie queue, but for educational content. Casilli and Hickey note how digital badges already support this goal. Two important features are that they provide choice by allowing learners to choose which badges to earn and they allow flexibility by providing different routes for the learners to earn them. Some badging systems also support personalization by allowing individuals to choose how to display their earned credentials.

For the authors of this book, personalized learning has always been an appealing area for digital badging research. Digital badges can serve as signposts to help orient learners in open digital learning environments. In Chapter 6, we briefly mentioned a course with these sorts of customizable learning pathways. This course was created with a choose-your-own-adventure structure designed with personalized learning in mind (Lindgren & McDaniel, 2012; McDaniel, Lindgren, & Friskics, 2012). Our idea was to develop a survey-based course for digital media covering different themes such as the history, application, and synthesis of digital technologies. Various modules were authored for each of these areas; for example, there were three different history of digital media modules and the students were required to choose at least one to complete. The instructors and the developers ceded some control over the educational progression in that they allowed students to choose particular modules to complete. This meant that students never viewed some of the course content that the designers produced – and that was okay. Rather, the important aspect was that students were exposed to *some* aspect of history and *some* domain of application. Further, they needed to have an opportunity to synthesize their knowledge in one direction or another, but the specific domain of application was less important to the learning objectives for this course. By yielding some authority over the authorship of the course to the students, the students were given an opportunity to personalize their learning in a fashion that many online courses do not allow. To help mediate the online interactions in such an environment, the authors used digital badges to reshape certain behaviors – such as social interaction or timely completion of tests and quizzes – in instructor-preferred directions.

Real-time methods for instructional support are the final grand challenge from the NSF report highlighted by Casilli and Hickey. In this case, the authors note that this problem requires infrastructure beyond what digital badging can provide on its own. They write, "these are precisely the sort of supports that are expected to follow when introduction and/or use of digital badges lead to broader transformations of programs, courses, schools, and other educational entities" (2016, p. 121). This is an important point. While badging can provide granular detail about performance and skill at the individual or group level, it is only one cog in a much larger educational machine. The monitoring of badge information is already a significant challenge in educational contexts, as supported by the many research studies we have reviewed throughout this book. Doing this in *real time*, however, is an even more significant challenge, particularly when the number of learners or users is high. It could be that human educators might need to rely on smart agents, machine learning, or other digital techniques to assist in the evaluation and proper provisioning of badge information as it becomes available in learning scenarios.

These examples show that the future of digital badges will not only involve new designs and implementations for these technologies, but also new configurations of people and procedures that will interpret and act upon their data. Some of this data might be motivational for the individuals earning the badges, but other data is also useful for the individuals or systems evaluating performance or learning. We might point digital badging systems of the future toward educational grand challenges, such as the three articulated by the National Science Foundation Cyberlearning Initiative report. Or, we might somehow tune badges to better operate in their existing contexts, to create more robust versions of already existing implementations. In any case, regardless of their specific purpose, understanding the detailed usage contexts for digital badges will be critical for properly building the necessary social and administrative support systems to maximize their impact.

Speculative Badging

In this final section, we use the term speculative to refer to those out-of-the-box ideas about digital badges that empower us to think about the technology without worrying too much about the details of their implementation, their cost, or their likelihood for success. We draw this term from speculative fiction, a genre of storytelling based in settings other than the real world. These stories often involve futuristic or imaginative elements. Speculative fiction began as a subgenre of science fiction, but has since expanded to encompass many other storytelling genres including gothic, dystopian, superhero-based, streampunk, and fantasy – essentially, any narratives that allow for alternate realties and support "a quest for the recovery of the sense of awe and wonder" (Oziewicz, 2017, para. 2). The goal in theorizing about speculative badging is not to create a category of unrealistic and non-implementable devices, but rather to use our imaginations to conjure up new imaginative possibilities for these technologies. What would digital badges that inspire awe and wonder look like, and how would they work?

Such rhetorical questions might, at first glance, seem patently unrealistic. Some might see such ideas as trespassing beyond the boundaries of respectable science and engineering. However, consider the ideas from speculative fiction that later became realities. Replicator technologies made famous in *Star Trek* are now becoming feasible, albeit at a more primitive level, through the use of three-dimensional printers. The handheld and wearable computers seen in early science fiction novels and television are now ubiquitous in many industrialized countries. And, as we discussed earlier in this chapter, VR devices, as seen in films such as *Strange Days* (Bigelow, 1995) and novels such as *Ready Player One* (Cline, 2011) are now both possible and affordable for everyday users. So, there is some value in thinking about this technology without worrying too much about the limits of our existing science and technology. This might provide us with a glimpse into the far future for digital badging.

One way of generating ideas for speculative badges is to assume significant technological process in other areas that has not yet occurred. This allows us to assume a hypothetical, fictional platform upon which our technology can exist. Again, while such an exercise might seem impractical, it is useful for projecting longer-term possibilities for digital badges. For example, we might think about artificial intelligence (AI) as being much more sophisticated than it is today. In fact, let us assume the field of AI has progressed to a point that allows machines to think at a level on par with human beings. AI theorists call this type of artificial intelligence strong AI. There are, of course, debates about whether or not such AI is even possible; here, though, we will assume for the sake of argument that it is, and that technologies can be developed that exhibit strong AI. We can then consider the implications of this underlying technology for digital badges. In this case, what would digital badging look like if sophisticated, intelligent computer algorithms could design and award badges rather than just human beings? It would be interesting to consider the particular ways in which badging might evolve based on that idea.

For one thing, there would be nothing preventing badges from being both designed and *earned* by autonomous computers, meaning that computers themselves could be adorned with various badges (perhaps by being particularly helpful, or for accomplishing complex tasks of note to other computers). Similarly, badges could be both awarded and earned very quickly, given the ultra-fast processing speed of computers. Triggers could be tuned to react on the scale of microseconds rather than seconds or minutes, allowing for a new classification of microbadges that could be chained together in complex configurations, creating interactions between badges that could propagate through an entire session of badge earning. These badges might create new opportunities for socialization among computing devices or they might steer computational behaviors toward more human-like behaviors and interactions, for example. Strong AI would also mean that computers could lie, cheat, and dishonestly acquire badges. Perhaps there would even be a black market for badges where digital objects of dubious legitimacy could be exchanged on the botnet. Finally, using peripheral sensors that provide data beyond what human sensory organs can process, artificially intelligent machines might also have entirely new parameters for what constitutes badge-worthy performance gleaned from that sensory data. An autonomous safety device in a building might be recognized for four consecutive years without a leaking pipe, for example.

There are of course a number of legitimate concerns we can raise with this example, not the least of which is why computers would care whether or not other computers earned badges. Remember, though, that we are talking about computers with strong AI. Not only are these computers advanced in terms of their processing power, but they are also more human-like in their thinking. This potentially opens them up to the same emotional and attitudinal registers as human beings. Accordingly, in a rich, data-driven environment, earning digital badges is one additional way in which aspects of performance or expertise can be drawn out of the larger data set and highlighted as a significant signpost of achievement. Perhaps they earn badges because they wish to impress humans or other computers!

Much like a computational system might focus on heat or vibration as external signals highlighting a need for maintenance attention, we can also imagine scenarios in which digital badges serve as flags to indicate useful data lines within certain machines or directories. If that seems too far a stretch, then consider the implications for humans monitoring computational systems. A badged system could make the system's capabilities and accomplishments more transparent to users, especially if Open Badges or a similarly open badging system are used. Within this scenario, users could learn more about the criteria for badge awarding and the evidence of the accomplishment and use that information to more quickly assess the structure and health of complex computational systems.

This example also leads us further down the path toward considering embodied AIs, or what we commonly refer to as robots. How might robots use digital badges? One area might be in robotic applications designed to directly support humans. For example, researchers are currently studying companion robots that can be designed to help the elderly, whether to help them remember to take their medications or simply to keep them company when they are lonely. However, what if such robots could also distribute badges, such as ones that could be awarded for taking medication for a given number of days in a row or for staying active? We can imagine situations in which insurance companies, hoping to keep costs down, subsidize certain types of badging initiatives in order to reduce the number of unnecessary procedures for their policyholders. This type of scenario is likely exciting for insurance companies, but is probably less so for the patients who want to have affordable coverage when they need it, regardless of their previously earned digital credentials. However, if these credentials also lead to specific types of rewards for the patients, such as discounted medication, there might be hope for both groups of stakeholders. A similar type of reward system has recently been implemented by some auto insurance companies who lower rates for documented safe driving behaviors.

This type of scenario has interesting implications for the ethical dimensions of badging. For example, are there certain contexts in which badges *should not be used*, particularly when there is a significant amount of computational autonomy involved in their distribution? Since researchers have not yet determined a way to install a moral reasoning engine inside of a robot, we can imagine how companionship robots or other caregiving computing devices might see badges as devices that are useful beyond just motivational purposes. We can imagine some situations where an elderly adult with dementia, for example, might have forgotten to take important medication and needs to be prodded by a caregiver to do so. In other situations, however, it could be that the medication causes side effects that a cognitively healthy adult simply does not wish to endure. If human will, whether justified or ill informed, is in opposition to the programming of a robot, could badges play a role in subtly redirecting them back on track? If so, when does such behavior move beyond what is acceptable and what is not for how these technologies are used? Who is ultimately responsible for defining what acceptable means in this context?

A third and final speculative example relates to the informational capabilities of digital badges. In a number of science fiction novels, perhaps most notably in author John Scalzi's *Old Man's War* series, it has become possible to remove human consciousness from one body and place it into another. In *Old Man's War* (Scalzi, 2005) and its sequels, this means taking an experienced consciousness from an elderly adult and placing it in a brand new, genetically engineered body. This type of arrangement has strategic military advantages – combining a wise consciousness with a powerful and young body makes for an elite soldier with both a seasoned intelligence and a robust biological body. This is a theme Scalzi continues to explore in *Lock In* (2014), a novel in which a segment of the population has been afflicted with a disease, Haden's Syndrome, disabling their ability to move their physical bodies. Instead, individuals are able to project their consciousness into robotic surrogates that allow them to experience the world through full, virtual, and robotic prostheses. So, while the human body is safely cradled in a medical unit back home, the robotic surrogate, paired with the biological human's consciousness, can be controlled and navigated in the outside world. The linked robot holding one's consciousness might go on grocery shopping trips, take trips to the library, or even pursue dangerous police missions. The latter is the case with the protagonist of *Lock In*, who happens to be a rookie FBI agent.

One interesting aspect of all of these novels is the role technology plays in sharing information in these new permutations of mind and biological body. In the *Old Man's War* series, Scalzi's super soldiers are able to communicate rapidly and beyond the natural boundaries of speech using embedded computers called BrainPals. In *Lock In*, it is possible – and considered polite – for robotic surrogates to broadcast identity information so that the human behind the prosthesis is recognizable. When human conventions such as social niceties and politeness are paired with the vast computational affordances of these embedded technologies, it makes for interesting ideas about communication and social interaction in hybrid computer/human contexts.

So, drawing inspiration and ideas from these fictional examples, how might our digital badges of tomorrow be used not only to display feats of earned accomplishment, but also as markers of everyday identity? Much like Microsoft's Gamerscore (discussed previously in Chapters 3 and 5), we can imagine how digital markers might be used to broadcast identity information in social gatherings where all parties are not immediately known to one another. Such a feature could also be useful in organizational dynamics, where ratings of particular skills or abilities would make certain activities, such as the formation of ad hoc teams, less time-intensive and perhaps more efficient. This type of identity projection and social rating system has also been explored in science fiction; one notable example is in Daniel Suarez's 2010 novel *Freedom*. Suarez's novel proposes a type of darknet in which participants continually broadcast a virtual reputation score to one another as they encounter each other in both physical and virtual spaces. In this type of configuration, then, digital badges could move beyond their current scope of application into more everyday types of scenarios. One master badge might be used to encapsulate salient aspects of one's identities and subthreads of information within this badge could be activated or made private as needed by one's owner.

We have explored three far-flung ideas in this section: advanced AI, caregiving robots, and distributed consciousness. From these thought experiments, however far removed they might seem from today's digital badging solutions, we can speculate about those aspects of these designs that are feasible and reasonable to pursue. In the first AI example, the idea of using external sensory arrays to monitor performance is in fact a useful way for thinking about digital badge triggers for future technologies. In our second speculative example, robots that do the types of jobs that humans are unwilling or unable to do at scale are certainly on our technological horizon and ask us to think carefully about the underlying moral complexities of digital badging. Understanding how AIs and machines might incorporate digital badging into their operation is helpful for highlighting both the ethical and practical dimensions of these technologies. Our third example asks us to think carefully about the potential for badges as informational devices that convey not only skills and knowledge, but also markers of identity. The trick in these exercises is to extract the information that is useful to future research and design on a shorter time horizon. Even these admittedly fantastic examples suggest directions for important underlying research questions about ethics, badge interactions, and the integration of digital badges with our everyday environments.

Conclusion: Why Digital Badges?

There are aspects of digital badging that are troublesome or problematic and we have addressed many of these concerns throughout this book. However, we have chosen to write a book on this subject because we believe the potential advantages of this technology greatly outweigh the disadvantages. Digital badges open new opportunities for learning, provide us with methods to encourage productive changes in behavior, and allow us to credential and evaluate learning in ways compatible with future careers and educational aspirations of our students of tomorrow.

Although we have done our best throughout this book to cover the most salient research dealing with digital badges, it is impossible to cover every useful source on this topic. There are some other useful resources we recommend for the engaged reader, several of which we cite throughout our book. In particular, we encourage readers interested in this topic to review the two excellent edited collections *Digital Badges in Education: Trends, Issues, and Cases*, edited by Muilenburg and

Berge (2016) and *Foundations of Digital Badges and Microcredentials*, edited by Ifenthaler, Bellin-Mularski, and Mah (2016). The HASTAC organization also maintains an excellent annotated research bibliography about digital badges (Grant & Shawgo, 2013).

As we consider the reasons for our sustained interest in digital badges over many years of research and our writing of this book, the two ideas we keep returning to are: (1) the core simplicity of the badging idea, and (2) the underlying power of these objects. As we have seen over thousands of years of analog usage, the core idea behind badging is so basic and relatable that anyone can understand them, regardless of expertise. One who has earned a badge has done something special and has been recognized for doing so. However, this simple form belies a deep complexity and underlying mechanical infrastructure that allows for sophisticated behavioral modification, deep customization, and layered progress for specific tasks in communication, learning, and entertainment. It is this duality of simplicity and depth that makes digital badging so powerful. We hope our readers will find interest and delight equal to our own in continuing to push the envelope of what is possible with this technology.

References

Bigelow, K. (Director) (1995). *Strange days* [Motion Picture]. USA: Lightstorm Entertainment.

Bista, S. K., Nepal, S., Colineau, N., & Paris, C. (2012, October). Using gamification in an online community. In *2012 8th International Conference on Collaborative Computing: Networking, Applications and Worksharing (CollaborateCom)* (pp. 611–618). IEEE.

Borgman, C. L., Abelson, H., Dirks, L., Johnson, R., Linn, M., Lynch, C., . . . Szalay, A. (2008, June 24). Fostering learning in the networked world: The cyberlearning opportunity and challenge, a 21st century agenda for the National Science Foundation. Washington DC: National Science Foundation. Retrieved from www.nsf.gov/pubs/2008/nsf08204/nsf08204.pdf.

Casilli, C., & Hickey, D. (2016). Transcending conventional credentialing and assessment paradigms with information-rich digital badges. *The Information Society, 32*(2), 117–129.

Cline, E. (2011). *Ready player one*. New York: Broadway Books.

Fitzsimmons, M., & Lynch, G. (2018, May 30). Oculus Go review. *TechRadar*. Retrieved from www.techradar.com/reviews/oculus-go.

Glover, I. (2016). Student perceptions of digital badges as recognition of achievement and engagement in co-curricular activities. In D. Ifenthaler, N. Bellin-Mularski, & D. K. Mah (Eds.), *Foundation of digital badges and micro-credentials* (pp. 443–455). Switzerland: Springer International Publishing.

Grant, S., & Shawgo, K. E. (2013, Feb. 27). Digital badges: An annotated research bibliography. HASTAC. Retrieved from www.hastac.org/digital-badges-bibliography.

Hamari, J., & Eranti, V. (2011, Sept.). Framework for designing and evaluating game achievements. *Proceedings of DiGRA 2011*, Hilversum, the Netherlands.

Ifenthaler, D., Bellin-Mularski, N., & Mah, D. K. (2016). *Foundation of digital badges and micro-credentials.* Switzerland: Springer International Publishing.

Kappen, D. L., & Nacke, L. E. (2013, Oct.). The kaleidoscope of effective gamification: Deconstructing gamification in business applications. In *Proceedings of the First International Conference on Gameful Design, Research, and Applications* (pp. 119–122). ACM.

Kim, J. H., & Lee, K. P. (2005, Sept.). Cultural difference and mobile phone interface design: Icon recognition according to level of abstraction. In *Proceedings of the 7th International Conference on Human Computer Interaction with Mobile Devices & Services* (pp. 307–310). ACM.

Koivisto, J., & Hamari, J. (2014). Demographic differences in perceived benefits from gamification. *Computers in Human Behavior, 35,* 179–188.

Lindgren, R., & McDaniel, R. (2012). Transforming online learning through narrative and student agency. *Journal of Educational Technology & Society, 15*(4), 344–355.

McDaniel, R., & Fanfarelli, J. (2016). Building better digital badges: Pairing completion logic with psychological factors. *Simulation & Gaming, 47*(1), 73–102.

McDaniel, R., Lindgren, R., & Friskics, J. (2012, Oct.). Using badges for shaping interactions in online learning environments. In *Professional Communication Conference (IPCC), 2012 IEEE International* (pp. 1–4). IEEE.

Muilenburg, L. Y., & Berge, Z. L. (Eds.) (2016). *Digital badges in education: Trends, issues, and cases.* New York: Routledge.

Oziewicz, M. (2017, March). Speculative fiction. *Oxford research encyclopedias: Literature.* Retrieved from http://literature.oxfordre.com/view/10.1093/acrefore/9780190201098.001.0001/acrefore-9780190201098-e-78.

Park, S., Locher, I., Savvides, A., Srivastava, M. B., Chen, A., Muntz, R., & Yuen, S. (2002). Design of a wearable sensor badge for smart kindergarten. In *Proceedings of the Sixth International Symposium on Wearable Computers* (pp. 231–238). IEEE.

Pino, N. (2018, May 31). PlayStation VR review. *Techradar.* Retrieved from www.techradar.com/reviews/gaming/playstation-vr-1235379/review.

Posner, R. (2004). Basic tasks of cultural semiotics. In G. Withalm and J. Wallmannsberger (Eds.), *Signs of power, power of signs: Essays in honor of Jeff Bernard* (pp. 56–89). Vienna: INST Verlag.

Rughinis, R. (2013, April). Talkative objects in need of interpretation: Re-thinking digital badges in education. In *CHI'13 Extended Abstracts on Human Factors in Computing Systems* (pp. 2099–2108). ACM.

Rughinis, R., & Matei, S. (2016). A delayed badge is a worthy badge: Designing digital badge architectures based on academic delay of gratification. In L. Y. Muilenburg & Z. L. Berge (Eds.), *Digital badges in education: Trends, issues, and cases* (pp. 203–214). New York: Routledge.

Scalzi, J. (2005). *Old man's war.* New York: Tom Doherty Associates.

Scalzi, J. (2014). *Lock in.* New York: Tom Doherty Associates.

Suarez, D. (2010). *Freedom.* Dutton: New York.

Sullivan, M. (2013, March 27). New and alternative assessments, digital badges, and civics: An overview of emerging themes and promising directions. The Center for Information & Research on Civic Learning & Engagement (CIRCLE) Working Paper #77 (pp. 1–23). Retrieved from https://civicyouth.org/civics-digital-badges-and-alternative-assessment-preparing-students-to-be-engaged-citizens/.

Swales, J. M. (2009). Worlds of genre-metaphors of genre. In C. Bazerman, A. Bonini, & D. Figueiredo (Eds.), *Genre in a changing world* (pp. 3–16). Fort Collins, Colorado: The WAC Clearinghouse.

Vinichenko, M. V., Melnichuk, A. V., Kirillov, A. V., Makushkin, S. A., & Melnichuk, Y. A. (2016). Modern views on the gamification of business. *Journal of Internet Banking and Commerce*, *21*(S3). Retrieved from www.icommercecentral.com/open-access/modern-views-on-the-gamification-of-business.php?aid=71902.

Webb, G. I., Pazzani, M. J., & Billsus, D. (2001). Machine learning for user modeling. *User Modeling and User-adapted Interaction*, *11*(1–2), 19–29.

Index